Berkhamsted

An Illustrated History

Written and Edited by
Scott Hastie

Photography
David Spain

Project Management
Lynne Fletcher

ISBN: 0-9528631-1-1

Printed and Published in 1999
by Alpine Press
in association with the
Berkhamsted and District
Local History Society

Alpine Press
Station Road
Kings Langley
Hertfordshire
WD4 8LF
Tel: 01923 269777

Acknowledgements

Percy Birtchnell 1909-86.

No book published on the history of Berkhamsted can help but properly acknowledge the debt owed to the town's foremost historian during the second half of the twentieth century. P.C. Birtchnell's two books "Short History of Berkhamsted" and "Bygone Berkhamsted", first published in 1960 and 1975 respectively, have delighted and informed two generations of local people. The wide ranging scope of the several hundred historical articles that Percy Birchnell wrote, over a forty year period for the Parochial Review, have proved to be another important and enduring legacy.

Encouraged by Percy Birtchnell's pioneering work the Berkhamsted and District Local History Society has, since its inception in 1950, steadily accumulated an outstanding collection of documents, maps, illustrations and archive photographs which have proved invaluable in the compilation of this illustrated history.

In particular the authors would like to thank the President of the Society, Jenny Honour and Chairman, Mr. Leslie Mitchell, for the many months of support and friendly encouragement he has offered since we were first approached to undertake this project in the Autumn of 1996.

A special mention must also go to Eric Holland who for many years has done a superb job adding to and maintaining the Society's photographic collection. Eric's own documentary work, which has faithfully recorded the changing face of many local scenes, has also made an important contribution to the quality of this volume.

Our thanks must also go to the other mainstay members of the Berkhamsted and District Local History Society such as Jimmy Honour, Ann Nath, Ken Sherwood, Mike Browning, Cynthia Freeman and James Bullen who have all generously offered us their assistance throughout the two years that we have been working with the Society.

The Berkhamsted and District Local History Society would also like to acknowledge the assistance received from Assistant Heritage Officer, Mike Stanyon and Curator Matt Wheeler, who are based at the Dacorum Heritage Store in Berkhamsted. Sue Flood and Christine Shearman of Hertfordshire Archives and Local Studies at County Hall, Hertford have also been supportive to the project and offered the authors every possible assistance.

The authors would also like to express their gratitude to the following organisations:

Berkhamsted Amateur Operatic and Dramatic Society, Berkhamsted Art Society, Berkhamsted Arts Trust, Berkhamsted Choral Society, Berkhamsted Citizens Association, Cowper Society, Berkhamsted Cricket Club, Berkhamsted & District Archaeological Society, Berkhamsted Film Society, Berkhamsted Town Football Club, Berkhamsted Golf Club, Berkhamsted Jazz, Berkhamsted Lawn Tennis and Squash Rackets Club, Berkhamsted Music Society, Berkhamsted Red Cross, Berkhamsted Women's Institute, Northchurch Women's Institute

The following individuals have also made a contribution either by offering information and/or photographs which we have been able to incorporate within the publication:

Val Atkinson, Joyce Baker, Alan Batchelor, Mary Birch, Clive Blofield, Mike Bridges, Douglas Brightman, Joan Burch, Margaret Casserley, Richard Casserley, Roy Clarke, Peter Clayton, Frances Collier, John Cook, John H. G. Cook, Ken & Shirley Cordery of Boxmoor Framing, Alan Cox, Margaret Crichton, Alan Cummins, Colin Davies, F. Davis, Mrs. M. Dudlyke, Jeff Edwards, Alan Faulkner, Rev. Robin Figg, George Fletcher, Geoffrey Flanders, George Franks, William Frew, Peter Gent, Pauline Gibbons, Eric Gill, Joan Goode, Richard Dixon-Gough, Bob Grace, Father Peter Grant, Peter Grimer, Peter Halsey, Stuart Grant Hastie, Colin Hextell, Joan Hollingdale, Bert Hosier, Pat Johnson, Janet Mitchell, Rev. James Neve, Roger Osbourn, Ros Partridge, Mary Peacock, David Pearce, Anne Pike, John Pilgrim of BBC Three Counties Radio, Lt. Stephen Poxon, Tom Price of the Hemel Hempstead Gazette, Ailsa Ramsden, Dorothy Redding, Jon Richardson of Kodak Ltd.,Janet Robinson, Peter Smoker, Joy Sturges, Mrs. R. Ward, Bob Warren, Norman Warren, Mrs N. Boddam-Whetham, Bryan Wood, Francis Cory-Wright.

We are also grateful to several local photographers who have allowed us to reproduce some of their own photographs:
H.C. Casserley, C.R.L. Coles, R. Grace, J. Hobart, E. Holland, B. Hosier

David Spain would particularly like to thank Debbie Elborn for her assistance on this project and also Vicky Nunn and Lucy Lee for their help in the darkroom. Natalie Dibble of Adeyfield School and Clara Sherry of the Abbots Hill School Photographic Club have also helped on the project. In addition David wishes to specially acknowledge the generosity of Kodak Ltd, who have once again supplied all the photographic materials he required to prepare for the publication of "Berkhamsted: An Illustrated History".

Foreword

Berkhamsted has been acknowledged for centuries as a town which enjoys a rich and exceptional heritage. The principal editorial judgements required therefore centre around how much it is possible to include within the scope of any one publication. The story of the town's royal castle or medieval monastery at Ashridge, Berkhamsted's ancient schools and churches, its literary traditions or industrial past could all justify substantial volumes in their own right.

A wide ranging study such as ours is therefore not intended to be a definitive account. Instead we have tried to identify the principal themes woven into the development of Berkhamsted throughout the centuries and explain them clearly, within a historical context, for the general reader.

We are especially grateful to the Berkhamsted and District Local History Society whose full co-operation has allowed us to illustrate our story with an outstanding range of archive material. We hope that you enjoy this glimpse into the past of one of Hertfordshire's most historic towns.

*The final missing panel of the Bayeux Tapestry, re-created by Jan Messent © **Madeira Threads**.*
This section shows William the Conqueror accepting the surrender of the Saxon nobles at Berkhamsted and his subsequent coronation at Westminster Abbey.

N.º 253

Rock & Co. London.

Berkhamstead, Herts

Foreword

Berkhamsted has been acknowledged for centuries as a town which enjoys a rich and exceptional heritage. The principal editorial judgements required therefore centre around how much it is possible to include within the scope of any one publication. The story of the town's royal castle or medieval monastery at Ashridge, Berkhamsted's ancient schools and churches, its literary traditions or industrial past could all justify substantial volumes in their own right.

A wide ranging study such as ours is therefore not intended to be a definitive account. Instead we have tried to identify the principal themes woven into the development of Berkhamsted throughout the centuries and explain them clearly, within a historical context, for the general reader.

We are especially grateful to the Berkhamsted and District Local History Society whose full co-operation has allowed us to illustrate our story with an outstanding range of archive material. We hope that you enjoy this glimpse into the past of one of Hertfordshire's most historic towns.

*The final missing panel of the Bayeux Tapestry, re-created by Jan Messent © **Madeira Threads**.*
This section shows William the Conqueror accepting the surrender of the Saxon nobles at Berkhamsted
and his subsequent coronation at Westminster Abbey.

№ 253

Rock & Co London.

Berkhamstead, Herts

Contents

Chapter	Pages
Historical Background	7 - 10
Berkhamsted Castle	11 - 15
Early Religious Life	16 - 18
End of An Era (1495-1661)	19 - 21
Period of Decline (1662-1831)	22 - 23
Early Transport	24 - 26
The Canal	27 - 30
The Railway	31 - 35
Motor Transport	36 - 37
Industrial Growth	38 - 51
Houses and Estates	52 - 64
Town Development	65 - 73
Berkhamsted High Street	74 - 77
Shops and Traders	78 - 99
Religious Traditions	100 - 110
Education	111 - 123
Police and Fire Service	124 - 127
Wartime Berkhamsted	128 - 137
The Story of Northchurch	138 - 148
Literary Berkhamsted	149 - 153
Social Life	154 -169
Chronology	170 - 171
Bibliography	172
Index	173 - 176

Historical Background

The geography of Berkhamsted, with its combination of good soils, favourable climate and plentiful supplies of water has ensured a long and unbroken history of successful human habitation. Set in a fertile valley, left by the retreat of the last Ice Age some ten thousand years ago, the town's prosperity stems directly from its favoured location in pleasant countryside some thirty miles from London. The place name Berkhamsted, meaning 'birch grown homestead', is a clear reference to the densely wooded conditions that prevailed in the local area for thousands of years, prior to the intensive woodland clearances that gathered momentum throughout the medieval period.

In the town centre of Berkhamsted the River Bulbourne occupies the most spectacular valley in Hertfordshire, displaying impressive slopes which, at the narrowest point, rise three hundred feet on either side. Unfortunately, this once fine old river is now no more than an insignificant stream. The demands of a fast growing twentieth century population was always going to substantially lower the level of the local water table, but it was the arrival of the Grand Junction Canal in 1797 which really damaged the River Bulbourne by ruthlessly usurping the majority of its water supply. The River Bulbourne currently rises at a point near Cow Roast, some three miles from its original source at the small hamlet of Bulbourne, close to the border with Buckinghamshire. In its heyday, some eight hundred years ago, the Bulbourne was a fast flowing river, sufficiently powerful to drive several local water mills and provide the water defences for the great earthworks of the Norman Castle at Berkhamsted. At the beginning of this century it was still possible to fish for excellent specimens of both trout and golden carp in the River Bulbourne.

A fertile river valley like the Bulbourne would have been attractive to early man especially as it also provided him with a clear route north through the dense woodland then covering the hillsides. Unfortunately any archaeological evidence that could have survived to indicate the local presence of early Stone Age man from the Palaeolithic era, would almost certainly have been washed away by the flood waters which swept through the valley, following the last Ice Age some ten thousand years ago. The peoples of the later Mesolithic period (10,000-4,500 BC) were nomadic hunters and foragers who gradually moved northwards through the river valleys of south-east England. Unfortunately they left little evidence of their activities behind them and, although they liked to settle temporarily in the vicinity of rivers and lakes, they favoured upland sites. Here the soil was better drained and the woodland less dense. It was these early clearings on upland slopes which were also the sites favoured by the last Stone Age tribes from the Neolithic era (4,500-2,500 BC). As recently as only eight years ago it was thought unlikely that there could have been any such Neolithic settlement in the Bulbourne valley. No supporting evidence had ever been found and historians were confident that the clay topped hillsides would have been too heavy for Neolithic man to work, without the benefit of the improved tools introduced by the later Bronze and Iron Age civilisations. However these previously unchallenged theories had to be rapidly revised in 1990, when startling finds were made during the construction of over eleven miles of dual-carriageway for the A41 By-pass which now runs between Tring and Kings Langley.

The first Neolithic site to be excavated on the Berkhamsted stretch of the By-pass was an area adjacent to Hamberlins Wood, some two miles west of Berkhamsted. Here, together with numerous finds from the later Iron Age period, examples of worked flint were found. The two substantial sub-circular shaft like pits uncovered were comparable, both in size and depth, to Neolithic flint mines already discovered in the north of Hertfordshire. At Bottom House Lane a series of over forty ditches, all aligned east to west, were excavated and plentiful evidence of multi-phased activity was found on the site, dating from the early Neolithic period to the Iron Age. A little further south at Crawleys Lane, the earthworks revealed another high concentration of prehistoric features, involving twenty-one post and stake holes with an overall diameter of five metres. Closer still to Berkhamsted, additional evidence of early man was also discovered at Oakwood, which proved to be the site of another large circular building of probable Neolithic date. As a result of the long promised roadworks, we can now be certain that Neolithic man was once living in a series of small settlements along the slopes of the valley at Berkhamsted.

It was not unusual for areas settled during the later Neolithic period to be inherited by the peoples of the Bronze Age (2,500-700 BC). Bronze Age settlements usually involved a group of timber built round houses, with a series of

Ancient pollarded beeches on Berkhamsted Common, photographed in 1965.

surrounding fields, banks and ditches which comprised the farm area. A typical indication of the presence of early Bronze Age civilisation is the existence of round barrows which they built as funerary monuments. Locally a good example of one such bowl barrow has been found on the Ashridge estate in Great Frithsden copse. Metalwork also made its first appearance during the Bronze Age period, but the copper and bronze implements produced were too soft to have been any practical use for agriculture. Because of this any surviving artefacts found tend to be of a more ceremonial nature, such as small weapons or decorative jewellery. From 1200 BC the later Bronze Age communities were living in circular fenced compounds, known as ring works. These were usually built around a central feature of one large rectangular communal grain store. This period is also characterised by the first appearance of banks and dykes marking out the tribal territories established, now that the previous nomadic style of life had been replaced by a pattern of more permanent settlement. By this time the earlier Bronze Age tradition of creating burial mounds had been replaced by a ritual cult based on rivers and wet places, no doubt making the river valley at Berkhamsted all the more attractive to early settlers.

From around 600 BC the knowledge of iron working spread into the local area and the introduction of more durable tools helped early farmers to clear the fields and cultivate the soil. Certainly the archaeological evidence of significant iron smelting both at Cow Roast and on the Ashridge estate suggests, from the amount of charcoal produced, that substantial woodland clearance was now taking place. The tribal chieftains consolidated their power by building a series of hill forts across the countryside which became a principal characteristic of the Iron Age period. The need for natural boundary markers and defensive positions could well be part of the explanation for Grims Dyke, which stretches across the Chiltern Hills and is the collective name for a group of ditches, portions of which still flank the Bulbourne valley. A well preserved section of the ditch can still be found close to the neighbouring village of Potten End, from where it runs across the Common towards the Frithsden Road. Beyond this point it veers towards Berkhamsted and disappears, on leaving the Common, a short distance below New Road. The dyke then appears again on the south side of the valley, where it runs parallel some three hundred yards below Shootersway. Further long and well preserved stretches of Grims Dyke can also be found further to the north-west at Wigginton.

Leading historians have speculated that such remains could be part of a much later sixth century line of demarcation separating the peoples of East Anglia from those living closer to London. However it is possible that Grims Dyke could have been much earlier, dating from the late Bronze Age or Iron Age periods. In the Berkhamsted area, traces of Iron Age pottery have been found in the basal fill of the ditch. When complete, Grims Dyke would have been an impressive feature of the local landscape, being a deep ditch 35 ft. wide, surmounted by bracken covered ramparts 15 ft. high.

The first recorded invasion of Britain occurred around 159 BC, when powerful tribes from the Marne valley, near Paris, crossed the English Channel and invaded south-east Britain. This Belgic tribe, known to the Romans as the Catuvellauni, gradually took control of the local area, extending their influence from the major settlements they established in the Wheathampstead and St Albans area. The majority of gold, silver or bronze Iron Age coins found in the Bulbourne Valley date from the reign of the Catuvellaunian King Tasciovanus, circa 20 BC, or his son Cunobelin AD 10-43. A fine example of a Tasciovanus silver unit was found at Great Gaddesden and to date some twenty Celtic coins have also been unearthed at Cow Roast. Nearer to the town, a gold stater was unearthed at the top of Gravel Path and a bronze coin featuring another Celtic chief, Addedomaros, has since been found in Lower Kings Road. It was during the late Iron Age that dramatic changes took place, transforming the local area from a relative back water to one of the most economically significant areas in Britain. The principal reason for this was the growing contacts established between southern England and the rapidly expanding Roman Empire. This process intensified following the expeditions of Julius Caesar to Britain in 55 and 54 BC. However before they could begin to introduce their civilisation, the Romans had to first defeat the resistance of the Belgic tribes and the Catuvellauni in particular. Roman ascendancy was achieved in a series of pitched battles, the nearest of which it has been suggested could have occurred either at Wheathampstead or around the Iron Age fort at the Aubreys, near Redbourn. Once subjugated trading activities between the Romans and the Iron Age chiefs continued until the full scale Roman invasion of Britain took place in AD 43.

A tableau of participants in the historical pageant held at Berkhamsted Castle in 1922.

Stimulated by the Roman influence, it was during the first century BC that the first industrial and trading areas began to appear. It is now accepted that an important local site of economic activity existed at the Cow Roast. Following a series of excavations conducted since 1972, the whole area is now protected and has been officially designated as an early Roman town. Significant quantities of pottery have been removed from the marina and orchard sites at the Cow Roast. There are also clear indications of the industrial production of iron with fourteen separate well shafts for water and, to date, two tons of iron slag and cinders have already been discovered on the site. Finds of Roman coinage dating from Claudius (AD 41-54) to Honorius (AD 395-423) indicate an unbroken sequence of Roman occupation of around 400 years at Cow Roast.

Under the Roman influence, the fertile lands of the Bulbourne valley quickly became a highly organised and important agricultural area, supplying the major Roman city of Verulamium. The Romans also exploited the Bulbourne valley as part of the route for one of their principal highways, Akeman Street. They split the local countryside into a series of estates, each of which had a substantial villa as its operational centre. Archaeological evidence suggests that these villas were regularly spaced about two miles apart along the valley floor. The villas that date from the earlier Roman period were often half timbered, with painted plaster walls, and flanked by corridors. By the second century such buildings were often replaced on the same site by more substantial masonry structures, featuring decorative mosaic floors and under floor (hypocaust) heating systems. In addition to the important villa and bathing pool discovered in Gadebridge Park, Hemel Hempstead in 1963, another Roman villa site was uncovered at Northchurch in 1973, prior to housing development for the Springwood estate. Roman occupation on this site was found to date from the first century AD and the remains indicated an eight-roomed villa, which featured two wing rooms at the end of the corridor. Substantial rebuilding took place on the site after AD 339 when a small bath house was added, together with some mosaics and painted plasterwork. Considerable evidence of mixed farming was found indicating the husbandry of cattle, sheep, pigs, goats, horses and ducks. There were also indications that this riverside villa at Northchurch was involved in the farming of trout, oysters and fresh water mussels.

In 1927 part of the substructure of another Roman building was revealed when the Golf Club was making a new green on the Common, near Frithsden Beeches. This building featured flint walls, tessellated pavements and a hypocaust heating system. Subsequent re-excavations have confirmed that this was indeed a sizeable villa, likely to date from the second century AD. There have been numerous other local finds of Roman pottery, coins and funerary urns made on various sites on Berkhamsted Common. In addition, when land was being cleared for the construction of the Castle Hill estate during the 1930's, many oyster shells, light pottery and other Roman remains were found. Nearer to the centre of modern Berkhamsted, finds of Roman tiles and bricks have also been discovered on land between the canal and the railway, close to St Johns Well Lane.

When the Roman military occupation of Britain came to an end in AD 410, Saxons from the harsher climate of Northern Europe gradually began to settle in Britain, intermingling their stock with the declining native population. The more aggressive of these Nordic raiders drove out any remaining Celtic tribes from Hertfordshire and systematically destroyed all the Roman buildings in order to introduce their own way of life. The river valley at Berkhamsted provided one of the entry routes for these Saxon colonists who began to settle in the area, clearing woodland and energetically draining waterlogged ground. The Saxons lived in family based clans and introduced their open field system of agriculture to Britain. They grew oats, barley and wheat on land ploughed by oxen and reared pigs semi-wild in the woodland. In stark contrast to the former Roman estate owners, they lived in huts built of mud and sticks, which were often sunk into the ground for warmth. However unlike the much earlier primitive settlements, located on higher ground, the chosen sites of the Anglo Saxons tended to be on the gravel terraces along the valley floor. Indeed it was these early Saxon settlements which were destined to form the pattern of modern communities in the valley today. With the exception of a circular bronze brooch and a mid-ninth century Christian seal found at Witchcraft Bottom in Little Gaddesden, the only definite local Saxon remains, as yet discovered, are portions of the south and west walls of St Mary's Parish Church in Northchurch. As early as AD 527 the local area was included in the Kingdom of East Saxony, ruled by King Erkewin. Immediately prior to the Norman Conquest Edmar, a Thane surviving under King Harold, was encamped at Berkhamsted from where he ruled the local area.

Berkhamsted Castle

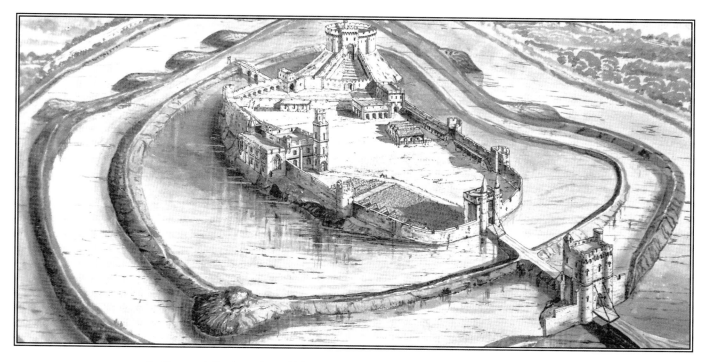

Berkhamsted Castle, as it could have looked in the time of King Edward IV (1442-83).

Following his defeat of King Harold's army at the Battle of Hastings in 1066, William the Conqueror broke his journey at Berkhamsted, where he met with the Saxon noblemen to acknowledge their defeat. Having accepted their surrender, he then proceeded to Westminster Abbey where he was crowned on Christmas Day by Alfred, Archbishop of York. As Lord and Master of his new kingdom, the Manor of Berkhamsted was among the many grants of land William awarded to his half-brother, Robert Count of Mortain. The Count quickly recognised the strategic importance of Berkhamsted, where there was already a Saxon encampment guarding the main route north through the valley. He soon set about constructing a strongly fortified castle, built to a traditional Norman plan of defensive motte and bailey earthworks. Many writers have speculated that this Norman castle could have been built on the site of an existing Saxon fort, although no actual archaeological evidence has ever been found to support this theory. Other local historians have suggested it is more likely that the original Saxon encampment was higher on top of the hill to the west, where Berkhamsted Place was built some 560 years later.

Following the construction of the castle, Berkhamsted became an important centre of Norman power, from which all the lands owned by the Count were administered. These included a wide swathe of territories, some of which were as far away as Northamptonshire. However nothing of this first wooden Norman castle remains today because the Count's son, William, having duly inherited all his father's lands and estates, unwisely led a rebellion against Henry I. This ended in ignominious failure and, as a punishment, William's eyes were burned out, all his estates confiscated and his castle completely razed to the ground. Having taken revenge and re-asserted his power, King Henry then granted the Manor of Berkhamsted to his Chancellor, Randolph, in 1104. Almost immediately the Chancellor started to rebuild Berkhamsted Castle and it is fragments of this second structure that remain with us today. There is sufficient surviving stonework to indicate that the main courtyard or 'bailey' of the Chancellor's castle was rectangular in shape, with dimensions of 300 ft. x 450 ft. approximately. These stone built curtain walls were originally 20 ft. high and 7 ft. thick and within the protected bailey area a series of apartments, workshops, barns and stables were built against this strong outer wall. Traces of some fireplaces and ovens can still be found within the remains and, close to the Keeper's lodge house, foundations of the small castle chapel are still clearly visible. At the northern sheltered end of the bailey was an inner ward, providing a safer and more privileged position for the castle's most favoured inhabitants. The entire castle community within the bailey was overlooked by a three storey tower or keep, which stood on a man-made hill or 'motte' 45 ft. high. This Keep was strongly fortified with walls eight feet thick and served as the last place of refuge in the event of siege. It

The bailey area of Berkhamsted Castle, as it would have been approached from the main entrance, also showing the motte to the rear, 1995.

Atmospheric view of the Castle motte, 1984.

The remains of the Castle Chapel and Palace, 1984.

The inner ditch and moat on the eastern side of the Castle, 1984.

was also provided with its own well, sunk right down through the centre of the motte. This well shaft can still be viewed by those prepared to climb the steep steps to the top of what is now known as Tower Hill.

A wide moat was built around the bailey area and a second huge ditch and moat also surrounded the entire castle site. Further massive earthworks produced additional great bastions at the north and east end of the site, in order to further strengthen the defences close to the Keep. The original gateway or barbican of the castle was considerably further east than the current visitors' entrance. In earlier times the main approach to the great stone barbican of the Norman castle would have been straight ahead from the top of Castle Street, across what was then low and marshy ground beyond the River Bulbourne. From this barbican a great drawbridge was lowered across the front of the outer moat, which has now become the road behind the railway. A middle gateway provided another drawbridge which spanned an inner ditch, giving access to a grand entrance through which the bailey was finally entered. Substantial remains of the Castle's impressive barbican survived until it was tragically demolished when the railway embankment was built in 1835. The middle gateway also survived as a significant ruin until well into Victorian times. Thankfully what remained of the Castle ruins at the beginning of the twentieth century was eventually placed under the care of the Ministry of Public Building and Works in 1930, thereby safeguarding the site from further deterioration.

Between 1155-65 Berkhamsted Castle was occupied by Thomas á Becket who spent enormous sums of money on extensive repairs and maintenance to the impressive stone structure that had been provided by Chancellor Randolph some fifty years earlier. King Henry II spent a considerable amount of time at the Castle, which became his favoured residence. This was very fortunate for Berkhamsted because the Monarch showed his approval by awarding a valuable charter to the merchants of the town in 1156. Berkhamsted was already enjoying the commercial benefits generated by a permanent royal retinue and the King's award effectively sealed the early prosperity of the town. The charter granted complete exemption for Berkhamsted traders from all taxes, tolls and duties when travelling with their merchandise in England, Normandy, Aquitaine and Anjou. By 1189 Berkhamsted Castle had been granted in dower to Berengaria, Queen to Richard I, but she was soon dispossessed by Prince John (later King John) whilst his brother was away on the Crusades. However, as part of the widespread civil unrest that was precipitated by King John reneging on pledges made in the Magna Carta, the Castle was besieged in December 1216. Its attackers were disgruntled English barons who had joined forces with Prince Louis, the French Dauphin, to unseat the unpopular monarch. After a siege lasting two weeks, the castle finally fell to the foreign prince and his allies.

Once order had been restored to the Kingdom, for much of the remainder of the thirteenth century, Berkhamsted Castle was held in turn by two successive Earls of Cornwall. The first of these was Richard of Cornwall who was the second son of King John and the younger brother of King Henry III. This earl was said to be a man of great wealth and talent, who achieved fame both at home and abroad; he was elected King of the Romans at Aix La Chapelle in 1257. When in England, Richard spent much of his time at Berkhamsted Castle, where he built a lavishly decorated chapel and substantially enhanced the main hall and principal quarters. Following his death his son, Edward, Earl of Cornwall, duly inherited the Castle where he had been born in 1249. It was Edward who was later responsible, during his tenure of the Castle, for the foundation and endowment of an important monastery at nearby Ashridge (see p.17). Because the second Earl died without an heir, Berkhamsted Castle simply reverted to the reigning monarch Edward I, who by then had also established an impressive royal palace at Kings Langley. The manor then remained in the personal possession of the Crown until King Edward II granted it to his favourite courtier, Piers Gaveston. However it was not long before Gaveston met his end in 1315, at which point the Earldom was revived and the Castle awarded to John, brother of Edward III, who held it until his death in 1336.

The later reign of Edward III was perhaps the most glorious period in the Castle's history. The King first ordered an extensive survey and then carried out a major programme of refurbishment and repairs, before granting the building to his young son Edward, who was to become the first Duke of Cornwall in 1337. Only six years later Edward became Prince of Wales and was to become forever remembered in history as the valiant Black Prince. Once again it was to Berkhamsted's considerable advantage that the Castle became the favoured residence of this national hero. As a young man the Prince enjoyed a series of spectacular military successes against the French, first distinguishing himself with his bravery and leadership at the Battle of Crecy, when he was only sixteen years old! It was the Black Prince who brought back the defeated King John of France to be imprisoned at Berkhamsted Castle, following another glorious victory at the Battle of Poitiers in 1356. Henry of Berkhamsted was one of a small troop of local men who had fought bravely beside the Prince at this defining battle. On their return Henry, who had saved the Prince's baggage during the fighting, was rewarded with promotion from porter to Constable of the Castle. Henry died in 1398 and it is now believed that the knight's tomb in St Peter's Church (formerly known as the Torrington Tomb) belongs to this loyal soldier. Beyond his involvement in military matters, the Black Prince's affection for Berkhamsted was a matter of record and when he married Joan of Kent the couple spent their honeymoon in the area.

On the death of the Black Prince the Castle at Berkhamsted passed to his son, who was destined to become the betrayed Lancastrian King Richard II. It was during Richard II's reign that England's most celebrated early poet, Geoffrey Chaucer, is listed as being Clerk of

Works to Berkhamsted Castle. On his accession in 1399 Henry IV granted the Castle and estates to his son and heir, King Henry V, from whom it passed to Margaret of Anjou, Queen to Henry VI. Another landmark in the early commercial development of Berkhamsted occurred when Edward IV (1442-83) granted the town the benefits of a second highly important charter. This declared that no rival market could be set up within eleven miles of the town and ensured that Berkhamsted was in a favoured position to further develop its growing prosperity without effective competition. In 1469 King Edward granted the Castle to his mother, Cicely Duchess of York, who lived at Berkhamsted for the last twenty-six years of her life. Historically the Duchess remains a highly significant figure who was mother to two kings of England, Edward IV and Richard III. Her later years were marred by tragedy, when first her son Edward IV and grandson Edward V, both died in 1483 and her two younger grandsons were also smothered in the Tower of London. Two years later Richard III was killed at the Battle of Bosworth and Cicely's death in 1495 effectively marked the end of a dynasty. By this time the House of Tudor had become firmly established and Berkhamsted Castle was promptly deserted by the Royal Court.

The Prince of Wales visits Berkhamsted Castle in 1935.

Early Religious Life

Parish Church of St Peter

St Peter's was not the first parish church in the manor of Berkhamsted; this distinction belongs to the ancient Saxon church of St Mary's in Northchurch. However as the local community began to grow and develop during the twelfth century a separate parish, originally dedicated to St James, was established in Berkhamsted. It was at this point that the name Northchurch came into use; its church being to the north of what had now become the principal parish in the area. Although the early Church of St James was certainly in Berkhamsted, historians think it unlikely that this church was founded on the St Peter's site. Indeed it is considered more probable that it stood in the vicinity of St Johns Well Lane, on the current main post office site. Here there was also an early burial ground and medieval hospital founded circa 1213 by the Brotherhood of St John the Baptist. Despite the uncertainty surrounding the precise location and dates of the Chapel of St James, we do know that some surviving parts of the impressive structure of the Parish Church of St Peter date from the early thirteenth century. This fine old church, built to an Italian cross plan, has an official date of 1222, although some of the earliest work in the original chancel (now the Lady Chapel) dates from 1200. The lower stages of the nave and tower would have been constructed later than this, with the aisle being added to the nave in 1230. St Catherine's Chapel was built in 1320 and St John's Chantry (now part of the outer south aisle) followed in 1350. One hundred years later the addition of the clerestory further enlarged the building and, when the tower was raised to its present height of 85 ft. in 1545/46, the church had grown to its full dimensions.

St John's Well

During the eleventh and twelfth centuries a small community of monks lived close to an ancient spring that bubbled to the surface at St Johns Well Lane. It is thought that this early religious site was adjacent to today's modern post office building, which itself was built on land formerly belonging to Lane's Nurseries. Despite the constant lowering of the local water table, this 'holy spring' remained an intermittent stream into the 1940's. During the Middle Ages what was then an abundant spring became the town's principal source of drinking water and two wardens were employed to regulate and safeguard this valuable asset. There is a surviving local legend that St John the Baptist once visited the well to baptise Berkhamsted's early Christians and, from Saxon times, the waters of the spring were said to have great healing powers. Indeed, as late as the

The Parish Church of Berkhamsted St. Peter, an engraving by Robert Clutterbuck, 1815.

Victorian era, many people regularly visited the Berkhamsted springs to bathe their eyes in the 'holy water'. The Christian care earlier offered to local people by the medieval monks of St John's was also extended to crusading knights, many of whom returned from the Holy Land suffering from leprosy. The endowment which officially founded a hospital on this site was granted by Geoffrey Fitzpiers, the Earl of Essex. Both the Hospital of St John the Baptist and the Hospital of St John the Evangelist (for lepers) at Berkhamsted were granted by the Earl to the Brothers of St Thomas the Martyr of Acon in 1213. The exact site of the hospital, or indeed the early Church of St James which is thought to have been close by, has never been precisely determined. It seems certain however that the burial ground was close to the modern post office site, on the existing corner of St Johns Well Lane and the High Street. It is here that numerous finds of skulls and early human remains have been found. The monks of St John's benefited from the later support of Henry II and Queen Isabella, the widow of King John, who also awarded them substantial grants including the tithes of all the mills in Berkhamsted and Hemel Hempstead. Under the umbrella of this royal patronage, the monks of St John's Well prospered for three hundred years. When the hospitals were eventually disbanded in 1516, their combined revenues were used by John Incent, later Dean of St Paul's, to help provide an endowment for the foundation of Berkhamsted School in 1544.

Ashridge Monastery

In 1275 Edmund, Earl of Cornwall, who was then in possession of Berkhamsted Castle, ordered a religious house to be built in a clearing in the woods at Little Gaddesden. Some years earlier Edmund, or more probably his father Richard I, acquired a casket whilst travelling in Saxony. This devotional object was a holy relic, said to contain the blood of Christ. It was Edmund's intention to install a group of grey monks at Ashridge, bound by the strictest of Augustinian rules, and charge them with protecting and promoting the precious relic his family had rescued. Building work began on the monastery in 1276 and the institution was finally dedicated in 1286. The initial establishment consisted of no more than a rector and a supporting body of nineteen French brethren, who together became known as the College of Bonhommes. Once the monastery was established King Edward I visited for an extended stay and he even held a Parliament there in 1290. When King Edward died in 1300, we are told that "his bowels were

immediately buried and his heart was placed with a drop of Christ's blood in the golden tabernacle at Ashridge". The second member of the royal family who was a great benefactor to the Monastery was the eldest son of King Edward III, the Black Prince. He too made Berkhamsted Castle his favoured residence and in his declining years developed an increasing attachment to the monastery. Shortly before his death in 1376 he endowed the altar at Ashridge with a great table of gold and silver, set with a fabulous selection of rubies, emeralds and pearls.

For two and a half centuries the monks of Ashridge prospered, making the 'holy blood' available to countless pilgrims who travelled from far and wide. The relic was so highly treasured that many leading members of the nobility asked to be buried at Ashridge. Despite their accumulated wealth, the monks continued their strict adherence to the rules of their order, wearing only ash grey tunics and cloaks. With the honourable exception of the Queen, no women were ever allowed on the premises. As the prosperity of the monastery continued, so the buildings grew in number. There was a great hall, an infirmary, a chapter house and cloisters, all built around a church which itself was 132 ft. in length; the monastery was also provided with a very handsome gateway. The Bishop of Winchester, who died in 1447, made substantial donations to the monastery which allowed for further improvements and by the end of the fifteenth century a large barn had also been built to house the monks' swelling harvests. All this accumulated wealth and earlier royal favours offered the monks little or no protection when, as part of the Dissolution of the Monasteries, King Henry VIII disbanded the community in 1539.

Ashridge now became a royal residence and three of the King's children, Edward, Mary and Elizabeth, divided their time between Ashridge and Hatfield House. It has been said that the western avenue at Ashridge, which is still known as 'Prince's Riding', was named after the young prince, later to become Edward VI (1547-1553) who was nursed at the great house. Evidence of religious tensions were soon to re-appear at Ashridge, following the accession of Mary Tudor to the throne in 1553. The estate had been bequeathed to Princess Elizabeth in her father's will of 1547 and it was here that she was arrested in February 1554 on the orders of her half sister Queen Mary. Elizabeth's crime was an alleged complicity in the revolt of Sir Thomas Wyatt against Mary's intended marriage to Phillip, King of Spain. Perhaps because of this unhappy memory, Queen Elizabeth never returned to Ashridge following her own accession to the throne in 1558. There was an impressive statue of Queen Elizabeth at Ashridge, which was later presented to Harrow Public School in 1925. The statue remains there to this day, on the outside wall of the famous speech room, and a replica has since been made which now stands in a niche overlooking the lawns at Ashridge. In 1604 Ashridge was acquired by Thomas Egerton who served as Lord Keeper to Elizabeth I and later as Lord Chancellor to James I. The newly elevated Thomas Egerton, who was to become Baron Ellesmere and Viscount Brackley, considered Ashridge as the ideal base to establish a permanent family seat for himself and his descendants. In 1643 the house and estate at Ashridge were comprehensively sacked by Cromwell's Roundhead soldiers and the Viscount's son, the first Earl of Bridgewater, was later rewarded as one of the leading Royalist families who had suffered during the Civil War. John Egerton, the third Earl (1646-1701) proved to be another distinguished servant of the Crown who was subsequently awarded the Order of Bath for his loyal service. It was John Egerton's son Scroop, who became the first Duke of Bridgewater in 1720 and cemented the family's fortunes by his two favourable marriages: the first being into the family of the Great Duke of Marlborough, the second uniting him with the family of the Duke of Bedford. The story of how his descendent, the third Duke of Bridgewater, first made himself a vast new fortune and then created plans to turn Ashridge into one of the most impressive stately homes in the Country, is told in a later chapter devoted to the houses and estates of Berkhamsted.

An engraving showing the monastery at Ashridge, first published in 1790.

End of An Era

View of Berkhamsted High Street, showing the old Market House, 1832.

Given the attractions of the Royal Court and the important monastery at Ashridge, it is not difficult to imagine just what a bustling place Berkhamsted would have been in its heyday during the fourteenth and fifteenth centuries. The pathway we now know as Castle Street would then have catered for a steady stream of royal processions, courtiers, merchants and pilgrims, most of them travelling to and from London and bringing with them undreamt of prosperity and commercial opportunity for the local people. It is, of course, tempting for local historians to overstate the historical importance of Berkhamsted Castle. However there can be no denying the key role this site played in an exciting and formative period of the nation's history, which stretches from the time of the Norman invasion until the end of the Plantagenet period. More importantly, from Berkhamsted's point of view, the two royal charters awarded by Henry II and Edward IV, provided the town with important commercial advantages and allowed it to develop relatively unchallenged for almost three hundred years as the economic centre of this part of West Hertfordshire. Unfortunately this extended period of grace for the town came to a sudden end following the death of Cicely, Duchess of York, in 1495. Berkhamsted Castle was then abandoned by the royal court, its large

domestic staff summarily dismissed and the buildings left to fall into disrepair. The economic effects of this wholesale withdrawal of the royal establishment must have been devastating for the town. By this time principal residences close to the Capital had become more exclusively favoured by the royal family and castles such as Berkhamsted had simply become outdated, uncomfortable and too expensive to maintain. However Berkhamsted Castle still appears in royal records and we know that in 1503 the Underkeeper sent a buck to Windsor for the Queen of Henry VII, but she never once came to visit the town. Subsequently the Manor of Berkhamsted was granted in turn to three wives of King Henry VIII: Catherine of Aragon, Ann Boleyn and Jane Seymour. However the Castle was by now a sad looking ruin, which was of no interest to any of them.

Worse was to follow for Berkhamsted, when the great Tudor monarch Henry VIII found favour with the neighbouring town of Hemel Hempstead. In 1539 the King awarded an important market charter to this town and the new Burgers of Hemel Hempstead seized their opportunity to become the agricultural trading centre of the district. Despite the fact that Berkhamsted's earlier royal charter had been confirmed by

Elizabeth I in 1598, and a second more limited charter awarded by James I in 1618, the townspeople of Berkhamsted remained unimpressed. They did not take their slide from royal favour with good grace and, by the time of the Civil Wars, Berkhamsted's support for the royal family was at best luke warm. The town refused to pay Charles I's ship money tax of £25 levied on the Borough in 1636 and suspicions developed that some of the Civic leaders of Berkhamsted had distinct Parliamentarian sympathies. It therefore came as no real surprise when the Charter of Incorporation was withdrawn from the town, two years after the restoration of Charles II in 1660. By this time the castle had become a complete ruin; unlike many such castles it had not been spoilt by the ravages of war, but instead robbed of much of its stonework by Sir Edward Carey, who was Keeper of the Jewels to Elizabeth I. In 1580 Sir Edward helped himself to a large quantity of masonry from the derelict castle and set about building a fine mansion at the top of the hill overlooking the royal site. By 1662 this house, which later became known as Berkhamsted Place, had become home to John Sayer who, as Chief Cook to Charles II, was another favoured royal courtier.

Market House

In the fourteenth century, when the royal castle was in its prime, Berkhamsted had the reputation as being one of the very best market towns in the Country. When the royal family was not in residence a large staff of courtiers remained and this favoured group would have been some of the very few people in the kingdom wealthy enough to afford the luxuries of life. Consequently merchants from far and wide were not slow to recognise that Berkhamsted would be a highly profitable place to sell their silks, spices and other costly wares. Almost a century after the departure of the royal court, the civic leaders attempted to restore the town's fast fading status as a trading centre, by erecting a substantial new market house in the town centre. This was built around 1583 on the roadside waste about two hundred yards west of St Peter's Parish Church. A typical sixteenth century market house, it was a brick and timber structure which stood on stilts. It had twenty great oak posts supporting the main building, which was used primarily for the storage of corn to be sold at the market. The lower portion of the market house was open on all four sides, offering some market vendors at least partial shelter from the elements. The earlier trading outlets adjacent to the new market house developed into the assorted buildings of Church Lane (formerly known as Back Lane). These shops obscured the finer properties, including the Court House, which had previously fronted onto the High Street. The town's stocks and whipping post were later positioned in front of the new market house and when the High Street was widened the main public right of way actually ran underneath this old building. By the middle of the nineteenth century the market house had become something of a dilapidated anachronism, which only served to narrow the main road through the centre of the town. Consequently few local people were sorry when it was completely destroyed by fire, one night in August 1854.

Court House

In contrast its companion building, the Court House, is one of the oldest surviving buildings in Berkhamsted and dates from the Tudor period. This attractive half-timbered structure was formerly two storied and, within surviving elements of its original roof, there are still some impressive oak beams which once supported the floor of the great loft. In essence the Court House was the town's first Civic Centre and it was here that, empowered by the royal charter issued by James I on 18th July 1618, the town's council met to deliberate. The Common Council was then made up of a Bailiff or Mayor and twelve chief burgesses, who were elected annually. This Council also had the services of a full time recorder and together this group was known as the Corporation. The last royal charter issued by James I granted the town the right to hold a Court of Records at the Court House, where the Corporation also kept the standard weights and measures used to help settle trading disputes. The courts of the Manor and Honour of Berkhamsted, held traditionally on Whit Tuesday and on the Tuesday after Michaelmas, were convened to hear "all pleas, actions, suites or offences against the laws and liberty of the manor". Thirty-eight years before the Urban District Council was formed in 1898, Lord Brownlow of Ashridge became the owner of the Court House, when he paid £43,682 for the Manor and Honour of Berkhamsted. However he immediately let it back to various trustees, at a nominal rent and from 1838 the building had become part of the National School. The adjoining house, originally built for the headmaster of the National School, later became home to the verger of St Peter's Church. Both Dean Incent's and the Court House are of key architectural significance, because these two old buildings represent a surviving link with Berkhamsted's Elizabethan past.

Dean Incent's House

The carefully restored structure of Dean Incent's is a picturesque half-timbered house, built in the latter half of the fifteenth century, and is certainly the oldest domestic building in the High Street. Furthermore, to the rear of the property, there are remains which indicate that an earlier medieval house is likely to have stood at right angles to the High Street on this site. The front of this earlier structure was then incorporated into the later Tudor house which was built to face the main road. The property has since had the minor addition of a small south-west wing, dating from the eighteenth century. It is thought that Dean Incent's may first have been used as a medieval hall or public meeting place, prior to the existence of the Court House. In the fifteenth century, the house was home to Robert Incent, who served the royal court at Berkhamsted Castle as Secretary to Cicely, Duchess of York. It is therefore very likely that Dean Incent's was also the birthplace of Robert's son, John Incent, who became President of the Brotherhood of St John the Baptist and was responsible for the founding of Berkhamsted School. John Incent also served as Dean of St Paul's Cathedral from 1540. Traditionally his arms as Dean have hung outside the house, which many will remember providing the town with a charming old-world coffee shop between 1930 and 1970. More recently the house has been used as masters' accommodation for Berkhamsted School and one of those masters, David Sherratt, has since discovered some interesting wall paintings at Dean Incent's, which are considered by experts to date from either the late Tudor or early Jacobean periods.

The Court House, circa 1980.

Period of Decline

The withdrawal of the royal charter by Charles II in 1662 was the final straw for the now impoverished town of Berkhamsted. So many local families had been decimated by the plague in 1643 that the parish authorities were forced to beg for help from neighbouring towns. In the absence of a Borough Council empowered by royal charter, the responsibility for maintaining the local community passed to the Vestry. This body was charged with administering the parish and raising the necessary revenues to provide local services. It was however handicapped in that its powers extended over a very small area, which then did not even include Northchurch, and this severely limited its tax raising potential. Furthermore, exacerbated by neighbouring Hemel Hempstead's success, the market at Berkhamsted had now declined to the point where revenues were virtually nil. Efforts to rehabilitate the town were further undermined by a series of smallpox epidemics and local outbreaks of cholera. This confirmed that, by the beginning of the eighteenth century, in addition to being a very poor community, Berkhamsted had become a singularly unhealthy town. Indeed one contemporary account declares with scorn that Berkhamsted was a truly miserable place to live - "stretching as it did along the southern side of a swamp". This was a far cry from the halcyon days of old when in 1337 and 1341, Berkhamsted was considered sufficiently prosperous to warrant returning its very own Member of Parliament.

Against this backdrop, it was the Parish Vestry which faced the daunting task of overseeing the development of Berkhamsted until the end of the nineteenth century. Amongst the Vestry's principal responsibilities were public health and the relief of the poor. During its lifetime it maintained a local workhouse and pest house, as well as struggling to administer some form of basic education and law and order. Since the first Poor Law Act was passed in 1601, local parishes had been compelled to provide work for all unemployed able-bodied adults. They were also made responsible for the welfare of all the aged and incapacitated people in their district. With the limited revenues of a small and by now impoverished parish, the Berkhamsted Vestry faced an uphill struggle to finance these statutory commitments. Altogether they amounted to a municipal burden which would have been completely insupportable, had it not been for the various charities and endowments that were fortunately bequeathed to the town.

Poverty and the Workhouse

In 1620 Charles I, then Prince of Wales, offered an endowment of £82 for the benefit of the poor of Berkhamsted. This sum of money helped to fund a ramshackle row of cottages for the homeless, which stood at the corner of Kitsbury Road and soon became known as "Ragged Row". Later in 1696 Edward Salter bequeathed the Park View Road site, together with other properties, stipulating that their combined rents were to be used for the "benefit of the industrious and laborious poor". The principal building on this plot of land was converted into a workhouse and very soon became filled to capacity. Surviving records tell us that in 1767 George Hoar had been appointed Governor of the Workhouse. He was given £28 per calendar month, with which he had to feed and clothe all the inmates, pay for their medicines and undertake "to deliver them up to the parish authorities in a good condition for work". Whilst a fortunate few may have enjoyed disproportionate wealth and an elegant lifestyle, life for the ordinary folk of Berkhamsted during the eighteenth century was a story of unrelieved ill health, grinding poverty and misery. The workhouse, together with most of the paupers' tenements, was situated in the west end of the town which by now had become a district of almost unimaginable squalor.

By the beginning of the nineteenth century there was a growing determination to improve conditions for the poor, partly because the overcrowded straw thatched workhouse had become a verminous and unsanitary disgrace, which one Victorian writer described as "one of the most wretched hovels in the town". Once again charity came to the rescue, this time in the form of a substantial bequest of £1200 left by the Rev. George Nugent. Surprisingly George Nugent was in fact Rector of Bygrave, near Baldock, but he preferred to live at the Red House in Berkhamsted. Whilst staying in the town he had become appalled by the living conditions endured by the poor of Berkhamsted. Consequently he left a substantial sum towards the cost of providing a new workhouse. In 1833 the old workhouse was pulled down and replaced by Berkhamsted's first elementary school. An alternative site for the new workhouse was created by demolishing 'Ragged Row'. This new building was a very considerable improvement, when compared to its predecessor and soon became known as Nugent House in recognition of its principal benefactor. The census records of 1851 reveal that the new workhouse was the most densely populated dwelling in the parish, being home to the official keeper, James Badderly and his family, together with a total of 61 inmates. Copies of the local newspaper, the Berkhamsted Times dating from 1871, tell us of another local charity which offered vital sustenance to the poor during the winter season. Balshaw's charity provided one pound of bread and a pint of soup to the poor of the parish, distributed from the castle grounds. As an indication of the surviving deprivation in the area, between three and four hundred families turned up every Wednesday and

Saturday; some travelling from as far away as Potten End. Certainly the sheer scale of poverty in Berkhamsted at this time would be rather shocking to any late twentieth century resident, such has been the transformation in the town's fortunes during the last one hundred years. As late as 1887 no fewer than 488 people in the town received out-relief and there were still 39 men, 9 women and 22 children in the workhouse. However just as its former period of glory had come to a sudden end at the beginning of the sixteenth century, so the first sign of an economic upturn had now arrived in the unlikely shape of the Grand Junction Canal. It was the construction of this commercially important waterway which lowered the water table and thereby helped to reduce flooding in the town. This was of great significance at a time when there was still no proper drainage systems and rotting waste, together with raw sewage, was left to run freely in the streets. Beginning in 1793 it was not the patronage of the royal family, but a series of transport developments that slowly but surely came to the town's rescue. First by helping to create a healthier environment and then, gradually producing a sustained economic revival which led directly to the prosperous, late twentieth century community we know today.

The old buildings of Northchurch Workhouse, demolished in the early 1960's.

View of Back Lane at the turn of the century.

Early Transport

Berkhamsted High Street is part of an ancient track which ran through the valley to join the Icknield Way at Tring. This was an important route used by the late Bronze Age tribes to link the more industrialised areas of East Anglia to the cultural and religious centres established at Glastonbury and Avebury. The straightness of Berkhamsted High Street, as well as the stretch of the A41 road further west, connecting Tring to Aylesbury, is considered to be a legacy of the Roman occupation during the first century AD. We know that the main route through the Bulbourne valley at Berkhamsted became part of Akeman Street, which the Romans built linking Verulamium (St Albans) to the other major cities established in the West Country at Cirencester and Bath. In many areas the road network they created defined the pattern of national transport links for centuries to come. Another important local Roman road was Watling Street, part of which ran from Verulamium to Dunstable, following a course similar to today's A5 main road. Certainly from the time of the Norman Conquest to the mid fifteenth century, the town's High Street would have been part of the main route towards Berkhamsted Castle. This ensured it was a busy thoroughfare, carrying a regular flow of visitors and deliveries to the royal court, in addition to the steady stream of pilgrims on their journey to the monastery at Ashridge.

However it is worth remembering that, during the medieval period, what was then considered a main road was little more than a well trodden right of way, linking one town or hamlet to another. Furthermore travellers also had the right to diverge from the main track during poor weather and such journeys through open countryside and woodland were unpoliced and often dangerous. Travel was made more difficult by the fact that early carts and carriages were cumbersome and badly designed contraptions. Most journeys were therefore made very slowly,

only adding to the travellers' vulnerability. In an attempt to improve matters a statute was issued by Edward I in 1285. It decreed that all main highways were to be widened, with bordering land cleared for 200 ft. on either side. Medieval guilds were also involved in the upkeep of some of the more important routes, like the road from London to Berkhamsted, but maintenance levels remained nominal. By 1555 all able-bodied men were required by statute to work four days a year on the roads, or supply an alternative labourer. Such piecemeal arrangements continued throughout the Tudor and Stuart periods, when road conditions still left much to be desired. It was not really until the eighteenth century that the first stirrings of nation-wide industrial development began to stimulate the beginnings of much needed improvements. The ancient obligation of statute labour did not officially come to an end until the General Highways Act was passed in 1835, although by then paid labour had already taken over the maintenance of all main roads.

The Sparrows Herne Turnpike Trust was formed in 1762 and given the power to "amend, widen, alter and keep in repair" a twenty-seven mile stretch of road which ran from the south end of Sparrows Herne at Bushey Heath, through Watford, Berkhamsted and Tring, before terminating on the outskirts of Aylesbury. Four tollgates were erected; two outside Watford, another at Newground (between Berkhamsted and Tring) and a further gate was built at Aston Clinton. Some historians have suggested that there was also a tollgate at the eastern end of Berkhamsted, near Bank Mill. A painted iron post bearing the name of the Turnpike Trust can still be seen close to the pavement, in front of the Standard Tyres Depot, on the corner of Park Street. Tolls were collected every six or seven miles. Cattle and sheep were an important source of revenue for the Trust, when farmers from

Examples of principal horse-drawn road vehicles (from left-right) stagecoaches, operating from 1650, a Square Landau, circa 1780 and a Brougham, circa 1839.

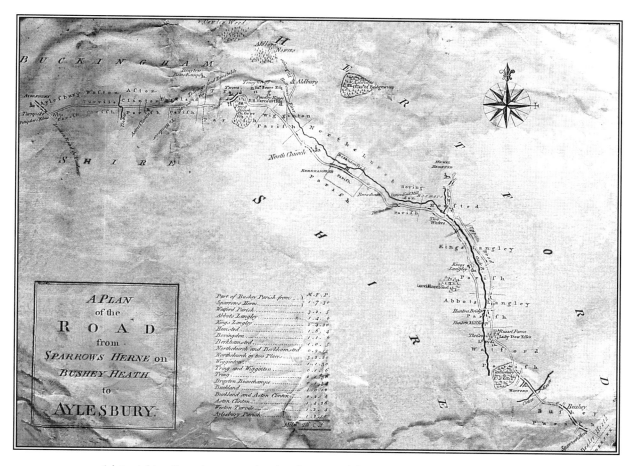

A late eighteenth century map showing the route of the Sparrows Herne Turnpike Trust.

Wales and the Midlands used the Sparrows Herne highway to take their livestock to the London markets. They often rested their animals in the large paddock provided at Cow Roast (formerly the Cows' Rest) near Tring; there were also similar but smaller enclosures behind the Goat Inn in Berkhamsted High Street. The appointment of James McAdam, later Sir James McAdam, as the main surveyor for the Sparrows Herne Turnpike Trust in 1821 made an immediate and positive impact. He supervised a new round of road improvements which ensured that all the road surfaces maintained by the Trust were made up of a compacted layer of small flints, one foot deep. In 1823 toll rates were set as follows: 4½d for a horse drawn coach, 1½d for a laden pack horse, other beasts (not laden) 1d, 10d per score for a drove of oxen or cows and 2½d per score for a drove of calves or pigs. The Sparrows Herne Trust was operating what was then one of the busiest highways into London and was therefore able to collect plenty of revenue. An Act of Parliament in 1832 raised tolls still further and gave additional powers to the Trust, which began to lease out the toll gates. Road maintenance had now become a professional business and the toll gates at Watford were then generating an impressive annual revenue of £2500. As the economic benefits of good transport links

became apparent, a system of hired labour and paid officials was put in place. However road conditions in the nineteenth century were far from ideal. There were still no drainage systems in place and as a result, roads were often waterlogged in bad weather and made all the more unpleasant by effluent cast out into the streets.

Age of the Stagecoach

Road conditions improved from the mid-eighteenth century and stagecoach services quickly became established along all the main roads into London. At this time stagecoach travel was the fastest mode of transport available and the best carriages with a full set of horses could manage an average of twelve miles-per-hour on long journeys. Not that the stagecoaches were a cheap method of travel. As early as 1792 one company was charging 8s 'inside' and 6s 'outside' the coach, as the fare from Berkhamsted to London, when the average weekly working wage was less than one pound per week. By 1836 the journey from Tring to London took three hours and the costing structure had been adapted to 12s sitting inside the coach, with a fare as low as 2s for those who braved the elements outside. Berkhamsted had now become an important posting town, situated on a main coaching route.

In 1824 there were two passenger coaches travelling to London at 7.00 and 8.00 in the morning. The London mail coach arrived at midnight, departing again at 3.00 in the morning, following a change of horses at the Kings Arms. Because Berkhamsted stood on one of the most important routes to Aylesbury and the Midlands, private coaches were also a familiar site clattering through the High Street. These were usually yellow post chaises, with brightly coloured postillions and were drawn by either two or four horses. A leading firm of Berkhamsted coach builders, E. King & Son, operated from High Street premises which were later to become the offices of the local builder, Donald Lockhart & Son and are now home to Sumner & Tabor, a firm of solicitors. There were two other coach builders in the town, Mr. Pethybridge who had a workshop near Cowper Road and a Mr. Holliday, who later became a cycle dealer. The constant stream of stage coaches brought considerable levels of custom to a variety of other tradesmen in the town. In 1792 there were three blacksmiths, two saddlers and collar makers, a wheelwright, a stage waggoner and a keeper of post horses, all trading successfully in Berkhamsted. However it was the many local inn keepers beside the main road who profited the most, because road conditions were still arduous and road travellers would usually stop every ten miles or so for refreshment. It was also normal practice for at least one of the team of four horses to be changed at every stop and the larger inns like the Kings Arms offered stabling for up to forty horses.

The stagecoach mainly transported people and perishables and, because of this, the arrival of the Grand Junction Canal in the town in 1797 made little impact on the economic success of the turnpike system. The chief benefit of the canal was the cost-efficient method it offered for the long haul transport of heavy goods and bulk loads of raw materials. This was more of an industrial role, which the road system in the nineteenth century was still totally ill equipped to deal with. It was really the arrival of the railway in Berkhamsted in 1837 that transformed the situation, offering an alternative and far quicker method whereby passengers and perishable goods, as well as heavy freight could be safely delivered into London and other major cities. Competition from the railways had the effect of halving toll rates by the end of the 1850's and the days of the Sparrows Herne Turnpike Trust finally came to an end on 1st November 1873.

A local London and North Western Railway horsedrawn bus, pre 1880, travelling through Hockeridge Woods towards Ashley Green.

The Canal

View of the canal by the Crystal Palace, circa 1893.

It was the invention of the steam engine in 1763 that marked the beginning of the Industrial Revolution in this Country. Industrial location was no longer entirely driven by environmental factors and factories could now be built wherever manpower and raw materials could be assembled. Because the best of the turnpike roads of the late eighteenth century were still unable to cope with heavy freight, there was now an urgency to find new ways of delivering bulk supplies to these industrial centres. To help fulfil this need, a system of inland waterways was devised and this became the first principal method of providing industrial transportation. Quite apart from the fact that a major canal was eventually built through Berkhamsted, the town's connection with this nationally significant transport development was reinforced by its relationship with the neighbouring Ashridge estate. Francis Henry Egerton (1736-1803) who was later to become known as 'the Father of Inland Navigation', had inherited Ashridge as his family home, on becoming the Third Duke of Bridgewater in 1747. Surviving accounts reveal that Francis Egerton grew up to be a rather odd and introverted character, who became obsessed with the idea of engineering a vast network of canals across the country. At first people

questioned his sanity, given the very considerable capital outlay involved in creating even a short length of canal. However Egerton was sufficiently confident to guarantee that the construction of his first new waterway, the Bridgewater Canal, would enable him to deliver coal to Manchester at half the previous cost. He had also calculated that, on their return journey, the same canal boats could be used to carry away large quantities of finished industrial products such as iron, bricks and tiles. These could then be delivered to towns for building works and also to the sea ports for export.

It was not long before the economic advantages of this novel form of transport became obvious and Britain's new entrepreneurs, together with many of the aristocracy were now clamouring to invest in this potentially lucrative business. By 1780 two thousand miles of new canal works had been sub-contracted across the Country, at an average cost of £3323 per mile. What became known as 'Canal Mania' reached its peak in March 1793, when a total of 48 new canal schemes were put before Parliament. A plan for the Grand Junction Canal was one of these and it was officially sanctioned by an Act of Parliament dated 1793. The initial capital raised was

£350,000, with a route carefully planned to provide a direct and cost effective link between London and the Midlands. This would be used primarily for the delivery of coal south towards the Capital. William Jessop was the appointed surveyor for the scheme and he estimated a total cost of £372,275 to complete the job. Work began on the local stretch in May 1793 and by the end of that year 3000 men were on the payroll, working simultaneously on different sections. Construction along the floors of the Gade and Bulbourne valleys was achieved in phases. King Langley was reached from the Thames by 1797, the canal was extended to Berkhamsted by 1798 and was running through Tring by 1799. Work on the Tring Summit, which had to carry the canal to 405 ft. above sea level, had already been completed in advance. This involved the creation of an impressive cutting, over 1½ miles long and over 30 ft. deep in places, achieving the highest canal level anywhere in the Country. This was one of the outstanding engineering feats of its day, when one considers that it was dug by teams of men using only pick and shovel. In several areas the clay dug from the pits close to the canal was also used to 'puddle' or line the bottom and sides of the channel, which helped to waterproof the canal.

Altogether it took twelve years to establish a fully operational waterway linking London to Birmingham. When completed the Grand Junction Canal was 137 miles long and had been provided with 101 locks. The geography of the Chiltern Hills dictated that the majority of locks were at the southern, Berkhamsted, end of the canal. In the one stretch between Boxmoor and Tring there were no fewer than 20 of the 55 locks required to carry the canal from the Thames to the Chiltern Gap at Tring. Every boat crossing the Tring Summit uses 200,000 gallons of water to achieve its height. It was this factor which made the canal's feeder branch from Wendover an essential feature. In order to safeguard supplies of water for this stretch of the canal during dry spells, a series of large reservoirs were also built around Tring at Wilstone, Marsworth, Tringford and Startopsend. As soon as the canal opened it proved to be a commercial success with heavy goods being moved up and down the Country with a cheapness and speed never known before. The positive effects on the economy in Berkhamsted were felt immediately, with local farmers and millers now able to receive double the price for their premium produce by selling it in London. Busy canal side wharves near Castle Street and Ravens Lane were soon dealing with daily deliveries of coal, for both domestic and industrial use. For the first time fuel could now be delivered to the town at reasonable prices, a feature that was to prove beneficial to the Berkhampstead Gas Company which was formed in 1849. In return for supplies of coal, the Gas Company despatched crude tar by-products by wideboat for distribution in the London area. Soon local timber merchants, notably Keys (later Alsford's) at Castle Street and Job East at Gossoms End made good use of the canal side wharves as their businesses developed. The Cooper factory at Ravens Lane also used two wharves, one to unload supplies of coal and other chemicals required in the production of its world renowned sheep dip and the other to despatch finished goods. The town's blacksmiths prospered, helping to maintain early fleets of horse-drawn wideboats, as did the publicans at canal-side taverns such as the Crooked Billet, The Boat and the Crystal Palace. In addition to providing refreshment for the navvies, these hostelries also offered stabling for the working horses. Another local inn, the Rising Sun, still has its front door opening on to the tow path. The largest local blacksmith's operation was run by Pocock's of Dudswell who shod hundreds of barge horses at the turn of the century.

At maximum speed a horse-drawn flyboat, with a crew of three men and a twenty ton load, could manage the entire canal journey from the Paddington Basin to Birmingham in 36 hours. An important feature of the Grand Junction Canal was that it had been built wide enough to accommodate two narrow boats side by side; the southern stretch from Berkhamsted to London was broad enough to cope with huge seventy ton wideboats which were 70 ft. long and 14 ft. wide. In addition to grain and forage these wide boats also began to take away flour and malt from the local mills, returning laden with soots and dung from London which could be used to enrich the fields of Berkhamsted's farms. Given the presence of a local timber industry beside the canal, it is perhaps not surprising that a local boat building yard was established in the town. This yard was situated between the two coal wharves at Castle Street and Ravens Lane. In 1826 it was owned by Joseph Hatton, until William Edward Costin took over the boat building works in 1882. In its day the canal proved to be a huge financial success and ironically the very best year of business was 1836, when the railway was being built and the canal's revenues reached a peak of £198,086. Although it is true to say that the arrival of the London to Birmingham Railway marked the beginning of the end for the economic prosperity

The canal viewed from the bridge at Lower Kings Road, circa 1910 (The fields to the right are the town's former cricket ground).

The canal lock at Dudswell, 1935.

View from the bridge at Billet Lane, looking back towards Northchurch, 1993.

Modern narrow boats approaching New Road Bridge, Northchurch , 1993.

View of the canal bridge at Castle Street, showing the former Castle Hotel and the Alsford totem pole, 1985.

The premises of Bridgewater Boats, established in 1971 on the same site as Hatton's (later Costin's) wharf and boatyard.

of the canal system, it was a very gradual process. The railway did immediately capture the bulk of passenger traffic and also the transport of perishable goods. However this was a part of the market which, prior to the 1840's, had primarily been using road transport and therefore did not initially damage the canal's trade in heavy industrial materials. For much of the nineteenth century the canal continued to compete successfully with the railways, by slashing its charges for the transport of heavy freight. Rates quickly fell from a peak of 42d per ton in 1839 to as little as 5d per ton in 1851. By this method the total tonnage of freight carried by the canal system was able to expand until it reached a peak of 1,404,012 tons in 1868.

Despite this initial success in maintaining freight levels a gradual decline eventually took hold to such an extent that by 1900 the railways were carrying ten times more freight than the canal system. During the First World War the canals came under the control of the Board of Trade, but their decline still continued. Following the War it was thought that the acquisition of additional systems might help revive the Grand Junction. The eventual outcome of this new approach was that the Grand Union Canal was formed in 1923 when the Regents Canal and

Dock Company in London was merged with the Grand Junction which, amongst others, also purchased the Warwick Canal. In a fresh attempt to compete with the railway system, steam powered boats were also introduced, but these were soon supplanted by diesel engine boats in the 1930's. A further scheme of improvements, which included widening all the bridges to Birmingham, was financed in 1934, but despite this the canal's decline proved irreversible. The canal system was nationalised in 1948, eventually coming under the control of the British Transport Commission in 1962. The levels of freight carried were falling dramatically and the final commercial blow was delivered by the hard winters of 1962 and 1963, which caused the canals to freeze up altogether. The Transport Act of 1968 subsequently classified the Grand Union Canal as a recreational cruiseway and, from this time onwards, it ceased to be considered principally as a commercial waterway. It is rather alarming now to realise that at one time in the late 1960's complete closure of the network was considered. Thankfully this option was rejected and, given the contemporary focus on the environment, and the growing interest in leisure boating holidays, the canal has enjoyed something of a prolonged revival during the last thirty years.

The Railway

Construction work on the London to Birmingham Railway began in the Spring of 1834. It had been the original intention of the sole engineer, Robert Stephenson, to adopt the simplest and most straight forward route, which involved laying tracks from Watford, through the estates at Cassiobury, Grove Park and Langleybury. The line would have then proceeded straight along the Gade Valley from Hemel Hempstead to the Dagnall Gap, via Water End and Great Gaddesden. However these first plans had to be scrapped, following vehement objections from the major land owners in the valley. As a direct result of their intervention it was finally agreed that the new railway, just like the main road and canal before it, was to veer westwards and take an alternative route through the Bulbourne valley. This change was destined to bring substantial growth and economic benefits to Boxmoor, Berkhamsted and Tring. However the engineering challenges now facing the new railway were immense. At the southern end of the Gade valley successful objections from the Lords of Essex and Clarendon had required the construction of the Watford Tunnel and the Oxhey Cutting, in order to minimise disruption to their estates at Cassiobury and The Grove. Meanwhile at the other end of the valley, similar refusals from Sir

Astley Paston Cooper at Gadebridge and Lord Brownlow of the Ashridge estate, meant that the new more westward route they had forced along the Bulbourne valley, now had to tackle the summit of the Chiltern Hills at Tring. By any standards construction of the London to Birmingham Railway was a massive undertaking, however work proceeded at an impressive rate from the Spring of 1834. Contracts for various sections of the line were awarded on a competitive basis, with 112 miles of construction shared between 29 different contractors. By this method the railway company ensured that progress would be made simultaneously along the full route of the railway. Locally W. & L. Cubitt secured three contracts to lay just over nine miles of track from Kings Langley, through Berkhamsted to Tring station. The more dangerous job of digging the Tring Cutting was awarded to Mr. Townsend, an engineer from Smethwick who brought with him his own army of labourers.

During 1836 the average number of workmen employed on the line was 10,000, most of whom were then earning between 18 and 24 shillings per week. The number of labourers working locally reached 700 at the peak of the

Early engraving of Berkhamsted Station also showing the canal (right) circa 1840.

construction works. The largest undertaking of all on the local stretch of the line was the creation of the Tring Cutting. This was 2½ miles long and required the excavation of up to one and a half million cubic yards of chalk and soil, to carry the railway through the Chiltern Hills. It took 400 men, using only picks, shovels and horse-drawn barrows, 3½ years to dig this cutting. The ambitious nature of the railway's construction, which often operated on slopes 60-70 ft. high, meant that this too was very taxing and hazardous work. It is difficult to overstate the scale of the construction work undertaken to create the London to Birmingham Railway. For example, earlier written accounts estimate that the total amount of earth moved in only one three mile stretch of embankment was equivalent to the building of the Great Pyramids in Ancient Egypt. Altogether seven workmen were killed at Berkhamsted, a further four perished during the construction of the Northchurch Tunnel which was a quarter of a mile long. The digging of the Tring Cutting claimed another six lives, in addition to another thirty-seven serious injuries.

The London to Boxmoor stretch of the line was finally opened on 20th July 1837 and one year later on 17th September 1838, the line was clear for through traffic from Euston to Birmingham. The total cost of constructing this railway had been two and a half million pounds and the new service proved to be an immediate commercial success. In its first year of operation trains carried 39,855 passengers, with daily receipts averaging £153. First class passengers paid 8s for the single journey from Berkhamsted to London. They travelled at an average of twenty miles per hour in covered upholstered carriages, whilst second class passengers paid 6s 6d to ride in coaches which were open at the side. By February 1840 four of the ten trains, which ran between London and Birmingham on weekdays, stopped at Berkhamsted. Down trains, which left at 8.00 and 8.45 a.m. and 2.00 and 6.00 p.m. reached Berkhamsted in 80 minutes, stopping at Harrow, Watford and Boxmoor. However the up trains were slower, with the first train leaving Berkhamsted at 7.55 a.m. and not arriving until 9.30 a.m. In 1846 the London and Birmingham Railway was taken over by the London and North Western Railway (L.N.W.R.) as part of an amalgamation with four other railway companies. The new rapid expansion of freight traffic on the local stretch of the line now meant that a third line was needed in 1858, so that passenger services would not be disrupted. As business continued to grow, it became possible to reduce fares without damaging profit levels and by 1858

the charge for a journey from Berkhamsted to Euston had fallen to 5s for first class travel, 3s 6d for second class and 2s 4d for third class travel. The original station built at Berkhamsted in 1836 was an unusual and rather elegant structure, built in an Elizabethan style. It was also situated much closer to the castle than today's still rather distinctive building. This later station was built in 1875, with a new set of extensive sidings provided to replace the old goods yards that had occupied ground between the old station and Gravel Path. In the same year the railway's capacity was again increased when a fourth track was added to the line into Euston. Given this new development the faster passenger services could now be confined to the western tracks and the slower freight traffic restricted to the eastern lines, which ran alongside the goods sheds and sidings.

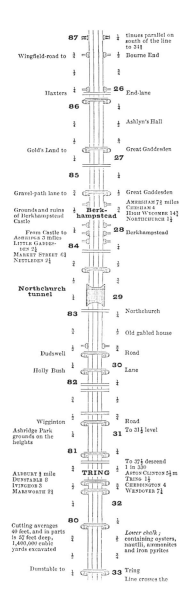

Plan of the local stretch of railway line, showing places of interest, 1840.

View of Berkhamsted Station, with the canal in the foreground, circa 1910.

Annual passenger bookings at Watford Junction had now reached 100,000, a level of custom which had more than trebled in the period 1845-75. The number of trains required to cope with this level of demand was creating something of a bottleneck in London, but the problem was alleviated by the construction of a double tunnel, just ahead of Euston Station at Primrose Hill. It was now far easier to maintain hourly passenger services for the growing number of commuters from towns like Berkhamsted. By 1887 services had improved to the extent that there were twelve 'up' trains and fifteen 'down' trains on weekdays, with the fastest train of the day leaving Berkhamsted at 8.45 a.m. and reaching Euston, in well under the hour, at 9.35 a.m. The L.N.W.R. became part of the London, Midland and Scottish Railway (L.M.S.) in 1923 and, following the railway's important contribution to the war effort, the company was nationalised to become part of British Railways in 1948. During the 1950's Government policy began to favour the development of diesel and electric locomotives and the phasing out of steam on the local line began in 1961. The progress of electrification proceeded from north to south down the line and by 1964 the old L.M.S. steam express locomotives had been banned north of Crewe. The overhead supply for the new electric engines operated at 2,500 volts A.C., drawn from the National Grid, and a full electric service from London commenced in January 1966. This began a period known as 'commuter paradise' and was in itself an important factor behind the continuing and rapid growth of Berkhamsted during the second half of the twentieth century. Now a prosperous country town offering a good range of schooling, its desirability had been reinforced by the introduction of high speed rail services. The town was now seen as the ideal location for the middle class professional to settle with his family. The local stretch of the railway line was now part of the important west coast route to Glasgow, which by 1970 had become the busiest trunk railway in the Country. With the introduction of four aspect colour signalling, clear headways of only three minutes were established between the trains on this route, each of which were now capable of travelling safely at up to one hundred miles per hour. The fastest train of the day currently leaves Berkhamsted at 8.09 a.m. and arrives at Euston 33 minutes later, stopping only at Hemel Hempstead. In 1996 privatisation was introduced on lines formerly operated by British Rail. The local service is currently run by Silverlink Train Services Ltd on lines provided by Railtrack who, in the Autumn of 1998, spent $430,000 on refurbishing Berkhamsted Station.

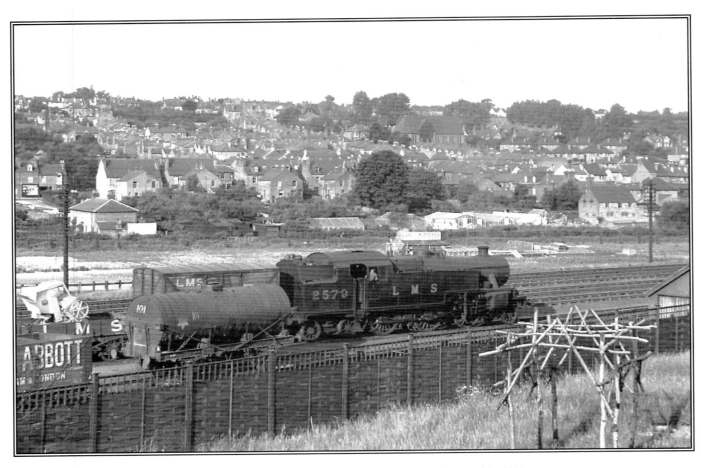

LMS Tank Engine hauling a goods train through Berkhamsted in 1939.

LMS City of Bradford Streamliner passing through Berkhamsted Station in the 1930's.

Local passenger train waiting by the goods sheds at Berkhamsted Station in 1935.

Goods train leaving the Northchurch Tunnel on the slow line, circa 1947.

The Euston to Carlisle Sunday train leaving Northchurch, November 1956.

Princess Class Engine 6210 with northbound express approaching Berkhamsted Station, June 1939.

Royal Scot hauled express passing Berkhamsted Gas Works, April 1955.

Motor Transport

Despite the transport developments of the nineteenth century, horse-drawn carts were still a common sight travelling through Berkhamsted as late as the 1930's. The very slow road speed of 4 m.p.h., laid down by the Red Flag Act of 1865, had discouraged the development of steam powered road transport and, following the First World War, stringent speed and weight restrictions were still imposed on all motor vehicles. These remained necessary in order to protect existing road surfaces, most of which still had sand and gravel dressings and were therefore unable to cope with heavy vehicles and solid tyres. From 1896 British motorists had been allowed freely on the road, subject to a maximum speed limit of 14 m.p.h.; this speed limit was subsequently raised to 20 m.p.h. in 1903. Colonel Wheatley, Lord Brownlow's Estate Agent, was the proud owner of Hertfordshire's first registration number which was AR1. One of the town's leading businessmen, ironmonger Mr. J. W. Wood, became another early local car owner when he bought a second hand Benz in 1897. In 1906 C. E. Southey & Co. cleaned and repaired cars and they also assembled their own make of motorbike in what was later to become Reynolds Garage and workshop, between Kings Road and Elm Grove. Southey & Co. also used part of what is now Birtchnell's gents outfitters as a High Street showroom for their bikes. Before the First World War, the Young family (later of Underhill and Young's Garage) started trading at the Kitsbury Cycle Works. Dwight's Garage in the High Street then offered garaging for ten cars, repairs and washdowns, in addition to driving lessons. It was this business which also introduced the town's first motorised taxi cab and Dwight's Taxis had their own stand at the railway station as early as 1913.

A key local transport problem at the end of the nineteenth century was the lack of an effective link between Chesham and Berkhamsted. It was then estimated to be costing £10,000 a year to carry goods between the two towns, using the laborious route via Kings Road. The Chesham and Hemel Hempstead Steam Tramway Company had been formed in 1887, with the intention of laying rails from the Marlowes in Hemel Hempstead to Bourne End and then along the Bourne Gutter to Chesham. Another tramway linking into this system, was also proposed to run along the main road from Aylesbury and Tring, then through Berkhamsted to connect up at Bourne End. It was even planned to provide a small branch line to link Berkhamsted railway station to this system, with an additional tramway laid along Lower Kings Road. After many years of delay such grandiose plans for a local tramway finally came to nothing, when the Government increased the maximum speed of buses with pneumatic tyres from 12 m.p.h. to 20 m.p.h. It was no longer cost effective to consider the capital outlay required for a tramway system, which had been planned to travel at only 8 m.p.h. on the roads and up to 25 m.p.h. across open countryside.

One of the earliest bus services in the Country was started by the London and North Western Railway Company in 1899, when one of their motor cars carried passengers between Berkhamsted and Chesham railway stations. The first regular motor omnibus service was introduced by an Aylesbury based firm in 1920. In 1921 the London and General Omnibus Service extended its Bushey-Boxmoor service to Berkhamsted and in 1923/24 a local service also started to run from Berkhamsted to Watford, via Chesham and Rickmansworth. This route was discontinued when a service to Windsor was established, running from Berkhamsted railway station. By 1925 the town had the advantage of two 'National' services to Watford, Aylesbury and Dunstable, operated by the Aylesbury Bus Company. In 1930 a new Road Traffic Act increased the maximum speed limit to 30 m.p.h. and the age of the motor bus had well and truly arrived. Consequently a proliferation of local operators sprang up to cash in on the boom in this favoured method of public transport. It was now possible to take a bus to Hemel Hempstead via Little Gaddesden and B & B Coaches, run by Mr. Barnard and Mr. Bedford, started to operate regular services between Berkhamsted and Potten End.

By 1930 the High Street at Berkhamsted was a fully made-up road and the main route through the valley had at last been provided with a reasonable road surface. The junction of Kings Road and the High Street was now sufficiently busy that Berkhamsted had become one of the first towns in Hertfordshire to have traffic lights installed. Following the Second World War the main A41 road was subject to a major scheme of improvements costing £800,000, designed to help it manage the increased traffic flow. However as car ownership continued to spread during the second half of the twentieth century, these old 'A' roads, which were still the main roads for all through traffic, became very congested.

Unfortunately the Government's response in introducing a nation-wide programme of motorway construction did nothing to help the local situation in Berkhamsted. If anything, the completion of the local stretch of the M1 motorway in 1958 only attracted more traffic on to the A41 through the town. However, despite increased levels of noise and air pollution, Berkhamsted's proximity to this improving national road network has certainly assisted in making it a highly desirable location. This process has accelerated during the last two decades; first with the construction of the M25 orbital motorway around London in 1986 and more recently with the long awaited opening of the A41 by-pass in 1993. Following the completion of this high speed link into the motorway system Berkhamsted High Street, which had formerly been part of the old A41 trunk road, was re-designated as the A4251. Just as the coming of the canal in 1797 and the arrival of the railway in 1837 first helped the town to revive its flagging fortunes, its strategic location close to current major road networks offers Berkhamsted some assurance of economic prosperity in the modern age.

Some employees depart from the Cooper Factory on a works outing, 1910.

View of the eastern end of Berkhamsted High Street, circa 1930.

Traffic in Berkhamsted town centre in the early 1960's.

Industrial Growth

Farming

Particularly as we view the urban sprawl of the late twentieth century, it is important to remember that historically Berkhamsted has always been a country town. First the Romans and then the Anglo Saxons established the local district as a well organised agricultural area. The dominant influence of farming extended into this century, as parent to most of the significant commercial activities which developed naturally in the town, both before and after the Industrial Revolution. The majority of significant industries that became successful in Berkhamsted were related, at least in part, to long standing locally established agricultural traditions. Seen from a national perspective, Hertfordshire summers have always been warmer than average, with a short but intense growing season which favours the harvesting of maximum yields. When compared to other areas of England, local soils are also particularly well drained and the combination of these two key environmental factors has helped to ensure that local farms have enjoyed particular success in the production of arable crops like wheat and barley. By 1822 the commentator William Cobbett was able to report that the lands of Hertfordshire were "very fine: featuring a red tenacious flinty loam, upon a bed of chalk, which makes it the very best corn land we have in England". As recently as 1850 no one could really doubt that Berkhamsted was essentially a farming community. The former lands of Kitsbury Farm ran very close to today's modern town centre, with sheep and cattle then grazing freely on meadows now occupied by Cowper Road and Torrington Road. A threshing barn stood on the corner of Rectory Lane, Lane's Nurseries were a major feature at the western end of the High Street and there were two water mills working in the town, grinding locally produced grain.

For the four hundred years that followed the Norman Conquest, it is likely that local farmers enjoyed a prosperity equal to any in the nation, as they struggled to satisfy the appetite of the wealthy royal court then established at Berkhamsted Castle. It was during this golden period in the town's history that sheep farming became a profitable activity. During the twelfth and thirteenth centuries, the quality of English wool was especially prized abroad and locally produced wool from Berkhamsted was then exported to the Low Countries. Chiefly in Flanders, it was made into fine cloths and then often imported back, until the highly skilled Flemish weavers were instead induced to settle in England and pass on their skills to local craftsmen. The decline in the town's wool industry took place in the early Tudor period, when a general collapse in the local economy had been caused by the royal court's sudden departure from Berkhamsted Castle in 1495. When Queen Elizabeth was on the throne, the town's principal industry was said to have become the manufacture of malt, from locally grown barley. By the sixteenth century, Berkhamsted was also beginning to develop a reputation for the production of woodenware. Increasing use was now being made of large horse-drawn wagons, as farmers could gain higher prices for their grain and straw by taking them to markets in London. Their carts would never return empty, but instead loaded with manure and 'night soils' collected in the City, which could be used as a powerful and highly effective fertiliser on the local fields. Despite the widespread poverty in the town between 1500 and 1900, Berkhamsted was fortunate to be largely self-sufficient in terms of basic commodities. The raw materials for food, drink, fuel, clothing, tools and building materials could all be found locally.

Examples of Berkhamsted's old historic farms are Cross Oak Farm and Broad Oak Farm, which are both listed in 1757. Broad Oak, which was near Ashlyns, was farmed by Robert Taylor who paid a £9 tithe for 90 acres, whilst Robert Ward paid £2 6s for the smaller 23 acre holding at Cross Oak. Kingshill was then a more substantial farm of 159 acres, for which William Chappell paid a tithe of £15 8s in 1778; larger still was Little Heath Farm where in 1851 Joseph Chennells employed 16 men on a farm of 235 acres. At this time Noah Newman of Castle Hill Farm employed five servants and fourteen labourers on a farm which ran to 310 acres and, closer to Ashridge, was the 266 acre Cold Harbour Farm which was then kept by Alfred Cooley and fourteen labourers. Just off the High Street was the site of a close or paddock, attached to the Goat Inn, where Welsh Cattle would be grazed and rested on their way to the Barnet Fair. It is also worth noting that, on a print dated 1724, a local windmill is clearly marked standing on White Hill, overlooking what is now Gravel Path. Although the windmills of Hertfordshire are well documented, nothing survived or is now known of this structure which was presumably demolished some time in the first half of the eighteenth century.

Harvesting at Tunnel Fields, circa 1920.

William George Bunting, 'Old Shep', Cooper's model sheep farmer, seen here in 1935.

The Market

What was once one of the richest markets in the kingdom soon collapsed, when the royal court deserted the town and left the Castle to turn to ruin. Soon the neighbouring town of Hemel Hempstead, empowered by Henry VIII's charter of 1539, began to capture most of the agricultural trade in the district. In comparison market activities in Berkhamsted dwindled to become a regular but insignificant affair. Despite the concerted attempts at a revival, instigated by the construction of a substantial new market house circa 1583 (see page 19) the presence of small pox and other infectious diseases in the town during the seventeenth century ensured that the town's market remained of little consequence to anyone other than the local inhabitants. By 1799 the writer Lipscomb was able to record in his 'Journeys' that the Berkhamsted market remained "shabby and decayed". Despite such difficulties, there was still sufficient spirit left in the town to organise and enjoy the ancient statute fair or 'statty' every Michaelmas. This was held in the High Street, between Kings Road and Water Lane, with the majority of the main highway being turned into a fairground for the day. In addition the town had always held a fair on St James' Day and the royal charter of 1619 allowed for another two fairs to take place on Shrove Monday and Whit Monday. The last recorded Whitsuntide Fair held in Berkhamsted took place in 1867. In 1882 Loosley's Trade Directory reveals that a cattle market was held in the town on alternate Wednesdays; there was still a straw plait market every Thursday and a miscellaneous market held on a Saturday. By the beginning of the twentieth century, this had evolved into a pattern of a vegetable market held every Tuesday, meat and flowers on Saturdays with a very small cattle market still surviving on alternate Fridays. The market rights, which had for many generations been vested in the owners of the Ashridge estate, were purchased for the benefit of the town from the trustees of Lord Brownlow's estate, following his death in 1922. These rights were subsequently transferred to the Urban District Council in 1972 and currently Berkhamsted's ancient market makes only one appearance a week on Saturdays, when various stalls line the northern side of the High Street.

Common and Parkland

Thankfully substantial portions of Berkhamsted Common survive today as a large and beautiful remnant of the former wasteland of the manor. Many hundreds of acres of gorse, fern and woodland still extend uninterrupted for nearly four miles, from Potten End into Northchurch and Dudswell. Although today its use is primarily recreational, until the beginning of the century Berkhamsted Common was prized by the local townsfolk for the practical and economic benefits it offered. Historically all common rights were granted by the Lord of the Manor to his tenants who could use the land freely to graze their sheep, cattle and pigs. Ordinary folk also had the right to take bracken, furze and broken wood from the common for fuel and dig on the land for supplies of sand and gravel. The tradition of using the common land was sustained in Northchurch far longer than in Berkhamsted and, before the First World War, it was not unusual to see winter fuel still being collected by villagers, and small flocks of sheep still being grazed on the Common. The Ashridge connection with Berkhamsted Common began in 1761, when the manor of Berkhamsted was leased by the Duchy of Cornwall to the Duke of Bridgewater. Eventually in 1860 Lord Brownlow, then resident at Ashridge, took the opportunity to purchase the Manor of Berkhamsted for the sum of £144,546, of which £43,682 was for 1,332 acres of waste or common land. Five years later advisers acting for Ashridge felt that they could exploit the General Enclosures Act to extend the estate, by enclosing this common land. In recognition of the historic rights of the townspeople, they were prepared to offer Berkhamsted in return a central recreation ground. This was to be on open land, then owned by the estate, which stretched along the High Street from Mill Street to Billet Lane. However local people, led by Augustus Smith of Ashlyns Hall, were outraged by this greedy aristocratic assault on their common rights. A gang of tough navvies from London, personally financed by Augustus Smith, travelled out to Berkhamsted one night in March 1866 and tore down over two miles of iron railings that had been erected on the orders of the Ashridge estate. Lord Brownlow's action was subsequently successfully challenged in the High Court and this attempt to enclose part of Berkhamsted Common thwarted forever.

Although large portions of ancient common land have survived into the twentieth century, there is little left of the choicer land of the manor that was once the royal estate and parkland. In 1302 a keeper called William was responsible for maintaining the royal park, for preserving the game and feeding the deer with hay in the winter. In 1335 the royal hunting park was completely fenced in by the Black Prince, who cut down hundreds of beech trees on the Common to finance the oak palings required. For many generations Berkhamsted Park provided good

Berkhamsted Common at the turn of the century.

sport and hunting for the royal family, who continued to hunt there well into the Stuart period. Following the demise of the castle, it was actually the residents of the mansion at Berkhamsted Place who maintained the parkland until it was bought from the Duchy of Cornwall in 1860. In 1627 authorisation had been granted to 'dispark' the land for agricultural purposes and the size of the park was reduced at a stroke from 1,132 to 375 acres. Gradually more and more of the parkland was taken for farming, until only a relatively small area below Berkhamsted Place survived as the Park. During the 1920's and 30's, a further portion was sacrificed to create the Castle Hill housing estate and the majority of the remaining land to the west was developed by the builder Constantine, starting with South Park Gardens in 1959. In 1914 the Inns of Court Officer Training Corps. camped and trained in the Park and the war-time name Kitchener's Field survives to this day. This small remnant of the former royal park is currently a sports ground with tennis courts and a bowling green; since 1983 it has also been home to the Berkhamsted Cricket Club.

Mills

As befits a farming town noted for its cereal production, there was once two working mills at

Berkhamsted. Upper Mill was located off Mill Street, on land subsequently redeveloped by Berkhamsted School in 1926. Its partner, Lower Mill, stood by Bank Mill Lane on a site marked today by the Old Mill House Hotel. A record of two working mills at Berkhamsted dates back to the Domesday Book, when there was also a series of other water driven corn mills, scattered along the floor of the Gade and Bulbourne valleys. In a survey of 1616, Upper Mill was said to be in the occupation of George Collins, whilst Richard Besouth was in charge at Lower Mill. William Archer is listed as the miller at Upper Mill in 1825 and by 1890 had been succeeded by Alfred Cook. It was another member of this family, George Cook and his son, who ran the mill until it closed in the 1920's. At Lower Mill William Parsons was miller in 1832; subsequently this mill was leased by the Ashridge estate to the Norris family. Lower Mill closed down earlier in 1900, not because there was insufficient work for two mills, but because the River Bulbourne was drying up at this point and there was no longer enough water to drive the wheel. A few years later there was a serious fire which destroyed much of the old building, but the great iron water wheel remained in place at Lower Mill until it was removed to help a war-time salvage campaign. There was a third much later mill,

Rear of Locke and Smith Brewery building in Water Lane, at the turn of the century.

Upper Mill in Mill Street at the turn of the century.

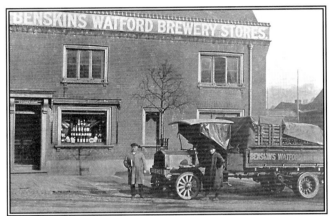

High Street frontage of Benskins Brewery, circa 1915.

which was built by the canal bridge at Lower Kings Road in 1910. This building was used for the manufacture of animal feeding stuffs by J. G. Knowles & Son, who dealt in corn forage and seeds. This mill, which also had the benefit of a small wharf for canal boats, ceased operating after the Second World War and has since been redeveloped to provide attractive canal-side office accommodation.

Brewing

Brewing, like milling, is another example of an industry which grew directly out of local farming activities. Encouraged by ready supplies of fresh water and good quality barley, both brewing and malting had taken a firm hold in the town by the sixteenth century. Pigot's Trade Directory tells us that by 1839 brewing, malting and straw plaiting had become the main industries of the town; it also reports that there were then two coopers and vat makers in Berkhamsted. Thomas Brinkman was situated in the High Street and Samuel Underwood was based in Grubbs Lane (now Chesham Road). Around 1800 John Page of the Kings Arms was brewing his own beer, using furze from the common for fuel. John Lane, who established a nursery business in the town in 1777, also had his own small brew house. In

these days it was not unusual for publicans to brew their own beer, until they found it cheaper and easier to buy from a larger locally established brewery. Initially the Swan Brewery in Chesham Road supplied only the Swan Inn. However the Foster family, the last owners of this independent brewery, expanded the business until it also supplied the Brownlow Arms and the Rose and Crown, as well as two off-licences in Berkhamsted. A second malting was located in Chapel Street and this building later became the headquarters of the local Boy Scout troop. The brewery suffered competition from larger companies until it was eventually bought out by the Chesham Brewery in 1897. Towards the end of the nineteenth century brewing was a significant industry in the town and as many as sixty men and boys were employed by local brewers in Berkhamsted. The largest of these was Locke and Smith which operated from a large brewery in Water Lane. This company supplied over forty local public houses in Berkhamsted and Northchurch including the Goat, Boat, Bell, Boot, White Hart, Stag, Crooked Billet and George and Dragon. Locke and Smith was taken over by Benskins of Watford and the old brewery at Berkhamsted eventually closed down in 1914.

Lace Making and Straw Plaiting

In the eighteenth century pillow lace making was a thriving cottage craft. An indication of Berkhamsted's importance in this industry was the issue of a trade token in 1794 by leading lace merchants Chambers, Langston, Hall & Co. This token bore the inscription: "pay at Leighton, Berkhamsted and London". Large quantities of froase lace were made by the women of Berkhamsted, until it was replaced by straw plaiting as the main cottage industry in the town during the nineteenth century. Straw plaiting was a highly successful by-product of the local agricultural emphasis on cereal production. From 1800 the large quantities of straw produced were diverted to satisfy what was becoming a heavy world-wide demand for quality straw plaits, used in the high fashion and hat industries. Weekly straw plait markets were held in Berkhamsted, Hemel Hempstead and Tring; frequented by hat merchants from Luton and Dunstable who were then entirely dependant on locally produced plaits. Straw plaiting, which could easily be done at home, only required three simple tools: a straw splitter, a splint mill and a yard measure. Usually the straw was made up into lengths of 20 yards known as scores. Several varieties of plait were used and those most generally produced for sale in Berkhamsted were called China Pearl, Rock, Coburg and Moss Edge. A good plaiter could make up to four scores a day, earning up to one pound per week. Significantly this meant that women could now earn more than their husbands who laboured all day in the fields. To further capitalise on this economic opportunity, children as young as three were sent to special plait schools which sprang up in Berkhamsted and at one time there were three such schools in Bridge Street alone. In the census of 1851 there were 441 straw plaiters recorded as working in the parish and plaiting had become the main occupation of the women in the village of Potten End. This charmed period, during which the average working family could transform their weekly income came to a rather abrupt end, with the encouragement of free trade and the repeal of protective duties in 1860. As a direct result of this legislation, imports of cheap plaits began flooding into the Country from Italy and the Far East. The enlightened social progress of the Victorian era also played a part in the decline of this industry, when the Education Act of 1870 effectively abolished the plait schools. Instead every child in the land now had the right to a basic education, offering them the opportunity of proper tuition in literacy and numeracy.

A rare photograph of local straw plaiters, circa 1890.

Timber Industry

From early days the town of Berkhamsted has always made good use of its ready supply of timber. Local craftsmen honed their skills on the nearby woodland's plentiful stock of beech and alder, woods which were comparatively soft and easy to turn. Consequently, from the days of the royal court to the beginning of this century, an endless variety of small wooden articles were manufactured locally. In the 1750's William Ellis, a leading agricultural commentator and farming pioneer from Little Gaddesden, states that: "alder poles were turned to great account amongst the Berkhamsted and Cheshunt turners of hollow ware, who in this commodity make more consumption of this wood and beech than any other two towns in Britain". He also recorded that the items then being made included dishes, bowls and many other serviceable goods including clogs, gate hurdles and small rafters. By 1792 the Universal British Directory indicates that the principal trade in Berkhamsted was now "woodworking, chiefly involving bowl turning with some shovel and spoon making". Prior to the Industrial Revolution most of this woodwork was undertaken by individual craftsmen, operating from their own small workshops. Sadly many of the old independent craftsmen in Berkhamsted, who had faithfully passed on their skills from generation to generation, were squeezed out of business when power driven machinery revolutionised the industry. During the Victorian era no less than five steam saw mills were established in the town, but at least they still offered good employment to those local woodworkers who could no longer compete with their economies of scale.

In addition to the timber required for these saw mills, there were also two coach builders in Berkhamsted, a barge building works by the canal and two coopers' yards, providing barrels for the three breweries in the town. Despite these larger industrial developments, some smaller scale activity was still possible. The 1851 census for Berkhamsted identifies several more local specialist traders such as a malt shovel maker, lath and hoop maker, plasterers' handle maker, rake maker, shaving box maker and chair maker. Brush making had also become a more significant offshoot of the local timber trade and was now employing over one hundred people in its own right. In George Street, T. H. Nash, a master brushmaker, employed up to 30 local people in a business which survived into the 1920's. His main competitor Mr. Goss owned a large brush works, coincidentally located at the western end of the High Street, near Gossoms

End. The sizeable Goss factory outlasted its rival by several years before this part of the local timber industry died out completely in the 1930's.

By the late nineteenth century Berkhamsted had become famous for its thriving and modernised timber industry. Trade had developed to the extent that there were now more than two hundred men and boys working in the local timber yards, with fifty more employed on coach works and a further sixteen building boats at Costin's yard by the canal. The man who was responsible for beginning the revolution in Berkhamsted's timber industry was Job East, a trader from Chesham, who arrived in the town in 1840 to take over a small shovel maker and turner's business. His original workshop stood on ground now occupied by today's BMG (formerly Castle's) Garage, at the western end of the High Street. Mr. East soon expanded and modernised the works, but complaints from Captain Constable Curtis of The Hall, concerning the smoke which billowed from the timber yard's new chimney, soon forced him to move his business to Gossoms End. This was probably a blessing in disguise, because his new site made it far easier to expand as the business became more successful. The onset of the Crimean War (1854-56) brought East's its first really large contract, with orders for thousands of lance poles, rammers and tent poles that were needed in this conflict. This one job alone allowed East's to employ up to one hundred extra local people and was the first of many Government contracts won by the company over the next one hundred years. By 1888, when Cornelius East was in charge, the timber yard was described as "the largest single handed business of its kind outside London".

Despite a serious fire in that same year, which destroyed the machine shop and badly damaged the beam engine, the firm's commercial momentum continued and the plant was soon repaired. The East family dynasty lasted until 1917 when Catherine East, the granddaughter of Job, sold the company to John Lenanton & Son Ltd. of Millwall, London. The original garden site was extended from $1\frac{1}{2}$ to 6 acres and the bulk of the yard's manufacturing capacity was now taken up with large Government contracts. In 1932, still trading as East & Son of Gossoms End, the company won a demanding contract to make and supply 202 lock gates, required for an extensive widening scheme on the Warwick to Birmingham section of the Grand Junction Canal. In more recent times the firm's finished timber work has made a contribution to several major buildings,

Sills' Timber Yard, in the 1890's (with John Sills standing left).

Sill's Timber Yard at the turn of the century.

such as London Airport and the Shell Centre on the South Bank in London. The yard finally closed down in the early 1990's and the area around Stag Lane is currently being redeveloped as a light industrial estate with warehousing capacity.

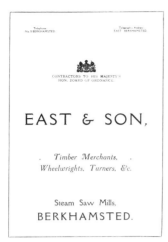

The Sills family ran another early timber yard in what is now Holliday Street and J. King established a specialist saw mill in George Street which made milk yolks, shovels, hoops, cricket bats and other similar items. However the other principal timber company in the town was Keys, first established on the site which later became Cooper's Technical Bureau and recreational ground. This business, started by William Key a former fencing contractor who had worked on the London to Birmingham Railway, was continued by his nephew Thomas Norris. In 1913 the firm's activities were transferred to a new site between Bridge Street and Castle Street, where Key's took over the old coal yard and wharf that had been used by the local coal merchant J. Hatton in the previous century. Although a smaller concern than East's, the yard flourished and continued to expand from its early days when it employed only 22 people. During the First World War the large sheds in Key's timber yard were used by the army as mess rooms, capable of accommodating up to 900 people. This business managed to continue trading into recent time as J. Alsford Ltd., who financed a modern range of buildings on the site in 1965. Only five years ago, the site was cleared and replaced by a smart modern canal-side residential development called Alsford's Wharf. Another reminder of its former industrial heritage remains close to the canal bridge in the striking form of a 27 ft. high totem pole which was brought into this country by a Director of Alsford's in June 1970. An impressive example of traditional Indian art from the north-west coast of Canada, it was carved from a single red cedar by Henry Hunt, a member of the Kwakiutl tribe.

Lane's Nurseries

Henry Lane founded his nursery business in 1777, originally specialising in hedging plants which by then were becoming very fashionable. The latter half of the eighteenth century produced a surge of interest in gardening throughout the nation and Henry Lane was able to capitalise on this to expand his business. By 1851 his son John had built large greenhouses on either side of St Johns Well Lane and was already one of the town's more significant employers, with 33 labourers on his staff. Roses and vines were added to the firm's specialities and Lane's even began exporting vines to France, Belgium and Germany. The apple, which became known as Lane's Prince Albert, offered the company its best nation-wide advertisement. This popular fruit, named in honour of a royal visit to the town on 26th July 1841, was first produced in the garden of 'The Homestead' at No 250 High Street. Its originator was an amateur gardener called Thomas Squire, who was Mr. Lane's neighbour. Unfortunately the original apple tree was cut down when The Homestead was demolished in 1958. As it prospered the firm, now known as Henry Lane & Son, expanded into three holdings: Home Nursery at Berkhamsted, Balshaw Nurseries at Potten End and Broadway Nurseries at Bourne End. In 1880 around 80 of the 140 acres then owned by Lane's were in Potten End, where the nurseries became famous for their collection of ornamental trees and shrubs. Lane & Son were adventurous pioneers, who played a major part in supporting the introduction of rhododendrons and azaleas to England. Some of these original stocks, imported from the Himalayas, can still be seen growing in various sites around the village of Potten End.

A map of Berkhamsted dated 1878 reveals that Lane & Son had already established nursery sites in the town on the west side of St Johns Well Lane, the west side of Park Street, the south side of Shrublands Road (then not built upon) and the west side of Cross Oak Road. Lane's were also using land between what was later to become Park View Road and Boxwell Road and on Canal Field they maintained a separate nursery devoted exclusively to roses. By this time several large greenhouses and the long run of wooden fencing near St Johns Well had become something of a local landmark, reinforcing the rural ambience of the town. In 1892 Lane's nurseries had reached the peak of their operations, employing over one hundred permanent staff with a further one hundred staff employed at harvest time. Although Lane's nurseries at Potten End survived until the 1950's it was really the prolonged depression

Fruit pickers at Lane's Nurseries, circa 1900.

following the First World War which prompted an irreversible decline in the prosperity of this local nursery business. A rather plain modern post office building, built in 1958, now dominates the former site of Lane & Son.

Watercress

The environment in Berkhamsted one hundred years ago was ripe for the sudden growth of another industry connected to local agriculture. Successful cress growing requires a set of very specific conditions, all of which could then be satisfied by the Bulbourne valley. A mild climate is essential combined with plentiful supplies of pure water, running at an even temperature of 50-52° Fahrenheit through shallow gravel beds. The Berkhamsted Times of 1883 congratulated Harry Bedford on converting "dirty ditches and offensive marshes into pleasing water courses, in which now grows a healthy product". The main cress beds in the town were situated between Billet Lane and St Johns Well Lane close to the river course. The abundant supplies of pure spring water then available in this area meant that the cress grown in Berkhamsted was of the highest quality. Cress was a plentiful crop which, if tended carefully, could produce up to ten yields a year. At the peak of their operations, Bedford's were sending approximately two tons of cress a

day by early morning train from Berkhamsted. There was then a high demand for good quality cress to be served fresh in the restaurants of the great hotels of London and the larger northern cities of Liverpool, Leeds and Manchester. Three generations of the Bedford family grew cress in Berkhamsted. Harry Bedford (both father and son) were succeeded by Dennis Bedford who was the last member of the family to grow cress in the town. His uncle, Frank Bedford, grew watercress at Dudswell and Northchurch. Given the rapidly dwindling supplies of natural water, the local cultivation of this highly nutritious crop did well to survive until the 1960's.

Wood's Ironworks

James Wood was raised on Marlin Chapel Farm in Northchurch, before coming to Berkhamsted to live with his family in Monks House (now Cafe Rouge) at the western end of the High Street. He was a highly skilled wire and iron worker, who in 1826 began manufacturing all kinds of ironwork in the yard adjacent to his property. Today the firm's modern premises still stands on the original site where Wood's glazed iron-framed showroom survived for over one hundred years, until it was sadly destroyed by fire in 1974. James Wood produced an innovative and varied range of ironware which included candle snuffers, rat traps, hurdles, skewers, meat safes, dish covers, cork drawers, fire guards and sieves. As his reputation for quality grew, he took on large contracts for garden greenhouses, fencing, ornamental gates and garden furniture. An important part of this business came from the leading land owners of the day and we know from surviving company records that James Wood undertook work for the Rothschild family, as well as for the Essex family at Cassiobury, the Bridgewaters at Ashridge and the Coopers at Gadebridge. However from 1849 it was Lord and Lady Brownlow, having succeeded the Bridgewaters at Ashridge, who became Wood's most important clients. James Wood died in 1861 and for a time the business was carried on by his widow, trading under the name of F. (Fanny) Wood & Son. Commercial activities are now more focused on a thriving nursery and giftware business, inheriting some of the traditions left by Lane & Son, who operated on the adjacent site now dominated by the main post office building. In 1996 Wood's celebrated 170 years of continuous trading in Berkhamsted.

Dwight's Pheasantries

It is thought that the pheasantries established at Berkhamsted in 1734 were the largest and oldest in England. Members of the Dwight family raised game in the town for many generations, with the business being handed down from father to son. William Dwight, who developed the business during the nineteenth century, was christened at St Mary's Church, Northchurch in 1843. He had three sons of his own: Percy, Sidney and Arthur, who were all educated locally at Berkhamsted School. It was Sidney who went on to live at the 'Pheasantries', a fine old house on the hill top in Ivy House Lane, whilst his brothers chose to stay at Little Heath Farm in Potten End. The arable side of the family's farms provided grain as foodstuffs for the pheasants and, although the extent of Dwight's total estates ran to several hundred acres, it was still necessary to rent additional land in the rearing season. Every year 20,000 young pheasants were raised at Berkhamsted and, in order to maintain a strain of strong and vigorous birds, a complete change of pure-breds was introduced into the stock every breeding season. Dwight's exported both pheasants and eggs in very large numbers to almost every part of the world. The success of the business is indicated by the fact that when William Dwight died, aged 74 on 18th February 1917, he left the highly impressive sum of £91,495 in his will. In 1934 the price for three thousand of

Dwight's Pheasantries, circa 1930.

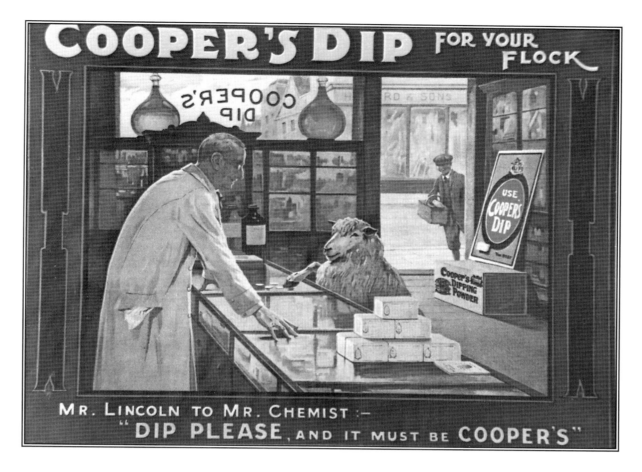

Cooper's distinctive style of advertising during the 1920's.

Dwight's pheasants eggs had reached £132, during the peak laying season April to May 12th. By the 1940's, Dwight's had three thousand brooding hens hatching pheasants' eggs and in 1965 their laying pheasants produced over 100,000 eggs in one single laying season. A modern housing development has since been built on the site of the former Pheasantries Farm at the top of Gravel Path; here construction work began on the Hunters Park housing estate in 1978.

Cooper's

William Cooper was born in Clunbury, Shropshire in 1813 and by 1843 had arrived at Berkhamsted where he established a small veterinary practice. In 1849 he became one of the first practitioners to qualify from the Royal College of Veterinary Surgeons. It is thought that at first he lived in a small cottage in Castle Street that was formerly The Sun public house, before moving to a small house in the High Street, from where he carried out a meticulous series of experiments. These mainly involved a combination of sulphur and arsenic and eventually led to the formulation of the world's most effective sheep dip. In 1852 he established a small factory in Ravens Lane, built on land he purchased from Frederick Miller who owned the Pilkington Manor estate. Here he

could manufacture his yellow powder-based dip and inside the factory there were initially horse powered mills for grinding the ingredients and great kilns for boiling up the mixture. It was this innovative sheep dip which was destined to become the foundation for one of the world's great veterinary and agricultural businesses. Steam powered machinery was introduced at Cooper's in 1864 and, as demand grew, the business expanded rapidly. A convenient dwelling place was important to a workaholic like William Cooper. He soon built Clunbury House, close to the Ravens Lane works and, as profits accumulated, the construction of Sibdon House was financed in 1869. The factory in Ravens Lane was also extended three times during the latter half of the nineteenth century. Teams of carpenters were now employed to make the boxes to carry the dip and William Cooper was one of the first manufacturers in the Country to establish his own lithographic printing works. It was the job of the Printing Department to produce the bold and distinctive labels which were to make his products uniquely identifiable.

As business continued to grow, William was joined by his nephews, William Farmer circa 1865 and Herbert Cooper in 1879. The company then traded as William Cooper and Nephews and by the time of his death, at his home 'The Poplars' in 1885, William Cooper was employing 120 men. He was sadly missed in the town because, although a strict task master, he treated his workers fairly and many employees remained with the company throughout their working lives. A team of Cooper's travelling salesmen ensured that Cooper's sheep dip enjoyed huge export markets all around the world and in 1880 a new, larger factory was built. This was called Lower Works and fronted on to the eastern end of the High Street, on a site which had formerly been Key's timber yard. To the rear of this new plant there was now a canal-side wharf, used for the unloading of the large quantities of coal, sulphur and arsenic required in the manufacturing process. In 1891 Richard Powell Cooper, who had joined the company on the death of William Farmer in 1882, became the sole owner of Cooper's and in 1898 he was joined by his eldest son, Richard Ashmole Cooper, as a partner in the business. It was R. A. Cooper who was instrumental in setting up the first Cooper's Research Laboratory in the office building at Ravens Lane. In 1905 Richard Powell Cooper was created a Baronet for services to industry. When R. A. Cooper eventually took over the business, following his father's death in 1913, he was also serving as a Member of Parliament for Walsall. Under his leadership the company continued to expand and diversify; the original factory had become offices, with manufacturing activity now centred on the newer High Street premises. By this time the family had purchased a large mansion known as Britwell, near Berkhamsted Golf Club. Built in 1906, this house had served as the last home of Sir John Evans (1823-1908) prior to being acquired after the First World War by the Cooper family who re-named it Shenstone Court.

In October 1925 Cooper's was merged with McDougall and Robertson to form the larger business of Cooper, McDougall and Robertson. From 1937 the company worked in association with I.C.I. to produce a range of horticultural products under the trade name of 'Plant Protection'. Since 1929 Coopers had also been running a programme of top quality stock breeding at Home Farm in Little Gaddesden and in 1940 a new purpose built Technical Bureau was constructed adjacent to the main factory site in the High Street. In order to maintain its position as a leader in the industry, the family home of Shenstone Court was converted for use as Berkhamsted Hill Research Station and the laboratory facilities, first established at Home Farm in the early 1930's, were moved here in 1952. The thriving printing department at Manor Street was now known as the Clunbury Press and began to undertake a variety of commercial work. During the immediate post-war period the first new synthetic insecticides began to appear and, as a result, the days of the powdered sheep dip were numbered. Production of the old powders ceased at Berkhamsted in 1952, but there was no danger of the company being left behind by its competitors, given the fact that it had invested so heavily in research and development. In fact the first aerosol filling line in the Country was designed and installed by McIntyre & Wallace in the Cooper's factory at Berkhamsted. 'Cooper's Fly Killer' and 'Household Aerosol' became successful brand names and the company soon diversified into other products like 'Freshaire' and 'Hi Fi Furniture Polish'. By 1965 the 100th million aerosol had been filled at Berkhamsted. The company had been sufficiently profitable to invest in social and recreational facilities for its workforce. Cooper's also had a thriving amateur dramatic group and back in 1922 a recreational club had been formed on land behind the newly built main factory. Here a large club house was provided in memory of R. P. Cooper and a bowling green was laid in 1932. Cooper's also ran a sports ground with facilities for cricket and tennis on Kitcheners Field at the bottom of Castle Hill.

The advent of mass production meant that Cooper's had to continue to expand to survive and in 1959 the business was acquired by the Wellcome Foundation. Following this take-over, the Cooper arm of Wellcome went on to enjoy further commercial success, with the development of anti-bacterial drugs for animals. However by 1962 much of the group's aerosol production had been switched to Kelvindale in Scotland and by the early 1970's only one in five of the Berkhamsted factory production lines was still in operation. By 1973 all former Cooper McDougall Robertson brands were being traded under the name of Wellcome. Cooper's old printing department, then called the Clunbury Cottrell Press, closed in 1979 and the Research Station at Berkhamsted Hill was sold to an American health company in the 1980's. In 1992 Wellcome sold its entire environmental health business, including the Berkhamsted site, to a French company, Roussel Uclaf. In 1995 the remaining group of Wellcome's companies were themselves acquired by Glaxo, to form what was then Britain's largest industrial concern. The Berkhamsted plant, which had been acquired in 1995 by the large chemical combine Agr-Evo UK, finally closed on 31st July 1997.

Early promotional photograph showing the use of sheep dip.

Production of sheep dip powders at Lower Works, 1953.

Cooper's delivery lorry at Lower Works, 1922.

Loaded canal boat leaving Cooper's Lower Works, 1922.

Laboratory staff at Berkhamsted Hill Research Station,1954.

Houses and Estates

Throughout the Georgian and early Victorian period, few localities attracted quite such a variety of fine houses and estates as Berkhamsted. During this time the principal demand from the wealthier and professional classes was for a pleasant rural environment, within easy reach of London. Although social conditions in Berkhamsted during the eighteenth and nineteenth centuries were very poor, this did not represent a serious disadvantage to the favoured few. Instead their estates, often with spectacular views, were carefully positioned high on the slopes of the valley, some considerable distance from the town centre. Given the widespread poverty at this time, there was also no shortage of local people prepared to take up employment, either labouring on the estate farmlands or helping to tend the extensive grounds which many of these fine houses enjoyed. There was however a fairly firm tradition of only employing indoor servants from outside the immediate area. This helped to reduce the possibility of unwanted gossip and scandalous rumours being spread amongst the common folk of the town! However many of the principal houses and estates established around Berkhamsted still have a fascinating story of their own to tell.

Ashridge

The establishment of the Ashridge estate dates back to the days of the medieval monastery, founded in the time of Edward I, and this aspect of its past is covered in an earlier chapter. Here we continue the story when the estate has been inherited by Francis Egerton, who became the Third Duke of Bridgewater at the age of eleven in 1747. Francis grew up to become a nationally important pioneer of inland waterways and although his ambitious schemes initially reduced him to a penniless state, financial success was assured when his new canals began to deliver huge savings in the cost of transporting coal and other industrial raw materials. Incoming revenues were accumulating so fast by 1796 that he was said to be earning £80,000 a year from the Bridgewater Canal alone. Flushed with success, Francis Egerton returned to Ashridge with ambitious plans to use some of his new fortune to rebuild the crumbling Ashridge mansion he had ignored for so long. However he died on the 8th March 1803, soon after his return and well before he could put his grandiose plans into effect. The 'Canal Duke' bequeathed £13,500 for a memorial obelisk to be erected, to his own design, bearing the inscription "Francis 3rd Duke of Bridgewater - Father of Inland Navigation". The monument's somewhat remote location in the parkland was dictated by Lady Bridgewater, who considered the design to be in poor taste and ensured that it was built well away from the main house. The monument is a 100 ft. Doric column, fluted in granite and has an internal spiral staircase with 172 steps leading to a viewing gallery. This offers an impressive panorama of the local countryside from 729 ft. above sea level.

Francis Egerton died without producing an heir, and much of his fortune was inherited by his cousin John Egerton, son of the Bishop of Durham, who became the 7th Earl of Bridgewater. It is perhaps fortunate that he carried out the Duke's plans for Ashridge so faithfully. All the grounds were re-landscaped under the direction of Humphrey Repton, a disciple of Capability Brown, whilst the construction of the new house was the responsibility of leading architect James Wyatt. Building work at Ashridge started in 1808 and by 1810 the main structure of the house had been completed, however much additional work remained. The new chapel at Ashridge was finished using fabulous fifteenth century glass, imported from Germany, which is now amongst the treasures kept at the Victoria and Albert Museum. The old 'holy well', formerly belonging to the monastery, was left intact beneath the south (chancel end) of the chapel. Rather unusually the walls of the well were lined with over two thousand cast iron pieces and it still has a depth of 224 ft. The interiors of the house were equally fine and had the benefit of the Canal Duke's impressive art collection, the majority of which had been purchased from the Duc D'Orleans. What is now sometimes referred to as the crypt is the only other part of the old monastic building left inside the main house. This chamber was actually the undercroft belonging to the monastery's great hall and the architect was able to utilise it in his design to provide a magnificent wine and beer cellar. By the end of 1817 further new extensions had been added to the building which doubled its length to 1000 ft. The total construction cost of the new Ashridge was in excess of £300,000 and the new frontage created was now the longest of any stately home in England. To achieve a consistent modern Gothic style, later designs and additions were made to the frontage by James Wyatt's nephew, Jeffrey Wyatville. Sir Matthew Digby Wyatt, who also worked on the restoration of Windsor Castle

Ashridge Management College in the 1960's.

Ashridge viewed from the east.

Monks' Garden at Ashridge.

Bridgewater Monument, 1937.

for George IV, remodelled the principal rooms at Ashridge between 1857 and 1863. His work, in an Italian style, featured marble fireplaces, as well as exquisitely painted ceilings with first class mouldings. He also introduced a good deal of superb panelling in Austrian walnut, some of which had been taken from the Tuileries in Paris. The decorative ceilings were the work of Francis Bernasconi, whose designs were directly inspired by the Scala D'Ora in the Doges Palace, Venice. Ashridge also had the benefit of the imposing grandeur of a modern baronial hall, whose ceilings rise to a height of nearly 100 ft.

The mansion's pleasure gardens were planned by Humphrey Repton in 1814 and included a circular rose garden and a monks' garden. As a feature to break up the level site, Repton also designed a mount garden, which was constructed using Hertfordshire pudding stone. Later additions were an Italian garden, contemporary with the Italian interiors of 1857-63, and a much more recent sunken rose garden, created by Malcolm Lingard in 1974-75. This new design now occupies the site of a former artificial lake created at Ashridge in the 1870's. Another principal feature of the estate, still enjoyed today, is the arboretum, with a formal avenue of wellingtonians, flanked by spectacular beds of richly coloured rhododendrons. The 7th Earl, who financed the construction of the new house, employed up to five hundred men helping to tend his estate and never refused work to any local man. Because of his support, he was well liked in the local community and when he died in 1823, the Duchess continued to live alone at Ashridge until her own death in 1849. As a result of the longevity of the 7th Earl's widow the 8th Earl of Bridgewater, Francis Henry Egerton, was never able to live at Ashridge and the title lapsed. The next significant figure was Lady Marion Alford, wife of Viscount Alford, who succeeded to the vacant Bridgewater estate as the 1st Earl Brownlow in 1849. However the 1st Earl died after only two years in residence at Ashridge and management of the estate then fell to Lady Alford, who remained at Ashridge until her death in 1888. It was Lady Marion who supervised the installation of the Italian style interiors of the house and she remained in authority during the minority of her eldest son's tragically short life. John William Spencer Egerton Cust, the 2nd Earl, died in 1867 at the age of 25. The second son Adelbert became the 3rd Earl Brownlow and in 1868 married Adelaide, the daughter of the 1st Earl of Salisbury. It was during the time of the 3rd Earl that Ashridge enjoyed its finest period as a fashionable high society retreat. To give some

idea of the gracious style of living then afforded at Ashridge, when in residence Lord and Lady Brownlow could call on thirty maids, two butlers and two footmen. They also employed twenty gardeners, fifteen keepers, three coachmen and seven stablemen. The house could cope comfortably with weekend parties of up to forty guests and Lord Brownlow's shooting parties often included members of the Royal Family. Queen Mary visited Ashridge, as did most of the nation's leading politicians: Benjamin Disraeli, William Gladstone and Stanley Baldwin. Country Life magazine described "one hundred acres of first class cover shooting at Ashridge, in which a team of eight guns can easily bag one thousand pheasants a day". The Shah of Persia was entertained at Ashridge in 1889 and famously Field Marshall Lord Kitchener was taking tea at Ashridge in 1914, when he received an urgent telegram informing him that war with Germany was imminent.

Countess Adelaide died in 1919 and when the 3rd Earl followed in 1921, the trustees of the estate were directed to sell Ashridge in order to meet the crippling cost of death duties. Thankfully, due to a great deal of well connected political lobbying and an anonymous donation of £20,000, a 'Save Ashridge' campaign managed to prevent the break up of the estate. This delay eventually enabled the National Trust to acquire 3,500 acres of the Ashridge parklands. In 1928 the house and 250 acres was bought by Mr. Urban Broughton. Together with J. C. C. Davidson, M.P. for Hemel Hempstead, he established a residential college at Ashridge, which became affiliated to the Conservative Party and known as Bonar Law College. During the Second World War Ashridge became an emergency annexe for both University College and Charing Cross Hospital in London and temporary ward blocks were erected in front of the house to cater for up to 1200 injured service men. Approximately 100 acres were leased to the Ashridge Golf Club in 1932 and the newly designed course was skilfully blended into the surrounding parkland. The first President of the Ashridge Golf Club was the 6th Earl of Roseberry (1932-74) and Henry Cotton, one of the greatest English golfers this century, was employed as the club's resident professional (1937-46). After the war, the house returned to its former role and the old ward blocks to the front of the mansion were then used to provide additional storage for the Public Record Office at Kew. In 1959 the College at Ashridge was finally shorn of its party political affiliations and is now an independent and prestigious management college, which enjoys an international reputation.

Berkhamsted Place

Sir Edward Carey, Keeper of the Jewels to Queen Elizabeth I, was granted the Manor of Berkhamsted in 1580. The Queen had rather playfully leased him the old ruined castle, at the nominal rent of one red rose, payable yearly on St John the Baptist's Day. Sir Edward built himself a fine mansion at the top of the hill, overlooking the castle and used much of the old stonework from its ruins in the construction of his new house. However in 1588 Sir Edward also took possession of the Manor of Aldenham and decided to live there instead, so his brother Sir Adolphus Carey became the first tenant of Berkhamsted Place. He in turn was succeeded by his son Sir Henry Carey, who later became Lord Falkland. The house was then used by various members of his family until it was purchased in 1612 by Henry, Prince of Wales for £4000. From Prince Henry the house eventually passed to his brother, Prince Charles (later King Charles I) who leased the property to his tutor and nurse, Thomas and Mary Murray. On 14th August 1616 Prince Charles visited the Murrays and spent the afternoon hunting in Berkhamsted Park. Their daughter Anne Murray (later Lady Halkett) became involved in a Royalist plot to save the young Duke of York and, following the execution of Charles I, fled from Berkhamsted Place fearing for her life. She was succeeded at the house by one of her natural opponents, Daniel Axtell, a ruthless Berkhamsted born soldier in Cromwell's army. Axtell succeeded in fighting his way up to become Lieutenant Colonel in a regiment of foot soldiers at the tender age of 26. However the pendulum of fate swung again when he was beheaded at Tyburn in 1660 and Anne Murray was later rewarded for her loyalty with a royal pension granted by James I. On the north wall of the chancel of St Peter's Church there is a beautiful monument to the memory of James and John Murray, "youths of the most winning disposition who lived and died at Berkhamsted Place".

In 1660 Berkhamsted Place was leased to the Lord Treasurer, the Earl of Portland and it was during his occupancy that two thirds of the mansion was destroyed by fire. The old house, which was faced with flints and Totternhoe stone in chequers seven inches square, was probably more attractive prior to this fire. However the substantial reconstruction work, financed by the next owner John Sayer, did manage to retain some of the original highly decorative flint and stone chequerwork on the north wall. John Sayer

Engraving of Berkhamsted Place, dated 1856.

Northern aspect of Berkhamsted Place, 1892.

Frontage of Berkhamsted Place, 1892.

Dining Room at Berkhamsted Place, 1950.

Hall Lounge of Berkhamsted Place, 1950.

was another favoured member of the Royal Court, being Chief Cook to Charles II. He was a very wealthy man and became a leading benefactor to the town. On his death in 1681 he left the substantial sum of £1,000 in trust "for the building of an alms house and the purchasing of lands for the relief of the poor in Berkhamsted St. Peter". His widow supervised the construction of a single storey almshouse, which then consisted of twelve rooms for the habitation of six poor widows. Each widow received two shillings a week and an allowance for fuel. These charming little cottages, with their lattice windows, are easy to find on the south-west of the High Street near Cowper Road and still bear an inscription which reads, "The Gift of John Sayer 1684".

From the Sayer family, Berkhamsted Place passed in 1716 to William Attwell and in 1718 he sold the property to John Roper, whose family remained in residence for almost one hundred years. The house then became home to another of Berkhamsted's great benefactors, General John Finch and his wife. Together they helped to rebuild the Bourne School and generously supported the Town Hall fund. The attractive avenue of lime trees that used to lead up the hill to Berkhamsted Place first appear on an old print of 1724 and may well have been re-planted by

General Finch. Following his tenure, the house then became the fashionable residence of Lady Sarah Spencer and Gertrude, Countess of Pembroke. Amongst their guests at Berkhamsted Place were the Duke of York (later George V) and the Prime Minister, Mr. Gladstone. After this period Berkhamsted Place became home to Mr. S. J. Ram K.C., who was followed by his son Sir Granville Ram, the First Parliamentary Counsel to the Treasury in 1937. However several years after the Second World War the house, which then offered nine bedrooms, three bathrooms and five staff bedrooms on the upper floor, was empty and up for sale. Maintenance costs for such a large property were now prohibitive and the mansion was converted into flats during the 1950's. However despite this investment the house once again ceased to be occupied in 1963. Berkhamsted Place was then left to fall into a state of such dereliction that its eventual demolition in 1967 was inevitable. For many years the surviving seventeenth century wing of Berkhamsted Place, 'Ash', was home and studio to the eminent sculptor, Reg Butler. He first achieved international recognition in 1953 when his sculpture, 'Unknown Political Prisoner', was awarded the Grand Prize in an open competition promoted by the Institute of Contemporary Art in London.

Ashlyns Hall

As early as 1314 Ashlyns Hall was listed as the home of a Robert Asselyn and it has been known as Ashlyns ever since. During the reign of Charles II this estate was home to Francis Wethered, who was then Comptroller of Works to the King. In 1764 Ashlyns passed to the Dorrien family when it was sold in Chancery for the sum of £4620. The estate then included nine acres of woodland and over 200 acres of arable and meadowland, in addition to gardens and orchards. The original manor house was replaced, towards the end of the eighteenth century, by the larger more distinctive mansion which survives today. This building features a Welsh slate roof and on its south-west gabled front there is a semi-circular bow with first floor cast iron verandah. In 1801 James Smith, a member of a leading Nottinghamshire banking family, bought the newly refurbished Ashlyns as his family home. Following the death of his first wife, he married a young woman called Mary Isabella Pechell, who was then living at Berkhamsted Place. She bore him five children, the eldest of whom, Augustus Smith, was born in 1804. Augustus was raised in Berkhamsted and, although he later settled at Tresco Abbey in the Scilly Isles, he remained very fond of the town. Augustus Smith played a leading role in the foundation of the town's first elementary school and was also instrumental in the revival of Berkhamsted School. Although he became M.P. for Truro in 1857, he retained a key interest in Berkhamsted's affairs. He was particularly outraged when he learnt that Lord Brownlow of Ashridge had enclosed 34 acres of Berkhamsted Common with iron railings and he personally financed the successful resistance to this attempt at enclosure of common land. When Augustus Smith died in 1872, a memorial fund was established which every year awarded annual book prizes to local school children.

Another notable resident of Ashlyns Hall was William Longman, who moved to Berkhamsted from Chorleywood in 1859. William's father, Thomas Norton Longman III, was the outstanding publisher of his time. William Longman died in 1877, aged 64, and Ashlyns subsequently became home to the Cooper and Kingsley families. In 1929 the bulk of the estate was bought by the Foundling Hospital, which later became Ashlyns School. For over 25 years there has been a nursing home for the elderly at Ashlyns Hall, built in the grounds of the former vegetable garden. The house itself has since been refurbished to provide deluxe business accommodation.

Ashlyns Hall 1977.

Haresfoot

A house was built at Haresfoot at the end of the eighteenth century. We know that the new house at Haresfoot very likely replaced a much older and smaller structure, because there is a mention of both 'Haresfordeshende' and 'Harefotehull' in early local documents, dated 1287 and 1357 respectively. The estate had much in common with Ashlyns Hall because it too became home to members of a wealthy banking family. Haresfoot was purchased by John Dorrien, whose father George Dorrien was Governor of the Bank of England 1818-19. The history of the two houses was to become inextricably linked when Robert Algernon Smith, the brother of Augustus Smith of Ashlyns Hall, married the granddaughter of John Dorrien. Robert later changed his name to Smith Dorrien and fathered fifteen children at Haresfoot. In 1851 the house had twelve servants to help cope with this growing family. Robert's eleventh child, born at Haresfoot in 1858, grew up to be General Sir Horace Dorrien Smith who distinguished himself as a military leader, first in the Boer War and then later in the terrible conflict of 1914-18. Following the Smith-Dorrien's, Haresfoot was home to another leading land-owning family in west Hertfordshire, the Blackwells. During the Second World War the old house was used to store art treasures for a major London gallery and was still standing in 1953. Nicholas Pevsner then described Haresfoot as a late Georgian house with five bays, noted for their stucco work. A portrait of Samual Smith, the noted goldsmith, then hung at the house. Unfortunately the old property at Haresfoot was damaged by fire no less than seven times after the war and a completely new house was built in 1962. In yet another link with its neighbour Ashlyns, the house and estate also became home to a local school. The independent school of Haresfoot was founded here, initially as a junior school only in 1985.

Amersfort

A house called Amersfort was commissioned by the Cohen banking family and built on Berkhamsted Common in 1911 by the architect Edward Willmott. The layout of the gardens was subject to a separate commission awarded to the leading designer of her day, Gertrude Jeykll. With Jeykll's reputation now secure, the gardens of Amersfort are becoming recognised as significant, being virtually unchanged from her original design. The Cohen family continued to live at Amersfort until 1960, when the house became a commune. In 1989 Amersfort was acquired to house the senior pupils of the expanding independent school at Haresfoot.

Rossway

The name 'Rossway' means a clearing and first appears in local documents dated 1432. It was then only a small manor of fifty acres located in the parish of Northchurch. By the early Stuart period, it was held by members of the Wethered family, who had been living at Ashlyns Hall for generations. By 1616 it was still a relatively small tenement, called Pratt's Place, owned by Russell Webb. This early property was later replaced by a farmhouse, which in turn was then enlarged to make a sizeable country seat. Rossway was purchased in 1802 by Robert Sutton, a London based mercer, who set about enlarging the estate and by the time of his death in 1848, it had grown to 570 acres. From Mr. Sutton, Rossway passed to Charles Stanton Hadden who purchased the estate of 577 acres for £34,500 in 1863. He built a new mansion close to the old house in 1866, however only 18 years later economic disaster struck the Haddens, when an outbreak of disease wiped out the family's extensive coffee plantations in Ceylon. The family could no longer afford to live on the estate and consequently Rossway was leased to George Frederick McCorquodale, the head of a large printing firm. However by 1903 the Hadden family were able to return to their country seat, when ownership was transferred by Charles Hadden to his distinguished son, Major General Sir Charles Frederick Hadden. The General and Lady Hadden soon began to play a full part in the social life of Berkhamsted and also succeeded in enlarging the estate to 1100 acres.

In 1949, following the death of Lady Hadden, Rossway passed to the General's son, Major Adrian Hadden Paton, who together with his wife continued the family's tradition of active involvement in the town's affairs. Major Adrian accepted the honour of being President of Berkhamsted's historic floodlit Pageant, held at the Castle to commemorate the 900th anniversary of the Norman invasion of Britain. During the 1960's Rossway was a frequent backdrop for many of the popular television series of the day and episodes of The Saint, The Avengers and Father Brown, as well as Harry Worth's and Jimmy Edward's comedy programmes, were all filmed at the house. Rossway is now a unique example of a leading local estate which has survived into modern times and remains in family hands. Major Adrian's son Nigel, together with his wife Bumble Hadden Paton, are now busy re-developing Rossway as a conference centre. It also offers a variety of top class accommodation for a range of business and family functions, as well as sporting and recreational facilities.

C. S. Hadden and family at the newly-built Rossway, 1863.

Rear of Haresfoot, 1908.

Rear view of Amersfort, 1998.

View of Pilkington Manor in Berkhamsted High Street, circa 1908.

Pilkington Manor

Despite its listing as a manor house of Berkhamsted, Pilkington Manor was situated too close to the town centre to be able to compete, in prestige terms, with the exceptionally fine houses elsewhere on the slopes of the valley. Despite this disadvantage, it was still home to some of the town's wealthiest families during the nineteenth century. The name Pilkington is mentioned in a local survey dated 1616 and the estate, established around this old manorial site, at one time stretched from the High Street to White Hill and from Castle Street to Ravens Lane. The building which survived into the twentieth century was an eighteenth century property and in 1775 Pilkington Manor, together with outbuildings, gardens, fish ponds and 13½ acres of meadowland were let to Samuel Simmons on a fourteen year lease for £70 per annum. By this time the house was of sufficient importance that a pew and vault were reserved at St Peter's Church for whoever was living at Pilkington Manor. Early in the nineteenth century, ownership of the estate passed from a London brewer named Joseph Kirkman to Charles Gordon, who made his fortune in Jamaica at the height of the slave trade. The house at this time had a large and impressive walled garden, stretching as far as the marsh in the valley where

there was also a large ornamental lake suitable for boating. When Gordon died in 1829, Pilkington Manor was bought by Frederick Miller who by 1852 had decided to take a profit on his investment and sell off a large part of the estate. The land of Pilkington Manor, which had previously been enclosed by a 12 ft. high wall, was then available for residential development. This enabled houses to be built in Ravens Lane, Chapel Street and Manor Street etc. In addition to helping satisfy the town's growing need for new housing, the sale also provided the site for the original Cooper's factory works. Some of the land was also used as a graveyard for the large Congregational Church on the corner of Chapel Street, of which Mr. Miller became a substantial benefactor. The rather elegant white house still in the High Street, which is now home to the Dower Gallery, is said to be the former dower house of Pilkington Manor. The estate's coachman used to live in the property which is now the corner shop in Castle Street and the head gardener's house later became the newsagent and sweet shop, further down the road opposite Berkhamsted School. The old manor house was demolished in 1959 and the site has since been re-developed to provide a run of modern shops which features, at its western end, the Happy Valley Beijin Restaurant.

Kingshill

The original structure of Kingshill, which later became known as Ernest Lindgren House, dates back to the seventeenth century. A large irregular two storey house, facing north, it was altered with wings to the north-west and north-east in the eighteenth century. Something of an architectural hotch-potch, it also has various nineteenth century additions, with a lower range extending to the south which is said to have been the ballroom for the once great house. Formerly one of the leading estates on the southern side of the valley, hundreds of acres of Kingshill land were eventually sold for development in 1888 and 1897. The break up of the Kingshill estate helped to provide many building plots for the rapid expansion of Berkhamsted that occurred during the late Victorian era. In 1886 Mrs. Lionel Lucas of Kingshill earned the town's eternal gratitude when, in order to protect it from development, she purchased Butts Meadow and presented it to the people of Berkhamsted. By her actions, she saved this important historic recreational space for the benefit of all. The site of the original butts in the meadow, where medieval archers once stood to practise, could still be found until 1932 when the meadow was levelled as a playing field. The old house of Kingshill, together with its stables, outhouses and adjoining farm buildings has since become home to the National Film Archive, run by the British Film Institute. The premises were officially opened on 28th May 1968 by Gwyneth Dunwoody M.P. and already holds a collection of over 300,000 films. Currently staff at the Archive work to ensure that old and important footage survives, by duplicating approximately three million feet of old nitrate film every year. Although initially named Ernest Lindgren House after a member of the British Film Institute, the establishment at Kingshill is now called The J. Paul Getty Jr. Conservation Centre, in respect of substantial endowments received from this leading benefactor of the arts. Recently in February 1997, the National Film Archive was successful in seeking a further £13,875,000 lottery grant which should ensure that its important work at Berkhamsted will continue.

The Hall

The Hall was a large but rather plain Georgian mansion, with a substantial estate, which in the earlier part of this century dominated the eastern approach to the town. The house had extensive cellars and earlier writers have documented a long standing local tradition that the house was

The Hall, circa 1910.

Kingshill as seen from the garden, 1998.

built on the foundations of a much earlier structure, which was used as a Royalist prison during the Civil War (1642-1661). Although the mansion itself was rather grey and gaunt, the Hall had magnificent gardens which were well hidden behind high brick walls. During its hey-day the estate provided employment to many local people, no more so than when the Hall was home to Thomas Halsey M.P. and his family. In 1851 they employed an indoor staff comprising a butler, footman, coachman, groom, housekeeper, cook, nurse, dairymaid, two laundry maids and two house maids. This was in addition to the significant gang of labourers and gardeners they also employed to tend the estate lands. Waverley House, next to the former Black Horse Inn, was home to the butler at the Hall, whilst the cottages opposite provided accommodation for some of the estate's gardeners and labourers. From the mid-Victorian period the Hall was home to the Curtis family; first Captain Constable Curtis and then his son the Rev. H. G. Constable Curtis, who was Rector of Berkhamsted in 1902-8. The internal accommodation in the Hall was truly impressive, offering both entrance and lounge halls, study and morning room, billiard room and no fewer than seventeen bedrooms. The Hall later became home to Mr. Edward Greene who was the brother of C. H. Greene, Headmaster of

Berkhamsted Boys School 1910-27. After the First World War much of the Hall's land was sold to provide badly needed council housing and this construction work was soon followed by the extensive private development of Hall Park Gardens, on estate land further to the east. Prior to this building work, the only property then standing on Swing Gate Lane was an attractive flint house, which was home to the head gardener. The final years of the house itself were spent as the preparatory department of Berkhamsted School. Although perfectly suited to this role, unfortunately the structure of the house became badly affected by dry rot. Finally the Hall was sold in 1937 and subsequently demolished.

Millfield

Overlooking the town from the southern side of the valley, Millfield was a late Georgian/early Victorian style structure, which took the form of a large square property with imposing chimneys, dormer windows and a Welsh slate roof. The house offered at least ten bedrooms and was situated in over six acres of garden, which featured an attractive rose terrace and two ornamental lily ponds. There were a further twelve acres of grassland and the grounds of Millfield originally stretched from what today is Gilpins Ride to the bottom of Gravel Path. From

View from the lawns of Millfield, circa 1920.

the first half of the nineteenth century the house was owned by members of the wealthy Pearson family, who soon established themselves as the Squires of the Sunnyside district of Berkhamsted. Edwin James Pearson, son of Sir Edwin Pearson and Emily Margaret Pearson (nee Valpy), was the first member of the family to be born at Millfield in 1842. In the latter part of his life he served as Churchwarden to the Rector of Sunnyside, until his death in 1906.

In its heyday five servants were employed at Millfield, which had its own stables, garages, grape and peach house, in addition to two other greenhouses. There were also two lodge houses and a coach house, with living quarters for the chauffeur and coach driver. A principal feature of the property was a huge glass verandah which stretched for over sixty feet, along the southern side of the house. The last resident of Millfield was Miss Mabel Anne Pearson who maintained an impressive collection of paintings at the house which included some work by the leading eighteenth century Spanish artist Francisco Goya. Miss Pearson also owned a splendid Rolls Royce which featured in the Automobile Show at Olympia in 1936. Miss Pearson, like her father, was a great supporter of Sunnyside Church and regular patron of the Sunday School. Following

the death of Miss Pearson, at the age of 88 on 22nd December 1957, Millfield was demolished.

Highfield House
Highfield House, which dated from the late eighteenth century, was a two storey structure, which featured plum and red chequered brickwork and a Welsh slate roof. This substantial house stood overlooking what was then a shorter Highfield Road, at the top of which was a tradesman's entrance to the estate. The main carriage drive serving the house was then accessed from Three Close Lane. At this time both Highfield Road and Victoria Road were cul-de-sacs and their extension was made possible when Highfield House and its many outbuildings were pulled down in the 1930's. The census of 1831 reveals that five servants were employed at Highfield House, then owned by John Hyde. A surviving plan of 1867 shows an impressive and well managed property, which then had the benefit of cottages, a coach house, stables and a harness room, laundry and billiards room, a paddock, lawn, vinery and large kitchen gardens. At this time Mr. Alfred Compigné lived on the estate. The last occupant of Highfield House was Mr. J. Whittal, prior to its demolition to make way for more housing. Another local estate had thereby fallen prey to local property developers.

Egerton House

It is now difficult to believe that Egerton House, with its attractive frontage, once stood on Berkhamsted High Street on the site of the now derelict Rex Cinema. What was originally a small but delightful Elizabethan mansion, at one time had gardens and orchards which stretched up the hillside towards the Ashlyns estate. In 1627 Edward Kellett of Egerton House was one of four leading property owners in the town and later Dr. Robert Brabant, Rector of St Peter's 1681-1722, owned the house in addition to Harriotts End Farm. Surviving land documents reveal that in 1757 a Mr. Lyttleton of Egerton House paid eight shillings for the orchard. Given its name, other early owners of the property could well have been members of the Egerton family, who are likely to have used it as a dower house for the Ashridge estate. In 1840 Egerton House was purchased for the sum of £700 by local Wesleyan Methodists, who opened it as a preaching house on June 20th 1841. However by 1846 it had been sold again for that same sum to Dr. Thomas Whately who lived there until his death in 1868. Egerton House was a two storey house with attics and between three distinctive gables it displayed two small gabled dormer windows and a steeply pitched tiled roof. The house was sold by auction at the Kings Arms on 3rd September 1895, with the property then offering three sitting rooms, a dining room, billiard room and conservatory, four bedrooms and four boxrooms, stabling and a large garden. Also included was Egerton Cottage for the gardener and a coach house which was approached from Rectory Lane. In 1904 Arthur Llewellyn Davis, his wife and five sons came to live at Egerton House. There is still a statue at the family's previous home in Kensington Park Gardens, which commemorates the occasion when the author J. M. Barrie first met two of Arthur's sons. These boys were to provide the inspiration for his famous tale of Peter Pan, which was a great success when first performed as a play at the Duke of York Theatre, London in 1904. Housed in the Rex Cinema, which replaced Egerton House on the site in 1938, was a commemorative plaque, unveiled by the actress Jane Asher on 14th February 1979. At the time Miss Asher was playing the title role of Peter Pan at the Shaftsbury Theatre in London. When the house was demolished some of its fine oak panelling was saved and transferred to the house called Four Oaks in Graemesdyke Road. Some panelling from Egerton House was also installed at Boxwell House, which was then the Rural District Council Office.

Egerton House, 1936.

The Red House

This red brick structure stands on the site of an earlier timber framed building and dates from the eighteenth century. It features a fine porch with Ionic columns and pediment, and large Venetian window above. One of the first occupants of the Red House was the Rev. George Nugent of Baldock who bequeathed £1000 to enable the town to build an improved workhouse in 1831. By 1841 the house was owned by a leading local Quaker, James Field. He let the house to the seemingly respectable John Tawell, who ingratiated himself into Berkhamsted society, only to be later uncovered as a fraud and a murderer. John Tawell was hanged at Aylesbury in 1845 for poisoning his former lover Sarah Hart with arsenic. James Field later sold the house to another wealthy local Quaker, Joseph Robinson, who pulled down the baker's shop next door and built an adjoining property. This became known as the White House and was built to house his sons, whilst his daughters lived in the Red House. Following the death of Joseph Robinson in 1883, the two houses, if they were ever joined, were certainly separated. The Red House then became home to William Paxton who was brother to Joseph Paxton, head gardener to the Duke of Devonshire at Chatsworth House. By 1898 the Red House was the residence of Canon Norman of Durham Cathedral. During the First World War Lieutenant Colonel F. H. L. Errington lived at the house, where he was succeeded by his son Mr. R. E. Errington. In 1946 the Red House became a smart private hotel, before conversion into attractive flats and offices now used by B. P. Saunders & Co. Ltd, Insurance Brokers.

Boxwell House

The structure of Boxwell House which survives today is a broad, three bay designed house built circa 1700. In 1757 the property was conveyed from Joseph and Elizabeth Knowles to Mrs Winnifred and Anne Noyes. By 1840 Boxwell House was to home to the curate of St Peter's Church, the Rev. James Caufield Brown. On Boxing Day 1843 the Rev. Brown sold the house to the notorious James Tawell who had earlier rented the Red House. The next owner was a wealthy local Quaker called Sarah Littleboy, but by 1879 the greater part of the estate had been sold for housing. In 1913 Boxwell House was purchased by Dr. Porter and subsequently sold to Dr. J. J. Rowlands in 1932, who lived and practised there until his retirement in 1963. The property was then used by the Berkhamsted Rural District Council and is now the offices of a leading firm of local solicitors, Harrowell and Atkins, established in 1948.

Cross Oak

Before the turn of the century this mansion was the family home of Mr. J. Berlein, the former Chairman of the Transvaal Gold Fields Ltd. and was later owned by Lieutenant Colonel and Mrs R. Humphrey Haslam. Cross Oak was built circa 1800 with some late Victorian extensions, however the farmhouse and outbuildings on the estate were much older than the main house and dated from the seventeenth century. This old farmstead could well have been built on an early site which provided a home to Robert de Cruce, who is mentioned in local documents dated 1307. Although it is possible that the name Cross Oak dates from this character, the long standing local belief is that the estate took its name from an ancient oak tree which formerly stood at the corner of Gillams Lane (later Cross Oak Road) and Shootersway. According to local legend, this tree was reported to have magical powers which could, for example, cure the old trembling disease known as 'ague'. Anyone suffering from this condition needed to first bore a hole in the tree trunk, peg a lock of hair into the hole, and then move suddenly away leaving the hair behind. Following the sale of Kitsbury Farm in 1868, the lands to the east of what is now Cross Oak Road were also sold in order to keep pace with the fast growing demand for new housing.

Although it is regrettable that many of these once fine properties are no longer with us today, it was the break up and sale of these estate lands between 1850 and 1950 that was to facilitate the urban development of Berkhamsted. During this time many hundreds of acres were gradually released to allow for the building of the numerous housing estates that were then required by a fast expanding population. The economic prosperity of the twentieth century, which fuelled this population growth, ensured that the benefits of social progress would be more equally distributed amongst the people of the town. However some legacy of the local gentry still lives on. In building up and maintaining such large holdings of land, they were protecting the natural environment, sustaining and enhancing the quality of the local countryside. For example, without the benefit of the Ashridge estate, it is doubtful whether what is now thousands of acres of invaluable National Trust land would have escaped the attention of the late Victorian property developers. Equally the Hadden Paton's Rossway estate is a rare example of a large holding which survives today, thereby safeguarding many acres of rolling countryside which still honours Berkhamsted's long standing rural and agricultural tradition.

Town Development

For much of the Victorian era Berkhamsted remained no more than a shabby run-down country town. It was during this period that the gradual effects of an improved transport infrastructure and new local industries, offering additional employment, first took hold. At the beginning of the nineteenth century Berkhamsted was still only a relatively small community of 1,690 inhabitants, but by 1851 this total had doubled to a population figure of 3,395, recorded in the census of that year. The largest increase in population occurred between 1831 and 1841, a period noted for the construction of the railway, the opening of two elementary local schools and the revival of Berkhamsted School. There was still appalling overcrowding, with almost the entire working population concentrated in a small area around the Parish Church. Apart from the workhouse in the shabby west end of town, most townsfolk still lived in a tight central quarter around the High Street, Castle Street, Mill Street, Water Lane, Back Lane and the Wilderness. At this time, with the exception of a few significant mansions and farm houses, there were hardly any properties built on the hillside south of the High Street and fewer still on the north side of the Bulbourne valley. Important

changes to the structure of local government, which helped stimulate improved standards of housing and fresh development in the town, did not take place until the end of the century. However, looking back, it is possible to recognise that the destruction of the old Market House and its replacement by an impressive Town Hall, marked the symbolically defining moment in the re-birth of the town's good fortunes.

Town Hall

Two months after the old Market House burnt down, a public meeting was held at the Kings Arms on 26th February 1856 to discuss provision of a new civic building "suitable for the increasing prosperity of the town". A leading grocer, William Hazell, had obtained a suitable site in the centre of the High Street at the cost of £823 and public subscriptions were invited to help finance an ambitious new building. In addition to a market house and corn store, this was also to house a town hall, a reading room for the Mechanics Institute, a magistrates chamber and several committee rooms. When completed the original building had cost £3291, with voluntary subscriptions contributing an impressive £2610 towards this total. Various

Berkhamsted Town Hall, circa 1915.

members of the local aristocracy such as Lord Brownlow, General Finch, Lady Alford and Mrs. Smith-Dorien had all contributed substantial sums to the fund and the majority of the shortfall was then made good from the proceeds of a Grand Bazaar, held in the castle grounds. The Town Hall was officially opened in August 1860 and, in order to protect the endowment made by the general public of Berkhamsted, the administration of the Hall was placed in the hands of a committee of trustees, to be elected annually by rate payers.

The distinctive design of the building was the subject of a competition won by a London based architect, Edward Buckton Lamb, whose decoratively carved initials can still be seen over the main entrance of the Town Hall. Later in his career Edward Lamb became a highly distinguished architect, who often took charge of the remodelling of historic churches and substantial country houses. One of his best known commissions being the re-modelling of Hughenden Manor for the Disraeli family. Berkhamsted Town Hall remains one of the few public buildings he ever designed and certainly the only one in such a decoratively Gothic style. The Town Hall was distinguished by a double staircase to the main hall and the unusual structure of the roof is the only one of its kind in Hertfordshire. In 1888 the Town Hall Committee purchased the two shops directly to the west of the Town Hall, in addition to land to the rear, on which the Session Halls and the Mechanics Institute's billiard room were built in 1890. Initially the main hall was used for the sale of corn and other produce, whilst the Institute rooms were home to a library and hosted many educational lectures. All council meetings were held in the Town Hall and over time it also became a popular venue for amateur dramatic performances, exhibitions, dinner dances and other social events. The Session Halls served as the magistrates' court for the town until the Civic Centre was built in 1938 and the Town Hall clock, one of the town's most familiar sights, was erected by public subscription. It was installed as a memorial to Thomas Read, who served the town for many years as Honorary Surveyor and died in 1897.

During the 1940's and 50's the building fulfilled a number of different roles supporting the local community. The Town Hall served as school classrooms and a British Restaurant during war time and later housed a parcel sorting office and public library. However these uses all took their toll on its physical condition and by the 1960's it

became obvious that the building was in serious need of repair and restoration. Unfortunately the necessary finances were not made available and because of this the Town Hall had to be closed in 1972. Despite its status as a Grade II listed building, it was the declared intention of the Dacorum District Council to demolish the Town Hall in 1975. This plan caused a huge public outcry, with the protest joined by national preservation societies and leading Berkhamstedians such as Graham Greene, Sir Hugh Greene and Antony Hopkins. A Rescue and Action Group was formed and early in 1979 the responsibility for the Town Hall was handed over by the town council to an interim group of trustees. These trustees were instrumental in first saving the building and then supporting the urgently needed programme of repairs and restoration. Under the auspices of the Charity Commission, the Berkhamsted Town Hall Trust was formally established on 12th February 1981 and the ground floor of the building has since been converted into an attractive shopping arcade, which opened in December 1983. The large hall above the arcade has been beautifully restored and the stalwart group of trustees have now been entirely vindicated by their hard fought success in safeguarding such a magnificent architectural asset in the very heart of the town. In October 1998, the Chairman of the Berkhamsted Town Hall Trust, Ken Sherwood, was able to announce that further progress was now possible, given the award of a £250,000 grant from the Heritage Lottery Fund. These new monies will enable further restoration work to be carried out, including a re-opening of the old Institute Rooms which have remained derelict since the early 1920's. Amongst other plans the ground floor shopping area is shortly due to be converted into impressive new accommodation for Caffe Uno, an Italian Restaurant.

Housing Development
The first significant expansion of housing stock took place at the eastern end of the town and was made possible by the sale of the Pilkington Manor estate in 1852. This created space for some industrial development and an entire new residential neighbourhood. On the opposite (southern) side of the High Street the break up of the Highfield House estate created further opportunities to provide new housing. It was during the period 1840-70 that this first phase of Berkhamsted's modern development took place, when the railway also brought with it many fresh commercial possibilities. In order to meet the basic housing needs of hundreds of new factory workers, several new residential streets soon

View of Berkhamsted from Gravel Path, circa 1860, prior to late Victorian housing development.

Charles Street, circa 1910.

Kitsbury Road, circa 1910.

*The corner of Cross Oak Road,
looking along Charles Street, 1897.*

Construction of Torrington Road, circa 1890.

appeared. These included Highfield Road and Victoria Road, as well as Bridge Street, Chapel Street, Manor Street, Ravens Lane, George Street and Holliday Street.

Following the sale of the large farming estate of Kitsbury in 1868, housing development could also begin in the west of the town. In addition to what is now Kitsbury Road, the land secured in the sale included farming meadows to the east of Gilhams Lane (now Cross Oak Road). This became more of a middle class area, where larger villas were built for the professional men and their families, now being attracted to Berkhamsted by its good schools and fast train service into London. In Victorian times the Kitsbury housing estate was regarded as the 'new town', because of the run of fields and meadows which, at that time, still separated it from the densely packed town centre. Over the next sixty years the progress of the house building, which began in Kitsbury, gradually extended eastwards towards the middle of the town. This expansion began with the development of the Boxwell estate in 1879 and continued with the sale of Steele's Meadow in 1887. A total of 108 plots were created with frontages onto new residential streets at Cowper Road, Torrington Road,

Montague Road and part of Charles Street. Most of the land between Charles Street and the High Street was now built upon and, with demand still increasing, there was no option but to spread further development higher up the valley slope. In 1888 the first part of the Kingshill estate, stretching from Kings Road to Cross Oak Road, was sold and a further part of the estate, which included what is now Doctors Commons Road, then became available eleven years later in 1897.

The town of Berkhamsted was now becoming economically prosperous again and attracting an ever increasing number of new residents, many of whom were commuting into London to work. Lower Kings Road was built by public subscription in 1885, in order to provide a more direct route to the new and enlarged railway station which had been built in 1875. Previously Castle Street had offered the only access, but whichever route was taken to the station there was still no avoiding the strong stench of a notorious open sewer, known as the Black Ditch, which was located close to the canal. If Berkhamsted was to continue its successful return to prosperity, now was the time for the civic authorities to invest significant amounts of money in public services.

Laying mains drainage in the High Street, circa 1898.

Berkhamsted Gas Works in Billet Lane, 1933.

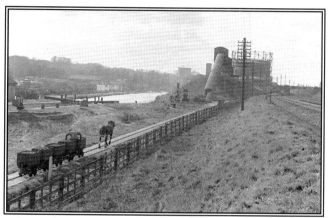

Horse-drawn coal delivery to Berkhamsted Gas Works, 1955.

Berkhamsted Water Tower near Shootersway, 1998.

Public Services

Gas light made its first appearance at Berkhamsted in 1849 when the local gas company was formed and the townspeople collected the sum of £106 as a contribution towards the street lights and piping. This meant that the Vestry only had to pay for the gas itself and any necessary maintenance work from the rates. Berkhamsted's gas supply was originally manufactured at a gas works located at the junction of Water Lane and the Wilderness. Although the coal originally arrived in Berkhamsted by canal boat, when the railway took over this important freight delivery a single track was laid from the station sidings to the gas works. In 1906 the gas works moved to Billet Lane and it was here that a faithful old horse called Ruby was employed to haul the coal in five small wagons. Ruby was succeeded by a small diesel engine which remained in service until the Berkhamsted Gas Works closed in August 1959. Gas for the town was then supplied via a pipeline from Boxmoor. Prior to the formation of the Great Berkhamsted Waterworks Company in 1864 the town had no piped water. At first the company used a small steam engine to raise water from a deep bore, twelve inches in diameter, to a high level reservoir at Kingshill. A

second low level reservoir was established in Green Lane, just off Chesham Road. As demand increased a new bore hole 200 ft. deep was sunk in 1903-4 and this was provided with a much larger engine, capable of raising 80,000 gallons an hour. In 1933 a new water tower was provided at Shootersway with a maximum capacity of 300,000 gallons. The water stored here can reach a depth of 30 ft., equal to 1,300 tons in weight.

The creation of the Rural Sanitary Authority in 1872 was a key step in the development of public services in the town. However, at first, this merely produced a further burden on the already hard pressed vestry guardians who, in addition to poor relief, now had a statutory responsibility for public health matters. Despite this, the local authority achieved an early success by building an isolation hospital near Aldbury. This was an important step at a time when the standard of public hygiene in the town was still very poor and it was difficult to prevent the spread of life threatening infections through the local population. In the nineteenth century there was no National Health Service to act as a safeguard and medical attention was only guaranteed for those who could afford it. In Victorian times local doctors like Dr. Steele, who lived at the large house called 'The Elms', were often important and wealthy members of the local community. Savings clubs were run by the parish church, whereby for the payment of a small weekly subscription ordinary families were offered some insurance against the costs incurred in the case of serious illness. In 1897 an appeal was launched for the Berkhamsted, Northchurch and District Ambulance Fund, so that a vehicle could be obtained to carry the seriously ill to the West Herts Infirmary which had opened in 1877. Under the auspices of St Peter's Parish Church, the Berkhamsted Nursing Association had been established in 1876. Terms for nursing in the home ranged from £1 1s a week for ordinary conditions, rising to £2 2s a week for smallpox and 'mental cases'. The first nursing home was established at Gossoms End in March 1880 and a three year lease was also taken out on a property in the High Street, opposite St Peter's Church.

At long last the civic burdens sustained by the vestry authorities were reduced by the Local Government Act of 1888, which transferred the functions of the local Justices of the Peace to the newly formed County Councils and County Boroughs. In 1894 another Act distributed the remaining work of the local authorities between existing boroughs and newly formed urban district councils. The Rural Sanitary Authority had now become the Rural District Council; however the Berkhamsted Urban District Council did not formally take up office until 15th April 1898. After much prevarication, one of the last acts of the Rural Sanitary Authority had been to spend £13,812 on providing a mains drainage system for Berkhamsted, but unfortunately much of this work proved faulty. In its first year of operation the newly formed Urban District Council therefore had no choice but to spend a further £8,645 on a more effective high level sewer for the town. This essential work at long last removed the blight which had quite literally plagued the town's prospects for several hundred years. The Black Ditch was now a thing of the past and the town could now expand and move ahead on a more modern footing.

Electric light first arrived in the town when it was used at the Mechanics Institute's Grand Exhibition, which was held at the Town Hall for ten days in 1886. Despite this relatively early appearance in Berkhamsted, it was twelve years later in 1898 before the North British Electric Company made the first formal application to supply electric light to the district. However they were turned down flat by the Berkhamsted Urban District Council, who insisted on retaining this right for themselves. Despite their laudable ambitions, the passage of time revealed that, in this respect, the council had overreached themselves. Without the resources to finance such an undertaking independently, they eventually bowed to the inevitable and granted the right to supply power to the town to another commercial concern, the Chesham Electric Light Company. An advertisement in the Berkhamsted Directory of 1929 confirms that electric light had reached the town and domestic wiring installations were now available for local householders. Another important step forward in the creation of a modern infrastructure for Berkhamsted had taken place in 1898, when the National Telephone Company began construction of the necessary 'telegraphic works' to connect up the town. Berkhamsted's first telephone

High Street offices of Berkhamsted Urban District Council, prior to the construction of the Civic Centre in 1937.

A meeting of Berkhamsted Urban District Council in the Civic Centre, 1945.

exchange was located in Chapel Street, however a private telephone number was then a service afforded by a privileged few and by 1906 there were still only 46 telephone numbers listed in the Berkhamsted and Tring district.

Twentieth Century Growth

Whilst the days of royal splendour were never likely to return, by the beginning of the current century conditions in the town were set fair. The main utilities were in place throughout the town, transport links were excellent and Berkhamsted was fast becoming economically prosperous again. In view of its long standing public hygiene problems, it is perhaps ironic to read in a magazine dated June 1909 that Berkhamsted was already being confidently advertised as a pleasant town on the fringes of London "which is a very healthy place to live, with pure bracing air". It may interest contemporary residents to know that the same article also reveals that household rents in the town then ranged upwards from about £30 per annum! By the end of the nineteenth century, the population of the Parish of St Peter had already grown to become three times as large as the figure of 1,690, registered in the census of 1801. However, given the formation of the Urban District Council in 1898, any analysis of census returns must be related to the new boundaries formed, which initially limited the new municipal area to only 1,035 acres. This was soon to change again with the addition of Sunnyside in 1909 and, with the subsequent inclusion of Northchurch in 1935, the size of the urban area eventually expanded to 1,982 acres. In direct contrast to its predecessor the Vestry, which for most of its life was handicapped by poor levels of income, the Urban District Council now had control of a much richer area of potential revenue, with a fast growing population of future rate payers.

During the first decade of the twentieth century, builders were again active in the western part of the town. In 1902 a start was made on Shrublands Avenue and there was further building work along Cross Oak Road, where allotments were being cleared to make way for what is now Queens Road. This decade also saw the beginnings of sustained development in the eastern hamlet of Sunnyside. However the First World War then put a significant brake on progress for the next ten years. With the tragic loss of life in this protracted conflict, the population of the town actually declined slightly from its 1911 level of 7,302 inhabitants and in 1921 there were only 23 more houses in the town than had been built by 1911. At the beginning of the decade there was a total housing stock of 1,700 homes in the town, of which over 1,200 were then being let for weekly rents ranging from 2s a week for a two roomed house, to 12s a week for a six roomed house. The vast majority of these houses had no bath or indoor lavatories and, thirty years later in 1951, there were still over 900 houses in Berkhamsted without a bath. At first, construction work recovered slowly with only 74 private houses being built between 1911 and 1924. Following the First World War there was still no council housing available and much of the older smaller private housing was in poor condition. Because of this men returning from the war often had a long wait for suitable family accommodation.

The need for further development was obvious and progress gathered pace again, with the first 50 council houses completed at Swing Gate Lane and Gossoms End by 1928. Building work at the eastern end of the town was now proceeding on a considerable scale, particularly around the Swing Gate Lane area. Development was taking place on land which had formerly been part of the estate belonging to the large mansion house known as The Hall. The fields further east of Swing Gate Lane were being developed by private contractors, whilst the land closer to the town was being used for council housing. During the 1930's a small neighbouring area of council housing was also developed when Highfield House was finally demolished and this enabled the extension of Highfield Road, Victoria Road and Three Close Lane. By 1939 the total of 1,690 houses available in 1921 had very nearly doubled to reach 3,000; although this was at least partly due to the inclusion of Northchurch within the Urban District. Between the wars the first development began on Ashlyns Road; Greenway and George Street were both extended and more houses were built in Shrublands Road. West Road, Anglefield Road, Kingsdale Road and Crossways were created and by this time the first houses had also started to appear on the Castle Hill and Dellfield estates. Already by 1939, the council had become the town's largest landlord; a role which gathered further momentum after the war, when a further 200 council houses were built on the Durrants estate and pre-fabricated dwellings were erected at Three Close Lane.

In 1960 the total population of the district had reached 12,000 and its rateable value had risen to £200,000. By the end of the decade the total stock of council houses was set to rise to around 1,100 dwellings, thanks largely to the completion of the Durrants, Westfield and Ashlyns estates. It was also during the early 1960's that the first part of a huge expansion of private housing stock began, with the development of the upper reaches of Bridgewater Road and South Park Gardens. The demolition of Berkhamsted Place in 1967 then cleared the way for further construction on the green fields and narrow strip of old woodland which lay behind the new houses in Bridgewater Road. In the local government reorganisation of 1974 Dacorum District Council replaced the old Urban District Council as the local planning authority. At first Berkhamsted was left with only a Parish Council, but only two years later this became a Town Council with the right to elect a Mayor. In a period of only twenty years the town's population had grown by over 40% from 10,785 in 1951 to 15,439 in 1971. However the pace of private housing development still continued to accelerate, particularly at the western end of the valley. Beginning at Billet Lane, the development of the vast Chiltern Park estate on the seventy acre site of Tunnel Fields continued westwards throughout the 1970's and 80's. This building work gradually eliminated the majority of green space that once separated the town of Berkhamsted from the fringes of common land at Northchurch. At the other end of town, a smaller housing estate called Hunters

Park was built in 1978 at the top of Gravel Path, on land formerly belonging to Berkhamsted Pheasantries.

As we reach the 1990's the balance between council housing and private housing stock has shifted further still. This has been encouraged by the national policies of the previous Conservative administration (1979 - 1997) which offered financial incentives to council tenants prepared to purchase their homes. Today the often rapid population growth that prevailed in the town for 200 years has finally slowed, inhibited by planning restrictions designed to protect the remaining green field sites. Having followed the development process carefully throughout the twentieth century, it has become clear how the expansion of the town, driven by economic prosperity, was only achieved at the expense of the many fine Georgian and Victorian houses and estates that formerly graced the hillsides. Pilkington Manor, Highfield House, The Hall, Cross Oak and Berkhamsted Place, together with the farmlands of Kingshill, Boxwell and Kitsbury were all casualties of this process of relentless urban expansion which fuelled a population explosion to the current levels, at the 1991 census, of 15,701 inhabitants.

The Shrublands area of Berkhamsted viewed from the north-east, 1967.

High Street

The Parish Church of St Peter, viewed from the eastern end of the High Street, circa 1912.

Looking towards Berkhamsted town centre from the east, circa 1910, with Dean Incents to the left.

Corner of Water Lane, clearly showing the old Tudor house and 'Graball Row', pre 1915.

The Court Theatre and Berkhamsted's War Memorial (extreme left) at the top of Water Lane, circa 1920.

Berkhamsted town centre circa 1912, clearly showing Hazell's Folly, then the International Stores.

View of Berkhamsted Town Hall looking east, circa 1920.

Berkhamsted High Street at the turn of the century, looking towards St Johns Well Lane.

A rare picture of Lane's Nurseries, looking east back towards the town centre, circa 1910.

Shops and Traders

The history of shopping in Berkhamsted can be traced back to 1357 when "Le Shopperowe" is mentioned in a register drawn up during the time of the Black Prince. Most of the town's early shops, inns and trading places were concentrated either in the High Street or along Castle Street, which at this time was the only other significant local thoroughfare. The importance of Castle Street initially stemmed from the fact that it was the main route into the royal establishment, as well as the principal crossing point over the River Bulbourne, where there was also a busy flour mill. It may be difficult for the modern resident to believe that, as late as 1882, there were thirty separate businesses still flourishing in Castle Street, which also played host to no less than seven inns and taverns. In the town centre a cluster of stalls and shambles evolved around the sixteenth century market house. Eventually an additional row of buildings developed which completely obscured this run of properties from the High Street. This run of shops, which began with the 'One Bell' public house and ran along towards St Peter's Church, became known as Middle Row or Graball Row. At the turn of the century they included local businesses such as Cheelds the grocers, Millen the shoemaker, Platt the wine merchant and Breeds the wool and toy shop. By divorcing important buildings such as the Court House from the High Street Graball Row had, in effect, created a new thoroughfare in the town centre. Formerly known as Back Lane, this historic side street has since been re-christened Church Lane.

The arrival of the railway in 1837, together with the Industrial Revolution it heralded, brought new levels of prosperity to Berkhamsted which stimulated rather sudden changes in the pattern of local shops and services. For example, between 1824 and 1839, the number of bakers increased from five to nine and grocers from ten to twenty-three. From this time, there was also a gradual decline in some of the older established local businesses such as saddlers, farriers, corn chandlers, hay merchants and wheelwrights, whose livelihoods all depended upon horse drawn traffic. In early Victorian times most of the local shops were located in the High Street or Castle Street and were simply the front parlours of cottages, some of which had the advantage of a bow window. Alternatively some traders would simply display their wares on trestle tables in front of the property. As the town developed during the second half of the eighteenth century, local craftsmen also began to run small businesses from properties in the newly built residential roads such as Ravens Lane, Highfield Road, Holliday Street and Chapel Street. It is also important to remember that the modern town's other main shopping thoroughfare, Lower Kings Road, did not exist until 1885, when it was built primarily to provide an improved link to Berkhamsted's busy railway station. The history of shops and traders in Berkhamsted is such a vast subject that it could easily justify a separate publication in its own right. Instead the following chapter includes a step by step tour which, along the way, aims to identify the more important historic businesses and fondly remembered shop keepers, locating them in relation to the current geography of the High Street. We begin at the eastern end of the town, following a main route which was established over 900 years ago to link London to the royal castle at Berkhamsted.

Swing Gate Lane to Castle Street (south)
At the bottom of Swing Gate Lane, the corner Tool Hire Shop was once Kempster's General Store and circa 1890 Charles Pocock ran a local forge from the adjacent property. The town's last traditional chimney sweep, William Olliffe, lived at the cottage at No.21 in 1930, whilst next door the Curry Garden Indian Restaurant, a property dating from the seventeenth century, was formerly the Black Horse public house. The large BMG Garage, formerly Castle's, is a business founded by George Callaghan who by 1935 was advertising as a haulage contractor and from 1949 was operating a petrol garage on the site. This land was previously the original timber yard established by Job East in the town from 1843. Beyond Ingleside, near to the corner of Highfield Road, is the interesting and charming structure of Pightle House, formerly known as Valhalla, when it provided billets for soldiers during the Second World War. The name Pightle is an old word meaning "a strip of meadowland between two copses". Its near neighbour at No.53 was previously the Queens Arms, a local Inn dating back to 1607 which surrendered its licence in 1968. Pightle House and the Queens Arms were one building until Victorian times, when the east end of the property was developed into a separate dwelling. At the top of Highfield Road was another early Inn, the Chaffcutters Arms, which by 1850 had been converted into two cottages. Beyond Highfield Road, Bygone Pine used to be Frederick Redding's grocers shop in 1934, while Coleshill was home to Paul Jay, an early Berkhamsted chiropractor. At one time the property known as the Poplars was the residence

of the important industrialist William Cooper and later the birthplace of one of the nation's most distinguished post-war actors, Sir Michael Hordern. The shops on the corner of Victoria Road, the Crystal Takeaway and J. L. Fitted Kitchens, used to be Batchelors wood/wallpaper shop and Alfred Geary's hairdressing salon which later became Smiddy's hairdressers. The Goat Inn is a nineteenth century re-building of a much earlier straw thatched inn, whose paddock made it a popular stopping off point for farmers taking their animals to market. The original horse trough, now filled in, still remains beside this public house. The mock Tudor buildings of Castle House and Chambers, built in 1865, dominate the corner site at Three Close Lane behind which was once the Lees Mineral Water plant, famous for its ginger beer.

Its hard to believe that until 1938 the delightful Egerton House occupied land now taken by a parade of boarded up shops and the derelict Rex cinema, which closed in 1973. The cinema itself remains a notable building and in 1988 the property was accorded listed status in respect of its stylish foyer and art deco interiors; it is the only cinema in Hertfordshire to achieve this distinction. When she was a pupil at Berkhamsted Girls School Clementine Hosier, later Lady Winston Churchill, lived at No.107 High Street. This property, now known as Churchill House, is used by Prestige Promotions and is part of Egerton Terrace, a well maintained Regency block currently providing deluxe office accommodation. Just beyond Rectory Lane is the distinctive Red House (see p.64) which was home to a leading Quaker Joseph Robinson in the 1850's. A wealthy man, he built the White House next door, which remains one of the more attractive buildings in the High Street and is now home to Gallery One Eleven. The offices of Wilding's the solicitors used to be Ripon's chemist shop as early as the 1870's, whilst a long standing dental practice continues to operate in Admiral House, the fine nineteenth century property which sits directly opposite Castle Street.

Swing Gate Lane to Castle Street (north)
By the mini-roundabout at the bottom of Swing Gate Lane, the small Vet's Surgery was formerly Whiting's sweet shop and post office in the 1930's; this later became Barlow's sweet shop. Beyond Rose Cottage at No.6, The Bull is another local pub which dates from the early seventeenth century. The next stretch of this side of the High Street is dominated by a run of buildings, all of which owe their origins to the chemical business founded by William Cooper in 1843. The now

deserted offices which formerly belonged to the Wellcome Foundation are followed by the large Technical Bureau, built by Cooper's in the 1940's. Next door to Putt's butchers, the Motorcycle Shop maintains a tradition established on the site by a local wheelwright whose presence can be traced back to 1839. The proprietor later became a cycle dealer and gave his name to Holliday Street. The High Street frontage between Holliday Street and Ravens Lane is taken up by the impressive Baptist Chapel, which was built for a flourishing local congregation in 1865. The construction of Sibdon Place in 1869 was funded by William Cooper as accommodation for senior workers employed at his original factory in Ravens Lane.

The shop front on the lower corner of Ravens Lane and Provident Place used to be a Co-op grocery store and later became Geary's shoe shop until the building was demolished in 1972. The High Street property now occupied by Country Desks and the Tangerine dress shop was built in 1863. At the turn of the century it used to be Woods Music Warehouse, which by 1929 had moved to Lower Kings Road. Bobby's newsagent and convenience store is housed in premises which were used as a war kitchen during the First World War. Its neighbour Tudor Antiques was formerly Cox fruiterers and Webster's off-licence during the 1930's. The properties on either side of Manor Street used to be an early Co-op general store and butcher, whilst the next run of shops was built in 1900 to replace a run of small semi-derelict cottages. At the end of this parade there was another Co-op store, which later became Verney's bakers shop. The art

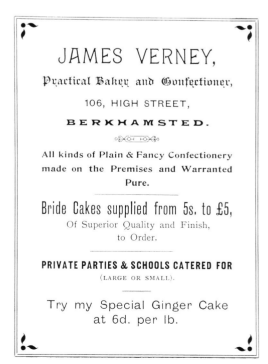

Early view of the eastern end of Berkhamsted High Street, showing East's timber yard and the Black Horse.

View approaching Berkhamsted from Bourne End circa 1860, the wall to the left belongs to the entrance of the Hall.

Looking back down the eastern end of the High Street, with the Black Horse now on the right.

The south side of the High Street, showing the Queens Arms (centre), circa 1860.

Pocock's blacksmith shop in the High Street, circa 1890.

Holliday's cycle shop on the corner of Ravens Lane in the 1920's.

gallery at No.108, previously Hutton Antiques in 1970, is housed in an attractive building which is thought to have been the dower house for the Pilkington Manor estate. Until the site of the old Pilkington Manor House was redeveloped in the 1950's to provide a range of shops, offices and flats, it dominated the view running up towards Castle Street, where the rather quaint eighteenth century structure of Gordon Cottage still survives on the corner.

Castle Street (east)

At the corner of Castle Street, opposite St Peter's Churchyard, the first property has a shop frontage shared by the Inside Track model shop and Mahoney plumbing. For many years this building was home to Bailey's watchmakers, a long standing local business established in 1872, which now enjoys a more central position in Lower Kings Road. Immediately beyond Yew Cottage, the house which was once Kathryn's ladies' hairdressers was formerly the only pawnbroker's shop in the town. This business was started in Victorian times by Mr. Chiltern and was continued by Mr. Gill until it eventually closed down in 1919. The row of five cottages that follow included accommodation for a tailoring business and Frank East's sweet shop. The next shop beyond the alley, until recently called Lollipops, will be remembered by many former Berkhamsted schoolboys as H. S. Brown's, a small newsagents and sweet shop. In the course of the construction of Manor Close during the 1930's, a rickety old cottage was demolished, which it is thought could well have been a former public house called The Sun. At the turn of the century, next door to the pair of Regency houses, now called Wits End and Peace Cottage, was a sports outfitters business run by the boys' school cricket coach, Isaac Evans. In 1929 Henry Nash the tailor ran his business from this property. The row of houses Nos.18-20 that run up towards Fiske House were owned by the large Congregational Church which until its demolition in 1972 dominated the corner of Chapel Street. On the opposite corner of Chapel Street there is a tall house which was formerly the Gardener's Arms public house which closed in 1967. In 1929 Edward Giddings the "baker, pastrycook and family miller" traded from the Castle Street Bakery at No.22 and this later became Foster's bakery in the 1940's. Past the picture framing shop, at No.23, is a property which was home to a nineteenth century leather business run by local shop keeper and champion of education, Henry Nash. Its neighbour, which is currently Heritage Antiques, used to be Everett's furnishing shop.

At the turn of the century the Stupples family ran two dairies in Berkhamsted; one of which was in Lower Kings Road, the other based at No.25 Castle Street. Next door to 'Waterhouse' was Packer's general store and beyond this a run of private houses (Nos.28-31) which lead up towards the entrance of the town's modern fire station. In the first half of this century, behind the properties of Buttermere and Whitemead, H. J. Matthews ran a large builders' yard and funeral directors which provided some of the ground for the new fire station site. Next is one of Berkhamsted's most picturesque properties, The Boote, which was built in 1605 and survived as a public house until 1920. For a period after the Second World War it was home to an antiques business. Immediately beyond the adjacent property at No.38 was an alleyway leading to a row of small cottages (now demolished) which stood at right angles to the road and this area was known as Happy Valley. Beyond Happy Valley is the town's former coal wharf, whose large corner site provided the ideal premises for Keys canal-side timber yard which moved here in 1913. The striking 27 ft. totem pole by the canal is a reminder of this flourishing business which traded successfully into modern times as J. Alsford & Son. The site has since been re-developed in 1994 to provide the attractive canal-side apartments of Alsford's Wharf. In earlier days a row of terraced cottages lined part of this site's frontage to Castle Street and closer to the railway bridge was another of Castle Street's old inns, the Railway Tavern, which closed in 1966. The Castle Hotel was another local hostelry on the opposite side of the canal bridge, but this ceased trading in 1968. However just beyond the canal the last of the three Inns built to serve the old railway station still survives. This distinctive looking tavern started life as a small beer house in one of two cottages. Re-built in 1854 and much altered in 1867-68, it owes its inspiration to the famous Crystal Palace, built for the Great Exhibition of 1851.

Castle Street (west)

The majority of the west side of Castle Street is dominated by St Peter's Churchyard and the buildings of Berkhamsted School. Viewed from the street the principal features of the Churchyard are the old yew tree, which has stood for hundreds of years at the corner near the High Street and the rather striking Smith-Dorrien monument, which is more centrally positioned. Erected in memory of Mary Ann Smith-Dorrien, who lived at the local estate of Haresfoot, it takes the form of a tall stone cross in the late Gothic style and is dated 1909. The original buildings of

The High Street end of Castle Street, with the Smith-Dorrien monument (left), circa 1912.

Brown's sweet shop in the 1930's.

St Peter's Sunday School outing leaving Castle Street, circa 1912.

The lower part of Castle Street, showing Brinklow's sweet shop, circa 1890.

Old cottages in Castle Street, seen here in the 1860's.

School House overlook the Churchyard and stand at right angles to Castle Street. Beyond the main entrance is an impressive school chapel, built in the time of Dr. J. C. Fry, Headmaster of Berkhamsted School 1887-1910. It was during Dr. Fry's tenure that the school's success was consolidated and several late Victorian buildings added around the quadrangle. Further down Castle Street, Deans Hall was also constructed during this important period of expansion. To the north of Deans Hall, Ward Cottage and the property known as St George's still survive in the midst of what is now an extended site for the school. In days gone by Ward Cottage used to be home to a local carrier and fishmonger's business, whilst St George's was formerly the George and Dragon temperance hotel and coffee tavern, established in 1879 with the support of Earl Brownlow. Next, where the school's fives courts have since been built, was a run of old cottages some of which dated from the late sixteenth century, but these had been pulled down by 1900. Beyond this another row of old cottages survived into more recent times, having become known locally as the 'sunken cottages', when the level of the road in front of these properties was raised to meet the canal bridge. This picturesque row of historic dwellings became rather dilapidated and they were finally demolished in 1963. Immediately beyond the school infirmary, the north end of Castle Street is still dominated by the large building which until 1968 was the Castle Hotel. This handsome property, together with its large yard and stable block, has recently been converted into deluxe residential accommodation.

Mill Street to Water Lane
At the top of Mill Street the old moor, which is now a pleasant park, is the likely site of what early historians referred to as the "Black Ditch". Encouraged by the valley's contours and the local water course, this was a notorious quagmire which was little more than an open sewer and the gathering point for much of the town's effluent, prior to the installation of mains drainage in 1898. On the other side of Mill Street stood Upper Mill, which together with several mill cottages, was demolished in 1926 to allow for the construction of a music department for Berkhamsted School. The old mill stone still survives as a feature of the garden area behind the fives courts and the line of the old mill race can still be clearly seen running beside the moor and beneath Mill Street. A curved wall has since been built over the mill race with a Latin inscription which reads in translation: "here for a thousand years the old mill stood and gave us

bread. Here now our school in rival motherhood feeds minds instead". A little further down Mill Street are the impressive range of school buildings known as Newcroft, which were officially opened by Her Majesty the Queen Mother in 1958. These were built on a small sports ground, which was formerly home to the school's tennis courts. On the opposite side of Mill Street, the house known as Westview is immediately adjacent to the site of the King Edward VI public house, which for a period was rather charmingly known as the Clown and Sausages. This old working men's Inn finally closed its doors in 1922. Beyond the school's modern fitness centre, the Jules Thorne block stands on land formerly occupied by a row of cottages, one of which was another public house called The Fish. This inn surrendered its licence in 1959 and was demolished in 1960.

The row of school workshops on the corner of Mill Street conceal Wilson House, the home of the Headmaster of Berkhamsted School. This house was built on the site of the second Baptist Church burial ground and gravestones still stand around the garden walls. On the opposite corner at the end of Mill Street is the property which, as Adelbert House, was home for many years to the manager of the local gas works. Behind Adelbert House there used to be a thatched sports pavilion belonging to Berkhamsted School. The gas works themselves, which were established in 1849, were situated at the lower end of the Wilderness, which is now part of the main car park behind the Tesco supermarket. Here behind the run of low school buildings which still mark the line of the Wilderness, was the burial ground for the early Baptist Chapel which stood nearby in Water Lane. In 1851 a total of 38 people lived in a row of eleven dilapidated cottages in the Wilderness, which closer to its junction with Back Lane (now Church Lane) was also home to various stables and slaughterhouses. Beyond the old Baptist Chapel, the top half of Water Lane was dominated by the large brewery works belonging to Messrs. Locke & Smith. This business closed down in 1914 and the premises, which then became Kepston's pulley works, was seriously damaged by fire in 1929. In earlier times this area, with its unfortunate combination of poor quality housing located close to a brewery, gas works, burial ground and slaughterhouses, had something of an unsavoury reputation. However the historic integrity of both Water Lane and the Wilderness, which survived into this century, was destroyed by the provision of a large car park for High Street shoppers which has truncated the length of both these early thoroughfares.

View of Mill Street at the turn of the century, showing the King Edward VI public house, which was demolished in 1922.

Lower part of Mill Street showing flooded meadow, circa 1900.

Newcroft, built for the Berkhamsted Boys School on the meadow in 1958.

Timber framed building which formerly stood at the junction of Water Lane and the Wilderness.

Castle Street to Kings Road (south)

Opposite St Peter's Church the Berkhamsted Delicatessen at No.125 was formerly home to a leading local ironmonger's business founded in 1820 by Ezra Miller's family. In turn this became Bligh's, Harper's and then Fox's ironmonger's, before becoming Kennett and Fox circa 1950. The house at No.127 used to be Watts china and glass store in 1943 and its historic neighbour, Dean Incent's House, dates from the late Tudor age and will be remembered by many as a delightful tea shop which offered refreshment 1930-70. At the turn of the century this ancient property was home to the noted local photographer J.T. Newman. On the corner of Chesham Road is the rather severe looking Overton House, which is owned by Berkhamsted School and has in the past been used to accommodate boarders. On the opposite corner of Chesham Road stands the large seventeenth century building which is now home to the Swan Youth Project and was formerly one of Berkhamsted's largest and most important public houses. As early as 1656 Michael Hancock was licensed to keep a 'wine tavern' at the Swan, an Inn which also had its own brewery run by the Foster family in the 1850's. In more recent times the Swan was also one of the principal hotels in the town run by Peter Caro. The property between the Swan and the Crown, now Regents Estates, was formerly Mitchell's and then Sanderson's shoe shop in 1958. Prior to this it used to be Daffy de Fraine's hairdressing salon, which was run by three generations of his family until 1930. Mr. de Fraine was a leading local Councillor who campaigned for the public swimming pool in the town, which eventually opened in 1923. The Crown itself, although much modernised, is a very early building which dates from the sixteenth century. Known as the Chaffcutter Arms in the first half of the nineteenth century, it re-adopted its former name of the Crown in 1852. Its near neighbour the Kings Arms is the third and most important historic public house in this stretch of the High Street. This large coaching inn, which once offered stabling for up to forty horses, dates from the reign of Queen Anne. Historically the most notable figure at the Kings Arms was John Page, innkeeper 1792-1840, who also served as local constable and post-master for the area. Rather famously the Kings Arms was the regular venue of a well documented romance between his daughter Polly and King Louis XVIII of France, who was exiled at Hartwell House, near Aylesbury 1807-14.

Of the two shops on the corner of Prince Edward Street, Henry's fish shop used to be one of

Berkhamsted's oldest multiple stores, Freeman, Hardy & Willis, a shoe shop which was established in the town before 1900. Taylors's estate agents at No.151 was Sprigg's outfitters in the early 1900's, later becoming Steven's gentleman's clothes shop and then Noel Sandall's outfitters in 1946. Prince Edward Street itself was not made up until 1888; formerly known as Snobs Alley, it was a well trodden trackway linking the High Street to Butts Meadow. A property then owned by greengrocer John Batchelor, with an upper storey which spanned the alley, was demolished when this new road was constructed. Prior to the opening of the Court Theatre in March 1917, one of the town's early cinemas, the Picture Playhouse, used to be in Prince Edward Street and this building survived as the Kings Hall, but has since been demolished to make way for a new office block. From June 1951, Prince Edward Street was also home to the town's public library until purpose built accommodation was officially opened in Kings Road on 22nd April 1965. Of the three properties before we reach the Civic Centre, the corner dress shop was home to Dick Wood's common carriers business in 1860. At this time its neighbour the Trio hairdressing salon used to belong to Johnny Walklate, saddler and harness maker, whose business was eventually taken over by Levi Newell and survived until 1946. Here also was one of the town's main post office sites, where Frederick Howard was the first post-master in 1891. The post office subsequently moved to newly-built premises in Lower Kings Road in 1909.

A house belonging to local builder William Nash was demolished in 1938 to make way for the Civic Centre. In the 1870's Mr. Nash, a staunch Wesleyan, provided a chapel in the yard behind the house for his fellow believers and this continued as a place of worship until the congregation moved to Cowper Road in 1887. Prior to the construction of the Civic Centre this building, which could seat up to 125 people, was used as a council chamber. On either side of the Civic Centre site was the Rock House fish shop and the former Five Bells public house which lost its licence in the 1870's. These premises later became an electrical business established by Norman Clarke in 1949. This venture later expanded and became known as Weatherhead's from 1966, when it operated from what now is Nicholl's brasserie at No.163. The offices of David Doyle's estate agents used to be occupied by Dwight's Garage, one of the town's first motor mechanics, who became established before the First World War. The Cutting Room at No.169 was an earlier site for W. H. Smith's newsagent shop, prior to its move to the modern re-development on the other side of the High Street. W. H. Smith first began trading in Berkhamsted with a stand at the railway station, before sharing High Street premises with Southey's Motorcycle Showroom in the building which is now Birtchnell's. It is hard to believe that Hubert Figg's long standing chemist business was also once split into two tiny premises shared by Mrs. Miekle's sweet shop and Bailey's watchmakers, prior to its move to Castle Street. Penny & Thorne solicitors' office used to be Spicer's baker's shop and the shoe repairers at No.177 will be remembered by many as Mr. Coughtrey's Chocolate Box, which traded from 1930 into the 1950's. The Adult Studies Centre was a drapery business run by the Robinson family, until it was sold in 1920 to become the Star Supply Stores. The Midland Bank was built circa 1939 on the site of another old Inn, The Red Lion, which ceased to be a public house in 1880. Close to the corner of Kings Road was Tompkins the butcher and Barbara's flower shop, prior to the modernisation and enlargement of the town's modern police station in 1972.

Castle Street to Kings Road (north)
Beyond St Peter's Church, the frontage of Brown & Merry estate agents still displays the only surviving fire mark in the town. Its next door neighbour, the gentleman's hairdressers, was a shoe shop established by George Loader, trading

at the turn of the century, before it became P. D. Millen & Co. and then White's shoe shop. Between these two properties it is still possible to see an old grapevine which has been growing in the High Street for well over 100 years. The large premises of the current Home and Colonial antique shop was for many years Brandon's and then later Neil's furniture shop. Godfrey solicitors at No.136 used to be Castle's off-licence and today's smart jeweller's shop, Phillip Kingh, is actually the original Home and Colonial Stores, as revealed by the painted sign on the western end of the building. What today is Castle's estate agent at No.148 was formerly Shambrook's wool shop, whilst its neighbour adjacent to the old 'Post Alley' at No.150 was previously an early home for the town's post office. George Scott was post-master here in 1839 and the post office remained on this site until it moved to the other side of the High Street in 1891. The Benetton clothes shop used to be first Farmer's and then Godden's the butcher. Farmer's was the largest butchers' shop in the town, with its own payment booth to keep the receipt of cash separate from the meat counter. A hundred years ago, the end of this run of shops was taken up by William Cheeld, the grocer and the One Bell public house. This old sixteenth century Inn survived until it was demolished in 1959 and the shop which replaced it became a Victoria Wine off-licence. Following a fire in 1969, Tesco's modern supermarket was built on the site of the Court Theatre, which presented its first performance in March 1917 and managed to survive as a cinema until Easter 1960. This imposing building, with its distinctive dome, was itself constructed on the former site of the old Tudor house, later the Stafford brush works.

The opposite corner of Water Lane was dominated by an old property which some residents will remember as being the Court Cafe and Ye Wool Shop. The town's war memorial once stood in front of these properties, until the re-development of Water Lane necessitated its removal to St Peter's Churchyard in 1952. Next came the offices of the local brewers Locke & Smith whose brewery was taken over by Benskins and closed in 1914. Until a serious fire in 1929 the old brewery buildings, then occupied by Kepston's pulley works, dominated the site which, following extensive re-development in the early 1970's, became Woolworths and Waitrose supermarket. At the time of the fire, this part of the High Street included several significant shops, the first of which belonged to W. F. Matchett the draper. Next came H. Kingham & Sons the grocer, followed by S. Howship's sweet

View of 'Graball Row' looking east, circa 1900.

Swan Hotel and Crown, 1935.

The staff of Berkhamsted Post Office in the High Street, circa 1895.

The One Bell, demolished in 1959.

Berkhamsted Town Hall circa 1900; also showing an early site for Timson's bakery.

View of the corner of Prince Edward Street looking east, circa 1910.

Striking display of meat at the Star Supply Stores.

Loosley's stationer's in the 1920's.

shop, a property which was used by Henry Gibbs the chemist circa 1890. At the turn of the century part of the re-developed area which is now W. H. Smith's store at No.178 was home to a leading grocers and wine merchants run by Charles Bishop Chasteney. The modern block of shops which today contain Lunn Poly travel agents, the Bakers Oven and Beaton's dry cleaners occupy the site of an earlier significant building known as Hazell's Folly. This was one of the tallest shops in the town and was built in the first half of the nineteenth century by an ambitious local tradesman, William Hazell, who was a grocer and pork butcher. From 1907 these large premises were taken over by the International Stores and were finally demolished in 1974. The yard belonging to one of the town's longest surviving businesses initially operated behind a small premises which had been demolished to build Hazell's Folly. Here James Nash first began trading as a farrier in 1793 and by 1915 the family were still in control, when Bert Nash took over the yard from his cousin William. The business was eventually run from a property situated behind the High Street overlooking the yard, called Farriers House. The property has since been re-built and is currently home to the British Legion. The next modern shop front of Boots the Chemist stands on ground formerly occupied by a private house, which became the White Hart Inn in 1861 and continued to offer refreshment next to the Town Hall until 1972.

The architectural jewel which is Berkhamsted Town Hall, (see p.65) was built in 1859 on a site secured for the town by William Hazell. Prior to the arrival of the railway, its central position had been used to great effect by a leading firm of London based carriers, King & Co. The office of the Halifax Building Society at No.198 used to be Wren's sports shop in 1967 and was formerly the Khaki Tea Shop, established during the First World War and run by Mrs. Potter in the 1920's. At the turn of the century, Clinton Cards was the offices of the solicitor W. J. Pitkin and many will remember the Berkhamsted Delicatessen who also ran a popular cafe above the properties during the late 1960's and early 70's. The Oxfam shop at No.204, formerly Curry's electrical store, was the principal site of another of Berkhamsted's important old businesses. Loosley's printers and stationers shop began trading here before the turn of the century. The corner site at Lower Kings Road has traditionally been a greengrocers and for many years was known by locals as Pike's corner, in memory of one of the shop's long standing greengrocers, Mr. David Pike who was trading here in 1895.

Lower Kings Road (east)
Just beyond Pike's corner is the current insurance office which was previously A. E. Williams & Son, men's outfitters in 1970, before becoming R. S. Wayman estate agents. The property at No.3, now Upper Cutz hairdressers, was formerly Frederick Moyle's radio shop before becoming a small gent's hairdressers run by Len Hornsby and then Bill Bailey. For many years the premises of Kitchen Plus used to be Elliott's dressmakers shop and prior to that provided accommodation for the exotically named Kiku No Chaya tea shop which was here throughout a period which spanned both World Wars. The modern premises of No.9 is now home to one of Berkhamsted's long established businesses, the jeweller Bailey & Sons, which began trading in the town back in 1872. The new red brick development called Claridge Court occupies a site formerly taken by the town's post office, which opened here in 1909 and remained until 1958, when the modern main post office was built close to St Johns Well Lane. The trade of the next two properties at Nos.13 & 15 has remained unchanged for a good number of years. In the early 1960's Clara Davidson was Lilian's florist shop, whilst Christopher John's salon was loudly advertised in the 1960's and 70's at the local Rex cinema as "Jean of Chesham for lovely hair".

La Fiorentina Italian restaurant has been established in the town since 1967. Mr. Vincenzo Iannone served as Head Chef at La Fiorentina from 1969-80 and is now the proprietor of this popular restaurant. The pet shop at No.27 used to be Mrs. Brown's toy shop and prior to this it was a shoe makers run by Mr. Meager. In 1929 Nos. 27-29 were a tailors/outfitters run by C. C. Macklin. The relatively modern premises of Classic Chassis was once an Iceland's frozen food store, established in what had been an indoor 'mini-market'. Prior to re-development, the rear of this site had been occupied by a warehouse belonging to the wholesale grocers, Alfred Button & Sons, as well as the local barracks of the Salvation Army. F. Saltmarsh's hardware store has been in Lower Kings Road for many years and during the 1950's operated from half its current shop front at No.35, when the other part of the premises was an art shop. Graham Webb's music shop was a piano showroom run by Malcolm Collins and the attractive new art gallery next door was a ladies fashion boutique during the 1960's. The rather unusual low building, which is now home to Stanley's florist was formerly Gilbert's TV and Radio repair shop, prior to its move to improved High Street premises in the 1950's. At the turn of the century

The junction of Lower Kings Road with the High Street in 1982.

this corner site was dominated by the large building of A. C. Meek's Livery and Hunting Stables.

Lower Kings Road (west)

Next to the corner site now occupied by Berkhamsted Fisheries, there used to be an attractive shop belonging to the local jeweller E. C. de Lisle and on the other side of Kings Chambers was a small office used by D. & A. Taxis. A local trade directory informs us that Woods Music Warehouse, formerly in the High Street, had moved to No.6 Lower Kings Road by 1929. The majority of the premises which is now Affordable Sounds was formerly Clement Clarke's the optician, whilst Traditional Interiors at No.16 was the base for Peter Ayres TV repair business. For many years Pretty Arty was Chown's (later Johnston's) newsagents and more recently it served a spell as an off-licence for the Peter Dominic chain. The shop at No.24, now Vogue Dresses, was formerly the offices of local coal merchants F. H. Woolsey, previously Brentnall & Cleland. The property used by Rickaby & Co. accountants at No.26 is important as a site of one of the two nineteenth century dairies run in the town by the Stupples family; more recently it has been a large pet shop called Pet World. At one time Stupples also used what is now the Bookstack in the High Street as a dairy shop. Today's smart pizza restaurant on the corner was formerly a home interiors and furnishing business which traded as Newman Smith. Prior to road widening at the entrance of Waitrose car park, there used to be another property on the end of this building, which in the 1950's was Maxine's wool shop. The area of the car park itself was home to a large Victorian factory built for H. G. Hughes & Co., costume manufacturers. In 1919 this building, also known as the Bulbourne Factory, was taken over by Corby, Palmer & Stewart who added extensions which expanded the factory space to 33,000 sq.ft. At one time the factory, which closed at Christmas 1969, employed up to 800 local people, making children's clothes and quality garments for ladies. On the other side of the car park entrance, the house at No.40 used to be King's printing works, founded by Arthur D. King in 1895. The refurbished office accommodation now provided by the White House was formerly the fondly remembered Tuckin Cafe. Here on the corner there also used to be Watts ironmongers and general store in 1950. The photography business at No.48, which formerly shared the property with a ladies' hairdressers, can be traced back to an advertisement for 'Photocraft', which appeared in a parish magazine dated 1957.

Berkhamsted town centre looking west, circa 1916, clearly showing Morris & Son watchmakers on the corner of Lower Kings Road and also Ward's drapers' shop beyond.

Burnham's greengrocer and fruiterers' shop, with the house known as the Elms clearly visible on the right.

Early view of the Sayer Almshouses, circa 1905.

The Royal Oak public house, demolished in 1908.

Kings Road to St Johns Well Lane (south)

The initial stretch of the High Street to the west of Kings Road became known locally as the 'Golden Hundred Yards' because of the three major banks which all became established here within a short distance of each other. Barclays Bank is housed in what was previously a substantial private house called Sidney House, built in the eighteenth century. For years the adjacent property was Rawlins ironmongers. It was later used by Basil Leatherdale as his stationery shop before he moved to Gossoms End, when Barclays Bank was extended circa 1960. In more recent times the property which is now Adams optician used to be showrooms for the Eastern Electricity Board. On the corner of Elm Grove is the long standing gents outfitters business which was established in 1938 by the town's leading historian, P. C. Birtchnell and moved to this site in November 1956. In the 1920's this building was the showroom for Southey's Motorcycle Manufacturers, whose works were located some way behind the building, whilst P. C. Birtchnell's first shop opened as one of the new shops in the parade attached to the Rex cinema, built in 1938. The fine property of Elm Grove House once occupied the site which is now shared by the Nationwide Building Society and Ash hairdressing salon. The old house was being used as a dental surgery by Pocock and Nash in 1935 and accommodated an earlier medical practice run by Dr. Bontor. The National Westminster Bank was built in the 1920's on a site which formerly contained a cottage and two shops, from which Mr. Christian the tailor and Mr. Burnham the fruiterer plied their trades. Burnham's greengrocers was previously home to the very first Co-op shop which opened in the town circa 1880. In common with Barclays, its near neighbour Lloyds Bank is located in what was earlier a substantial private property. This house was called The Elms and was home to one of the town's early Victorian doctors, Dr. Steele. The current Red Cross shop at No.207 was Dean's fruiterers in the 1950's and later became Gemma's clothes shop. The earlier property on this site had a late fifteenth century crown post roof and the present building is a re-build in the same style of the original structure which was demolished in the late 1980's.

The substantial building which stands next door to the Red Cross shop was originally built in 1933 as a large store for the Co-operative Society. This development necessitated the demolition of much older premises, used by the local firm of Pethybridge, later Pocock, the coach builders. The next run of shops originally featured a range of more specialist Co-op outlets, which initially included a butcher, a greengrocers and a hardware store. However, prior to the Co-op development, two of the earlier shops on this site were William Roberts the fishmonger and Joseph Callard the corn merchant, whose premises stood on the corner of Cowper Road. Cowper Road was also home to Berkhamsted's

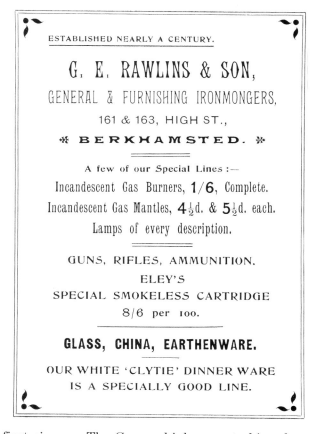

first cinema, The Gem, which operated in a large corrugated iron shed from the turn of the century. On the other side of Cowper Road the charming Sayers almshouses, built in 1684, still survive. However the adjacent property, which used to be the Gas Company's showrooms, and is now an Orange Balloon restaurant, was built on the site of another public house, The Royal Oak, which was demolished in 1908. During the 1890's one of the properties in Camilla Terrace was home to George Loader, who became the second chairman of the newly formed Berkhamsted Urban District Council. Next to this terraced row we can still find The George public house, which was listed as being kept by local nurseryman John Lane in 1853. The modern office block, Salter House on the corner of Park View Road, recalls the name of Edward Salter, whose bequest in 1696 helped fund the town's seventeenth century workhouse on this plot. Following demolition of this first workhouse in 1831, this site became home to the town's first 'free' state school which later to became Park View Primary School. On the other side of Park View Road, another modern office development now stands on the site where, until 1985, there used to be a small hairdressers shop called Hair Flair as well as Trina Tools the ironmongers. A leading firm of local lawyers, Harrowell & Atkins, still run their practice from the impressive premises of Boxwell House, on the corner of Boxwell Road. Beyond Boxwell Road is The Lamb public house and a small newsagents shop, that local people will remember trading for many years as Jennifer's.

Lower Kings Road to St Johns Well Lane (north)

Lower Kings Road was not built until 1885 and the entrance to this now important thoroughfare was once lined with a row of distinctive villas. Although the majority of these houses were demolished elements of two villas survive, their frontages now mainly hidden by High Street shops built in what was their front gardens. The prominent trading position occupied by the Berkhamsted Fisheries has an interesting and varied history. Although coincidentally it started life as a fishmongers, it later became the trading premises of the local watchmaker W. H. Morris until 1933 when the site was redeveloped. The new shop was used for a period by the town's leading tobacconists, Mayo's and more recently provided the initial premises for the Bookstack, which today remains Berkhamsted's leading independent book seller. Mackays department store occupies premises which were formerly part of a business developed by Jack Sharland and owed its traditions to one of the town's longest established trading concerns. This was Ward's drapers shop, which was located in the centre of the current site, and can be traced back to 1790. Mr Sharland financed a substantial extension of the building in the 1960's, which involved demolishing an old property at the east end. Despite this, its original timbers were retained in the new department store he created. The Britannia Building Society occupies the distinctive premises of the Bourne Charity School, which first opened in 1737. This building was later used by the Berkhamsted Girls School in 1888, before becoming the National Provincial Bank in 1902.

The lovingly maintained period shop front of the next property provides the clue that Dickman's the chemist, established in 1895, is another of Berkhamsted's leading historic businesses. However Dickman's first outlet was further up the High Street at what is now No.266 and the

HIGH-CLASS BAKER AND CONFECTIONER
AWARDED GOLD MEDAL FOR EXCELLENCE OF QUALITY

CRISP'S
MODEL BAKERY

Speciality: VIENNA BREAD AND ROLLS
made from an old Viennese Recipe
WEDDING & BIRTHDAY CAKES
DIABETIC BREADS

234 HIGH STREET, BERKHAMSTED
Telephone 70   Deliveries Daily

current chemist shop was originally built by Mr. W. Dickman as his private house. This property, which became a shop premises from 1914, originally had a small front garden facing onto the High Street. Coincidentally, almost a hundred years ago, what is now the Kodak shop at No.226 was a studio belonging to Thomas Banning, another of the town's nineteenth century photographers. A hundred years ago the Abbey National office was Timson's drapers shop, a property which was later re-built by Sainsbury in 1937 to establish one of their early traditional grocery stores. The attractive premises now occupied by the Wine Rack was formerly Mayo's, who ran an impressive specialist tobacconist business in the town for many years. Simmons at No.234 has been a baker's shop for several generations. Originally Timsons cake shop in the 1870's, many will remember it trading as Crisp's in the 1950's and more recently as Smith & Graver's. The next shop, currently occupied by Home Counties Property and David Paul opticians, is the site of another long standing local business where evidence of a stationers can be traced back to 1840. T. W. Bailey took over what had previously been Mrs. Greedy's stationery shop shortly before the First World War. Tom Bailey was subsequently elected Chairman of the Urban District Council and the business continued until 1971, when it was run by Mr. A. G. Fry. Gammon's newsagents at No.238 used to be Collins', previously Derrick's pork butchers shop, whose amusing adverts were a feature of the St Peter's Parish Magazine during the 1950's. Colton's, formerly Jones, has been a shoe shop for many years, whilst Mary Brooks at No.246 used to be Gilbert's TV and Radio shop. The current Bookstack premises has an interesting history, previously being home to Shuttleworth's cycle repair business, Stupples dairy shop and Buckland's fishmongers.

The next run of three shops occupy part of a site formerly taken by two houses, one of which was an important property known as the Homestead, demolished in 1958. In 1616 this house was home to Dr. Christopher Woodhouse, who was the last mayor of the town prior to the loss of its royal charter. In the nineteenth century the Homestead was owned by the Squire banking family whose

Roberts' fishmongers shop, circa 1910.

View of the Homestead (right) at No.250 High Street.

The far end of Berkhamsted High Street, with King's Coachworks (left), looking towards Gossoms End, circa 1910.

Woods Ironworks, circa 1910.

High Street frontage to Lane's Nurseries, circa 1910.

amateur gardening efforts produced the famous Prince Albert Apple which helped local nurseryman John Lane to make his fortune. At No.254 the offices of White Leaf House was the address used by the two Misses Loosley for their wool and material shop, which was also still advertising in 1955 as a registry office for servants. More recently this property was home to a local veterinary practice which has now re-located to a newly built property on the corner of St Johns Well Lane. Beyond the YMCA shop, which used to be Harts TV & Radio shop in 1950, was an old house which was formerly Timson's grocery shop. This property was subsequently rebuilt to become Lintott's, which was a popular local butchers shop during the 1950's and 60's. What is today the Highwayman restaurant used to be the home of early local photographer George Sills, whilst the Lace Collection, formerly Potters Pride, was the site of the original Dickman's chemist shop. The small post office shop at No.268 will be remembered by many as Barnard's toy and cycle shop and Atkins the bakers at No.270-272 used to be Manders ironmongers. Clare of Berkhamsted has previously been Pratt's watchmakers and the Co-op cake shop, whilst Johnston's betting office used to be Eliott's and then Davey's wool shop in 1950. These premises later offered 'massage, turkish baths and sunrays' as the Berkhamsted Sauna and Beauty Centre during the 1970's. To the rear of the funeral parlour at No.284 was Timson's coal and timber yard. This was being run by Leslie B. Good in 1966 and, at the turn of the century, the adjacent tyre yard was home to a business run by local auctioneer Joseph North. Woods garden nursery and gift centre are the surviving elements of an important ironworks business, established here by James Wood back in 1826. The distinctive building of Cafe Rouge, previously Flambards Restaurant in 1982, was formerly the properties known as Monks House and Monks Cottage. Griffin's fishmongers used to be here in 1905, but from 1914 the house became a doctors' surgery which was later used by Dr Charles Waterman and Dr Gwyn Rowlands until 1966. The Doctors then moved to 1a Boxwell Road where a new purpose-built surgery had been built in the gardens of Boxwell House. This practice was later enlarged with the purchase of No.1 Boxwell Road in 1981. The modern post office occupies land previously owned by Lane's nursery business and is thought to have been the ancient site of the town's medieval hospital, run by the Brotherhood of St John the Baptist. Also on the site was the early Chapel of St James which would have still served the hospital following the building of St Peter's Church.

St Johns Well Lane to Billet Lane (south)

This section of the High Street begins with the distinctive structure of the Quaker Meeting House which was built close to the main road in 1818. Beyond Prospect House are the solicitors' offices, which were once home to one of the town's better known post-war builders, Donald Lockhart. He took over premises that had formerly been the base for King's coach builders business until 1937. The dental surgery at No.301 used to be Pitkin's fishmongers, whilst the Venetian style villa next door was Berg's tailor shop. The small corner property at Kitsbury Road will be remembered by many as the premises used by West's shoe shop and later Willmore, the hairdresser. A little further up Kitsbury Road was the Kitsbury cycle works. This enterprise developed into the garage business which eventually became Underhill and Young's. The more modern run of shop fronts on the other side of Kitsbury Road stand on the site of the town's second workhouse which was built in 1831. This institution finally closed in 1935, when its remaining inhabitants were transferred to the workhouse at Hemel Hempstead. The old building was then demolished in 1937 to make way for a development of new shops. Some of the local traders people may remember being in this parade during the 1960's are Peter Mac's fancy goods shop, the Candy Box, Woolcraft and Eastwood's award winning family butchers, who still have their main premises in Gravel Path. Beyond the Unisex hairdresser the next modern block, now dominated by the Berkhamsted Tandori, used to be home to the Princess Launderette and the Blue Jade Chinese Restaurant in 1971.

Beyond Cross Oak Road is an old suburb of the town known as Gossoms End. For several hundred years this was one of the poorest quarters of Berkhamsted, until the arrival of East's timber yard circa 1850, when it began to develop as something of an industrial quarter. The extended corner site, now occupied by the Renault car showrooms, was at various times home to Brinkman's nursery and florist business, the Goss brush works which continued to flourish into the 1930's and Binge's fish and chip shop. Close by there was also the site of the Gossoms End infant school, built in 1844, which later became a domestic science block used by several local schools. On land now taken by the petrol station and developed by Underhill & Young, was Gibbs Dairy together with a row of old cottages which were eventually demolished to make way for the expanded garage site. The headquarters of the first Gossoms End Scout

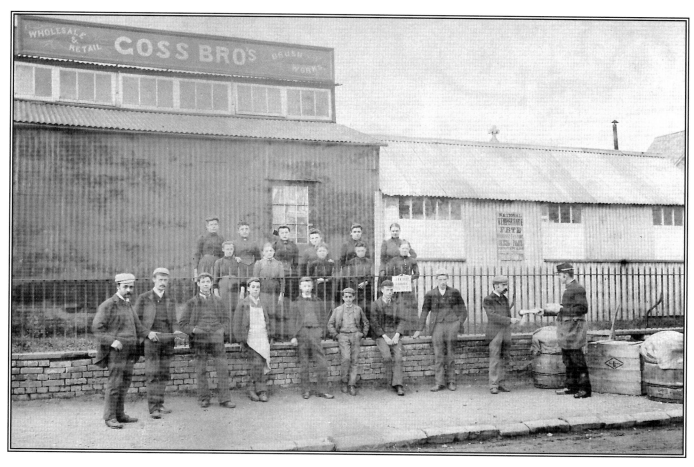

Goss Brushworks, circa 1890.

The original site of Underhill and Young's Garage, near Park Street, seen here in 1935.

of the Local Health Authority. A modern youth club opposite Billet Lane was built in 1991 on the former meadows of Lagley House and completes our tour of the southern side of Berkhamsted High Street.

St Johns Well Lane to Billet Lane (north)
The area immediately beyond St Johns Well Lane is still dominated by the rather elegant run of eight, three storey late Victorian/early Edwardian style town houses which were built in 1891. The first of these, on the corner, once served as offices for the Berkhamsted and District Building Society. At the turn of the century, the next three properties beyond the villas (Nos.340-344) were home to William Osbourn Norris, boot and shoe repairer, John Strange the butcher and Albert Snoad the baker. The site now taken by Avica House was occupied by the Primitive Methodist Church, established in 1867, and in a small shop adjacent to the church was Pike's grocery shop. The property which is now Pizza Express (formerly Park Street Antiques) was used by David Osbourne, the builder and stonemason, who was also the first Chairman of the Berkhamsted Urban District Council in 1898. Park Street was also the location of a public house called the Carpenters Arms and beside it was a tannery which can be traced back to the eighteenth century. This property was once used by the builder David Osbourne to produce the town's first concrete slabs. On the other side of Park Street, the premises of National Tyres was home to Underhill & Young's garage, prior to its move to a larger site on the other side of the main road. Part of the large frontage of Cook's Delight was once a small ladies/children's clothes shop. The property also housed another of Berkhamsted's well known businesses, Basil Leatherdale's stationery shop, which had moved here from its town centre site by 1960. Part of this building had previously been the Cross Oak Handy Stores in 1955. In the next run of properties No.368 was used by the Jones family, first as a greengrocer's and then as a funeral director and monumental masonry business. At No.372, which is now the Unicorn Chinese take-away, was formerly Walton's newsagents. Closer to the laundry, Barnett's baker's shop used to be Cripps baker's, which then included a small restaurant. The large laundry, which is still a going concern today, traded as Excelsior Laundry in the 1940's, but is still best known as the Berkhamsted Steam Laundry.

Group, which stands on higher ground above the corner of Queens Road, was built by the garage owners in partial compensation for the properties lost. To the west of Queens Road are a run of substantial private houses, the first of which 'Silverdale' is the family home and headquarters of another long established Berkhamsted business, S. Dell & Son Removals. Beyond Crab Tree Cottage there used to be three blocks of old council housing, built in the early 1930's, but these have since been demolished to make way for a range of more modern accommodation around Victory Road. At the heart of this stylish new development is the Gossoms End Elderly Care Unit at Gossoms Ryde, which is now run by the West Herts Community Health Trust and was designed by the same architect who was responsible for the improved Council housing. This impressive facility was officially opened on 21st July 1989 by Mr. Nick Tilley, former Chairman

On the corner of Stag Lane, the modern warehouse belonging to S. Dell & Son removal business was formerly the site of Gossoms End junior school, which closed in 1917. It then became a boys woodwork centre used by several local schools. On the other side of this road stood the tiny public house, The Stag, which gave the lane its name. This inn became a private house after the First World War and was finally demolished in 1971. The Stag stood on the end of a row of old properties which separated it from its rival public house the Rose and Crown. These were known as East's cottages and also included a seventeenth century farmhouse. The area which is now being re-developed between Stag Lane and Eddy Street is the site of East's timber yard, which until its demolition in 1990 was one of the town's principal industrial concerns. Although all the old cottages have now gone, the Rose and Crown still survives on the corner of Eddy Street, which is named after John Turpin Eddy, a local banker who lived at Gossoms Lodge circa 1850. Mr. Eddy was in partnership with William Squire of the Homestead and together they ran an early local bank called Eddy & Squires. The attractively renovated Gossoms Lodge was also once the family home of Cornelius East and its near neighbour Gossoms Cottage dates from 1691. Although the trading names may have varied, the small run of shops at Gossoms End have remained unchanged for many years and since

the war have always featured a small general store and transport cafe. Beyond this small parade of four shops is Dealey's motor repair works. The private cottage at No.65, on the corner of Norris Terrace, was once a small greengrocer's, before becoming the local Spar store. Eagle eyed visitors to Gossoms End will spot a small model cat on the roof of No.73, the quaintly named Mousehole Cottage. At the end of this run of surviving cottages in Gossoms End is the modern development of flats in Riverside Gardens. These were built in the early 1960's on the site formerly occupied by a group of timber framed buildings used as the Northchurch workhouse. This takes us as far as Billet Lane and on the other side of the lane, much closer to the corner, there used to be a small low building dating from the early eighteenth century. This was the original Crooked Billet public house, an old inn which was popular with the bargees because, in addition to food and lodgings, it also offered stabling for their horses. However it was demolished in 1964, as part of a road widening scheme and the modern Crooked Billet was built further back from the main A41 trunk road. Next to the original pub there also used to be two old cottages, which at one time served as a small hospital for the Northchurch workhouse.

The old cottages of Northchurch Workhouse (demolished in the early 1960's), now the site of Riverside Gardens.
The original Crooked Billet is also visible (left).

Religious Traditions

The Parish Church of St Peter

This substantial parish church was built to an Italian cross plan and has since been given an official date of 1222, although some of its architectural remains in the chancel date from 1200. Measuring an impressive 168 ft. from east window to west door and 90 ft. across its transepts, it is one of the largest churches in Hertfordshire with a total seating capacity of up to 1,100. The early architectural development of St Peter's concluded with the construction of the tower in 1544 and is discussed in more detail in an earlier chapter (see p.16). The first parish of Berkhamsted (St Mary) related very closely to the size and shape of the historic manorial boundaries. However, when St Peter's Church was built, a new parish of Berkhamsted St. Peter was created by taking some 4,000 acres from the middle of the original parish. For the majority of its life the parish of St Peter fell within the vast diocese accorded to Lincoln. However in 1843 all the local parishes were transferred to Rochester before passing to the See of St Albans in 1877.

As a building the Church of St Peter endured a gentle but protracted slide from its days of medieval splendour and was in need of some serious attention by the time that fundamental restoration work took place in the nineteenth century. The oldest surviving photographs of the church, pre 1870, reveal that it had become a rather dour and neglected looking building. The first unsatisfactory programme of work took place in 1820 and was supervised by Jeffrey Wyattville, a young architect with rather Gothic taste. His gratuitous and superficial meddling with the interior attacked the integrity of the church and his insistence on covering the church with stucco was certainly not to everyone's liking. However later in this century, a leading Victorian church restorer, William Butterfield, made some substantial improvements. Butterfield achieved an amazing transformation to the exterior appearance of St Peter's by skilfully re-facing the church with flint in 1870. Although his programme of interior restorations, which closed the church for a few months in 1870-71, were more appropriate than Wyattville's earlier attempts, they still involved the destruction of some original features. Under Butterfield's direction, both the floor and the roof of the chancel were raised and the roof of the south transept altered to its original pitch. The vestry was demolished and the old south porch was made part of the outer south aisle. He made it possible to extend the main aisles by knocking down the dividing walls of two chambers, one of which (at the south-west corner) had been used to store the town's fire engine! Wyattville's west gallery was unceremoniously replaced by the present gallery and the whole church was re-floored, with oak benches being substituted for the former pews. Another benefit of Butterfield's plan was that with new clear glass in the clerestory, more light was now shed on the interior of St Peter's. Flint gathered in the process of demolishing dividing walls, during the restoration work, was stored carefully in the local yard of Matthews the builder. These stones were later to be incorporated in the structure of Sunnyside Church, which was built in 1909. A later scheme of restoration work, costing £24,000, took place at St Peter's between 1956 and 1960. Under this programme of improvements the tower was given a new timber and lead roof and the roof of the nave was completely removed and covered with copper. The interior of the nave and St Catherine's Chapel were both thoroughly refurbished and the new arrangements also featured the provision of a new sanctuary in the tower crossing and the re-siting of the choir. More recently in 1984 the St Peter's Restoration Appeal was launched, with the declared objective of raising £150,000 over a period of three years. These plans, which included the restoration of some exterior stone work, the repair of various stained glass windows and the re-building and re-siting of the organ have all since been achieved.

The eight bells of St Peter's together weigh 3½ tons, but none are of any great age. In 1553 the tower held a peal of four bells, the largest of which weighed 18 cwt. However in 1837 the decision was taken to provide a new clock and ring of eight bells. With the addition of new metal, Mears and Stainbrook of Whitechapel, London, recast the bells at a total cost of £429 10s 9d. As befits the parish church of a town with such a rich history, St Peter's has many fascinating features, principal amongst which is the fourteenth century tomb of a knight and his lady. Situated on the north side of the church, close to the chancel, this was previously known as the Torrington tomb and is now thought to be the interment of Henry of Berkhamsted, who served as Constable to the Black Prince at Berkhamsted Castle. In St John the Baptist's Chauntry John Raven, another local servant of the Black Prince, can be found represented by a brass of a knight in armour which dates from 1385. There are also two memorial brasses to the parents of Dean Incent who founded

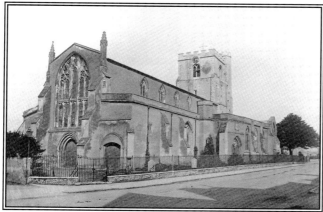

An early photograph of St. Peter's Church, prior to Butterfield's restoration of 1870.

St Peter's Church Choir in 1930, with the Rev. William Chipchase Stainsby (centre).

Interior of St Peter's Parish Church, circa 1920.

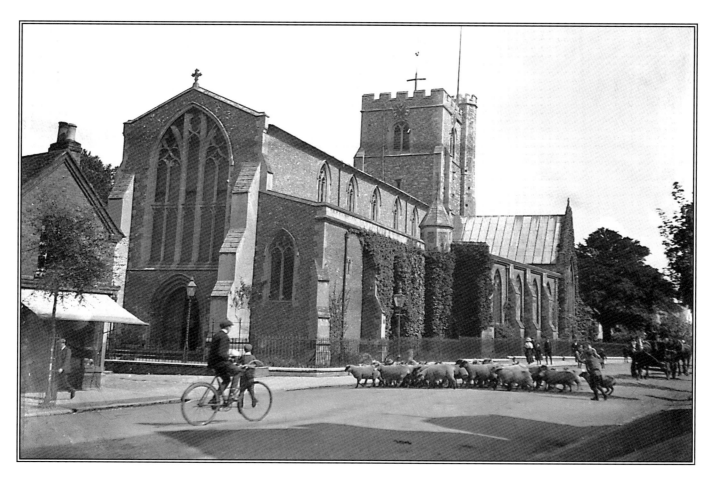

St Peter's Church, circa 1910.

Berkhamsted School. However the oldest brasses in the church are displayed in the south aisle; these belong to Richard and Margaret Torrington and date from 1356. St Peter's also houses historically important memorials to early residents of Berkhamsted Place. The large black marble topped tomb of John Sayer, who endowed the town's almshouses in 1684, is easy to find close to Henry of Berkhamsted's tomb and there is also a very fine monument to John and James Murray of Berkhamsted Place on the north wall of the chancel. On the south side of the church is a large stone memorial to Mary Isabella, wife of James Smith of Ashlyns Hall (1764-1843). It also commemorates other members of the Smith family, including Augustus Smith (1804-72) and some of the Smith-Dorriens of Haresfoot. An early vault belonging to John Dorrien and his family is located beneath the Lady Chapel and immediately behind the Sayer tomb there is a brass, dated 1782, recording this fact. The peaceful atmosphere of St Catherine's Chapel is enhanced by a stained glass window which depicts St Francis of Assisi and includes a verse by the poet Coleridge. Some surviving medieval glass at St Peter's was incorporated into the north lancet window of the chancel which depicts the arms of Richard III. Another attractive window can be found near the pulpit. Dating from 1871, this is a representation of two famous paintings by Holman Hunt called 'The Light of the World' and 'The Good Shepherd'; beneath this window is a memorial plaque to William Longman, who died at Ashlyns Hall in 1877. Another feature window in the north aisle was provided by the Cooper family in memory of local industrialist William Cooper (1813-85). At the beginning of the north aisle, close to the west door, it is possible to find another unique feature in the form of a painted board commemorating the death of Elizabeth I in 1601, which was repainted in 1797. One of Berkhamsted's most famous inhabitants, the celebrated eighteenth century poet William Cowper, is also honoured in St Peter's Church. William Cowper was born in the town and described his childhood, spent at the old rectory, as a "blissful time". In 1872 the Rev. J. W. Cobb raised the necessary funds to create a beautiful and permanent memorial to the life of William Cowper in the form of the large east window. Cowper's father, the Rev. John Cowper, served as Rector of Berkhamsted (1722-56) and it was here at St Peter's Church that his son, destined to become the nation's greatest eighteenth century poet, was baptised on 13th December 1731. William Cowper himself was later to describe his childhood, spent at the Rectory in Berkhamsted, as " a blissful time".

Rectors of St Peter's Parish Church

John Cowper	*1681*
John Jeffries	*1756*
Charles de Guiffardiere	*1798*
John Crofts	*1810*
James Hutchinson	*1851*
John Wolstenholme Cobb	*1871*
Arthur Johnson	*1883*
Henry G. Constable Curtis	*1902*
Reginald A. De Vere Hart-Davies	*1908*
William Chipchase Stainsby	*1920*
Horace Spence	*1948*
Robert Saville Brown	*1953*
Edward M. Norfolk	*1969*
H. Roger Davis	*1981*
Mark Bonny	*1996*

Baptists

The Baptist community in Berkhamsted is one of the oldest nationally recorded within the denomination and dates from 1640, when early Baptists would gather to worship in local houses or barns. Despite its early hold in the town, the practice of non-conformist beliefs could be a dangerous business in the second half of the seventeenth century. In 1662 the leader of Berkhamsted Baptists, Thomas Monke, was reported to the authorities for his religious work and actually sentenced to death. However he was later reprieved by Charles II, following representations by his son. The Conventicle Act of 1664, required everyone to conform to the worship of the parish church or run the risk of similar threats to their well-being. However this official discouragement seemed to have little impact locally in a town rapidly developing a strong non-conformist tradition. In 1676 the Baptist community was led by an Elder, John Russell, who was supported in his work by five or six deacons. A survey conducted in that same year tells us that in Berkhamsted St Peter there were then 400 conformists and 150 non-conformists, whilst in Berkhamsted St Mary (Northchurch) there were 236 conformists and 45 non-conformists. It is also worth noting that, given the continuing climate of state disapproval, this is likely to be an underestimate of the true extent of non-conformist belief in the town.

At the beginning of the eighteenth century there was sufficient confidence to worship more openly and by 1722 a site in Water Lane was purchased by the Baptists from two local grocers, George Topping and Benjamin Morley. Here a substantial chapel was built which had seating for 390 people and was to be in regular use for the next 140 years. This chapel also had its own small burial ground and stood on a site which is now part of the town's main car park, behind the former Waitrose supermarket building. At first the new chapel was strictly for the use of the 'Dissenting Protestants Baptised', a group which insisted upon whole body immersion during baptism. From around 1750 the church began to suffer from a drop in numbers and by 1780 there were only 112 members worshipping regularly at Water Lane. However in February 1802 Pastor Joseph Hobbs arrived to revitalise the Baptist community in Berkhamsted. He was also responsible for inspiring other local churches to become involved in education, by starting the first Sunday School in the town in 1810. With a resurgence in numbers the Chapel was enlarged and modernised in 1840, the year that Joseph Hobbs died aged 75. In 1838 the church had already found it necessary to obtain a second burial ground. The plot of land called Blackhouse Mead, near the Wilderness was purchased for this purpose and this ground now forms part of the garden of Wilson House, home to the Headmaster of Berkhamsted Boys School.

The Baptists continued to prosper in the town of Berkhamsted, but the area of Water Lane and the Wilderness was not really an ideal environment for a religious building. Early in the ministry of

Rev. John Lawton, it was acknowledged that both the Chapel and the Schoolroom urgently required improved accommodation. At a sale of land held at the Goat Inn in 1859, the Baptist community was fortunate to acquire a much improved site in the High Street, on the corner of Ravens Lane. Following several years of fund raising efforts, the cornerstone of the new Chapel was laid on 11th October 1864 and the opening ceremony took place on Tuesday, 1st August 1865. The total bill for the construction of the new church and schoolroom was only £1,600 which included the cost of the site. The Baptist's burial ground at the Wilderness continued to be used until 1889 and was subsequently sold to Berkhamsted Boys School in 1962. When the Chapel in Ravens Lane was renovated in 1903, the church had 215 members and continues to thrive today with many young families among its congregation. A recent programme of work has renovated the impressive spire and thoroughly cleaned the stonework of this historic church, which can now be seen to its best advantage. This initiative resulted in the Berkhamsted Baptists receiving a special 'Environment Award', which was presented to the current Minister, the Rev. James Neve by the Berkhamsted Citizens' Association on 26th March 1998.

Sunday School outing leaves the Baptist Church, circa 1910.

Quakers

A small Quaker community began to emerge in Berkhamsted during the second half of the seventeenth century when, despite the threat of prosecution, several strands of non-conformist belief were beginning to take hold in the town. One of the earliest Berkhamsted Quakers was Christopher Woodhouse, a leading member of the local community who lived at the Homestead in 1660. Despite this, surviving records tell us that in 1683 a local trader, who was a Quaker, still fell foul of the authorities, suffering 'distraint of goods'. In 1809 a Quaker sympathiser, Thomas Woodman of New Ground in Tring, sold a corner of the grounds belonging to Boxwell House to Anne Littleboy and the Squire family who were then living at the Homestead. For some time the local Quakers had been raising funds with the intention of building a Meeting House on this plot of land, which was already being used as a burial ground for the unmarked graves of non-conformists. Their plans were fully realised when a purpose built Meeting House opened in 1818. In addition to the Squire family, who were bankers, Joseph Robinson of the Red House was another wealthy Quaker who helped provide funds to finance this new building.

Originally the Meeting House faced towards Boxwell Road and was divided by a wooden partition so that, as was then the custom, men and women could gather separately for business meetings. It was unfortunate that this building suffered from damp which was rather ironically caused by the presence beneath its foundations of waters from the 'holy spring' which drained down the slope towards St Johns Well Lane. In 1930 the Meeting House was considered "too old and chilly for monthly meetings" and waggonettes were hired so that Berkhamsted Quakers could travel elsewhere to worship. Meetings were only held locally in the summer months of June and July and by then Berkhamsted had become an 'allowed meeting', which was now considered too small to operate independently. However during the war years the Meeting House was again in regular use every Sunday and there was a small but active group of twenty members in Berkhamsted. One local Quaker, Winifred Rawlins, joined the Peace Pledge Union and as a result spent a month in Holloway Prison for "refusing to register for war purposes". Undaunted by this experience, Winifred and her sister Kathleen rented a house in Charles Street where, at their own expense, they established a wartime hostel for thirty Jewish refugees. In keeping with their compassionate beliefs, after the War the Berkhamsted Friends also collected clothes and money for food to send to destitute families in Germany. A prolonged fund raising campaign finally enabled an extensive renovation of the damp old Meeting House to be conducted in 1964. During building work the Friends had use of the Red Cross premises in Kings Road for their meetings. In April 1965, newly encouraged by their improved accommodation, the Berkhamsted Quakers were successful in their application to become a 'preparative' rather than an 'allowed meeting'. A central tenet of the Quaker philosophy is good works for the benefit of others and the Friends at Berkhamsted remain active today, supporting international charities and helping to raise money for the Quaker Relief Fund.

Congregationalists

The Congregationalists in Berkhamsted are another early group and their presence in the town can be traced back to 1780. At this time the first meetings were held in Castle Street, in the parlour of a local lace merchant called Langston. This new non-conformist church proved very successful and it was soon necessary to switch the main services to a nearby barn as numbers grew. The Rev. W. Baker arrived to tend to the local congregation in 1790. A few years into his pastorate a small Gothic style church was built in Castle Street, which became known as the 'Countess of Huntingdon's' Chapel. In 1834, with overcrowding a continuing problem, it was necessary to replace this rather unusual building with an 'Independent Chapel', which stood on the corner of Chapel Street and Castle Street. Armed by the faith of a large congregation, the church became more ambitious and in 1867 this second chapel was demolished and replaced, on the same site, by the imposing Congregational Church which dominated the corner of Chapel Street. However 100 years later, the post-war decline in church congregations meant that a building on this impressive scale was no longer necessary. Consequently the decision was taken to demolish this spectacular monument to the faith of yesteryear and sell some of the church land to the Hanover House Housing Association. In 1974 the site was then used to create the modern sheltered housing development known as William Fiske House, which opened on 4th October 1978. To the rear of these new flats, a much smaller place of worship was provided for local Congregationalists who then joined forces with the Presbyterian Church. Quite recently, in November 1998, this modern church was re-christened and dedicated as St Andrew's United Reformed Church.

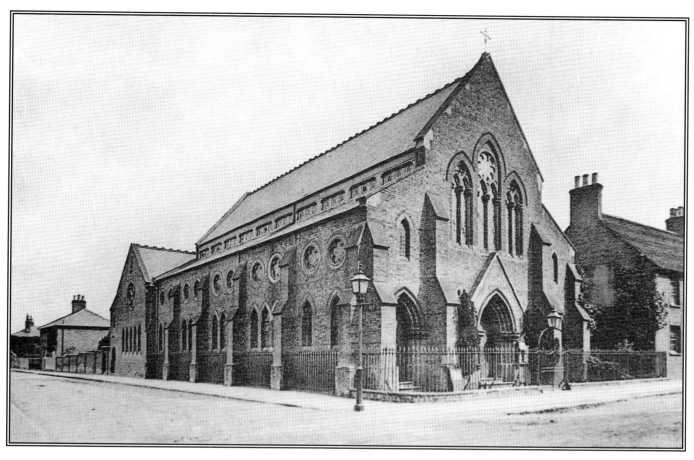

The imposing Congregational Church which formerly stood on the corner of Chapel Street and was demolished in 1974.

Methodists

The arrival of Wesleyan Methodism in the town can be traced back to 1837, when it was the popular creed of some of the many hundreds of workmen who descended on the area to help construct the London to Birmingham Railway. At first meetings were held in local cottages until 1840, when a fast growing Methodist community was able to purchase the fine property known as Egerton House. The ground floor of this spacious building was then used for religious services and the upper storey was let to the Berkhamsted Temperance Society for £5 per annum. However this arrangement was short-lived and in 1846 Egerton House reverted to a private house, when local Methodists re-sold the property. Temporary arrangements for worship were again introduced until a brand new structure, called the Prospect Place Chapel, was erected in Highfield Road at a cost of £240. However, only two years after its registration in 1854, this new chapel was offered for sale and was adopted by a group of Strict Baptists, who were later succeeded by the Plymouth Brethren. The early sale of this first purpose built chapel may well have been influenced by the fact that there was now a rival community in the town. Inspired and led by the fiery evangelist Thomas Russell, who was based in St Albans, this 'Primitive Methodist' group at first met in a house in Castle Street. Eventually in 1867, they gathered sufficient funds to build their own church in the High Street, opposite Cross Oak Road. The 'Prims', as they were then known, quickly became the dominant force in Berkhamsted and they succeeded in attracting regular congregations of over a hundred, then double the number of those attending the local Wesleyan services.

Fortunately for the earlier group, local builder William Nash was a staunch Wesleyan and was able to provide them with their own small chapel in his yard, behind the High Street. This sufficed until the Wesleyans were able to obtain another church in Cowper Road. This building, which was made of galvanised iron, had originally been erected in Hemel Hempstead and was brought to the town in 1887. It was subsequently provided with brick walls, a vestry and front porch in 1923. Meanwhile the Primitive Methodists continued to flourish, enlarging their premises in 1898 and later adding church halls to the original building. Although Methodist Union officially took place nationally in 1932, it was another 21 years before the Wesleyan and Primitives of Berkhamsted combined forces. Eventually in 1953 the Cowper Road church was sold to the Christian Scientist Movement and local Methodists at last

Methodist Church in the High Street, 1971.

Quaker Meeting House in 1985; also showing the gravestones of early non-conformists.

Kings Road Evangelical Church, 1983.

worshipped together in one chapel in the High Street. The current situation, whereby local Anglican and Methodist communities share the facilities provided by All Saints Church, began on 9th April 1976. Following the success of this arrangement, the Methodist Church buildings became redundant and have since been re-developed to provide the offices of Avica House. Today the Methodist community in Berkhamsted has 130 members and its work with young people in particular means that it remains an important part of community life.

Evangelists

This religious group began its life in Berkhamsted as part of the Plymouth Brethren, which traditionally has always been a lay ministry with no ordained minister. The early group used various buildings around the town. At first the Brethren met in a cottage in Castle Street and for a time used the Prospect Place Chapel, which had been built by the Wesleyan Methodists. Prior to building their own church they had no choice but to use the Town Hall for larger meetings, until Hope Hall opened in January 1875. From 1870 the local community was led by a gifted teacher and lay preacher called Samuel Alexander. The strength of this early evangelical

group is indicated by surviving church records which reveal that on Good Friday 3rd April 1874, "four hundred sat down to tea in the Town Hall and we had several good speakers in the evening". Alexander's own notebook revealed a heavy workload, which involved preaching to large congregations in places as far away as Newport Pagnell. Despite financial hardships, the church survived the next one hundred years and in 1969 Hope Hall was refurbished and re-christened the Kings Road Evangelical Church. This local evangelist group also use the old Beulah Chapel in Kings Road as a Sunday School and this property is currently rented from the Assemblies of God Pentecostal Church who originally built this place of worship. Most of the exclusive practices of the early Evangelical Church have since been discontinued and the building at Kings Road is now formally part of the Association of Berkhamsted Churches.

Roman Catholics

Historically, when compared to the early communities established by the local non-conformists, Catholicism has a limited tradition in Berkhamsted, where its impact remained minimal until the dawn of the twentieth century. The first small group of Catholics in

Berkhamsted worshipped in one of the middle cottages in the old 'sunken row' in Castle Street. This sufficed until the opening of the first Catholic Church in Park View Road in 1909. The founder of the original Sacred Heart Church in Berkhamsted was Father Henry Hardy M.A. who died in January 1918. It was here that General de Gaulle was a regular member of the congregation during his wartime exile in Berkhamsted (1941-42) and Catholic worship continued in this building until 1967. Its impressive successor, the Church of the Sacred Heart in Park Street now caters for a thriving Catholic community of around 800. Berkhamsted's new Catholic church was officially opened by Cardinal John Carmel Heenan, 8th Archbishop of Westminster on 4th June 1967 and finally consecrated by Cardinal George Basil Hume, the 9th Archbishop, on 15th September 1980.

A spacious and stylish building, the Church of the Sacred Heart is an exceptional example of modern church architecture, which optimises the use of light in its design. The huge central crucifix is adorned with an arc of small stained glass panels in bright red and yellow, cut through the outer wall of the church to create a stunning effect. The two large 'Star of Bethlehem'

windows, on either side of the church, combine to fill the building with light. The small Lady Chapel, with its blue stained glass, was funded with money raised by the children of the parish between 1936-57. An outstanding feature of the Church of the Sacred Heart are the Stations of the Cross, which have been sensitively fashioned in a unique design of wrought ironwork and copper. Worthy of note is a wooden crucifix, mounted in a small memorial garden to the front of the Presbytery. This came from the original church in Park View Road and is in memory of three Sisters: Julie of Gabriel, Mary of St Alban and Julie Joseph, whose work helped establish the early Catholic community in Berkhamsted between 1884 and 1934. From 1936 the Convent of Our Lady of the Sacred Heart, together with the first St Thomas More School, was established at No.1 Boxwell Road. William Campling M.B.E. served as the Catholic priest in Berkhamsted from 1963-85 and it was Father William who was responsible for securing the excellent plot of land for the Church of the Sacred Heart. It also worth noting that it was his brother, the architect Mr. Edward Campling, who designed the new church. In September 1997 Father Peter Grant succeeded Father Vincent Cummerford, who had served as Priest at the Church of the Sacred Heart from

The former Catholic Church in Park View Road, 1987.

Church of the Sacred Heart in Park Street, 1985.

Interior of the former Catholic Church, circa 1920.

1985 until his sudden death in 1997. Father Vincent, who also did much work for the diocese of Westminster, will be especially remembered locally for his commitment to Catholic education and his natural affinity for work with children.

All Saints Church
All Saints Church was built as a daughter church to Berkhamsted's Parish Church of St Peter. It was founded in 1906, in order to cater for the spiritual needs of the fast growing population in the west end of the town. All Saints opened its doors for the first time on the evening of Whit Sunday, when it was dedicated by the Bishop of St Albans, Edward Jacob. The new red brick building in Cross Oak Road replaced a neighbouring iron-framed structure, which had been used as a temporary Church and Sunday School since the 1890's. Housing development had begun in this area in 1868 and prior to the provision of the 'Iron Room', the first residents in this part of Berkhamsted could attend local services, held in a barn behind the town's old workhouse in Kitsbury Road. There is still a drawing in All Saints showing the full extent of the architect's plans for the new church, but these were never fully realised. Despite its now densely populated surroundings, the Church struggled to be successful and came near to closure in the 1920's. However a single weekly service, held at 8 o'clock on Sunday morning, helped maintain some momentum. In 1938, encouraged by the Rev. Chipchase Stainsby, All Saints found fresh impetus, providing much needed spiritual comfort during the war years and slowly began to flourish again. By the early 1970's the Anglican community of All Saints had the opportunity to reduce costs and also afford much needed improvements to the building, by sharing their facilities with local Methodists. This plan enabled the west end of the church to be completed and for modern committee rooms, halls and a kitchen to be added behind the new west hall. Following protracted discussions, the Methodist Church in the High Street was closed and the co-operative arrangement whereby both Anglican and Methodist congregations share All Saints as a place of worship began on 9th April 1976.

Salvation Army
The Berkhamsted Corps of the Salvation Army was first established in 1887, operating from a base in a small workshop in Back Lane. Here they had upstairs accommodation next to the old Tudor House, which used to stand close to the

All Saints Church, 1998.

Travelling preacher from the Salvation Army at the turn of the century.

junction with Water Lane. By 1898 the Salvation Army Barracks were listed as being in a hall in Lower Kings Road which became a more permanent headquarters. An enthusiastic member of the 'Sally Army' was local draper W. E. Timpson, who often led the band and became known locally as 'Alleluia Timpson'. The Corps closed down during the First World War, after which its presence in the town became rather fitful. The Army re-established themselves in the town, returning to Lower Kings Road in 1925, only to close down in 1947. Today the Salvation Army are active once again, renting accommodation either in the Court House or at the Town Hall for their meetings. The current work of the Corps in Berkhamsted is co-ordinated by Lieutenant Poxon who took up his local duties in 1994.

Church of St Michael and All Angels, Sunnyside

The Parish of St Mary, Northchurch, once extended around that of St Peter, Berkhamsted, to the north and the east. This situation remained until 1855 when a separate parish of St John, Broadway, was consecrated to serve the villagers of Bourne End and the growing community of Sunnyside. The beginnings of pastoral activity in the Sunnyside area itself owe their origins to the

Rev. A. F. Birch, Rector of Northchurch. He was fortunate to have been supported in his work by Mr. E. J. Pearson of Millfield House, who took responsibility for raising funds to establish a local place of worship. As a result of their efforts a wooden mission room opened in a converted barn at the end of George Street and the first service was held there on Good Friday, 1881. Under the leadership of lay reader, Mr. G. H. Siddons, the new congregation outgrew its first premises and a small iron church was built on land, donated by Earl Brownlow, just to the north of the railway. The cost of this new building was £400 and the original George Street premises then became the Parish Room. However, the 'Iron Church' which was dedicated on Michaelmas Day 29th September 1886, was only a temporary prefabricated structure and twenty years later ambitious plans were afoot for a more permanent building. A further plot of land was donated by Earl Brownlow, just to the north of the Iron Church and architects, Rew & Son, drew up plans for what was to eventually become the Parish Church of St Michael and All Angels. As befits its semi-rural location, the charming structure of this small church was deliberately based on a traditional design of Sussex church architecture, although the building was to be clad in local flint. The creation of such an impressive church proved to be an achievement for the whole community, with regular parishioners all involved helping to raise money, prepare the foundations and gather the necessary flints. The people of Sunnyside were doubly rewarded for their efforts by the creation of the Parish of Sunnyside and Broadway, when the Church was officially consecrated on 30th June 1909. The ecclesiastical parishes of Sunnyside and Bourne End were not finally separated until 1916.

The Parish Church of St Michael and All Angels consists of a nave with four bays, a chancel, vestry and south aisle, with a porch and bell turret at the west end. Subsequent additions have included attractive stained glass in the south aisle and baptistery, as well as the creation of a Lady Chapel in the south aisle, provided by the Mothers' Union in 1954. The construction of the chancel was funded by local industrialist Sir Richard Cooper, whose family remained for many years great benefactors to the Church. The first church wardens of St Michael and All Angels were local landowner Mr. W. Dwight of The Pheasantries and Mr. E. Mawley of Rosebank, President of the Rose Society. The east window in the south aisle is a memorial to Edward Mawley and is dated 1916. During his time as a

parishioner, Mr. Mawley also gave Sunnyside the benefit of his professional expertise by supervising a spectacular display of rose plantings around the original Iron Church. Today the Church of St Michael and All Angels houses a memorial brass plaque to George Henry Siddons who, beginning as a Lay Reader, served as the first Priest in Charge of the Parish 1888-1906. The community at the new Church of St Michael and All Angels was led by the Rev. R. A. Cattell, for whom the vicarage was built in 1911. By 1983 the old Iron Church, which had served for so many years as the Church Hall, had reached the end of its natural life. Consequently it was dismantled and the land used to provide the site for 'The Cedars', a development of flats in Ivy House Lane. A modern hall was then erected which featured a large lobby connecting it directly to the Church. This new and well equipped meeting place was dedicated by the Bishop of Hertford on 3rd March 1984. Although the Parish Church of St Michael and All Angels remains the town's newest Anglican Church, it does incorporate some thirteenth century flints within its structure. Appropriately these stones were saved from ancient walls in Berkhamsted, demolished during restoration work at the Parish Church of St Peter in 1870-71.

The old iron church at Sunnyside, 1888.

Interior of the old iron church, circa 1900.

The Parish Church of St Michael and All Angels, Sunnyside.

Education

Although Berkhamsted has an impressive educational tradition, which can be traced back to 1544 when John Incent founded Berkhamsted School, it is worth remembering that, until the 1830's, the vast majority of local children received no formal education whatsoever during the working week. However those youngsters who attended one of the early Sunday Schools in the town at least had the opportunity to gain some basic instruction in reading and writing. The role of the church, particularly the part played by non-conformist chapels, was pivotal in creating educational opportunities for working class children in Berkhamsted. The first such Sunday School in the town was established by Joseph Hobbs, the Pastor of the Baptist Church, and when it opened on 11th June 1810 was able to welcome 73 children. This school was also supported by the local Congregational Church and after several months its runaway success prompted the Church of England to open its own Sunday Schools in Berkhamsted and Northchurch. The local need for such facilities was obvious and soon these three new Sunday Schools were catering for a combined total of over 300 pupils. Numbers continued to increase to point where it became necessary for the Baptists and Congregationalists to run their own separate schools and brand new schoolrooms were later provided when these two flourishing local churches were both re-built in the 1860's.

Despite the church's efforts, until the educational reforms of the mid-nineteenth century, proper schooling was only available to those children whose parents could afford such a luxury. There was also a limited opportunity for a few fortunate pupils to attend endowed charity schools, such as the Bourne School which was established in the town in 1737. Berkhamsted offered a considerable choice to those whose wealth allowed them to educate their children independently. For example in 1824 there were no fewer than five small private schools or 'academies' established in the town. Three of these institutions catered for boys and two for girls. We also know that one of these academies was then charging fees higher than Berkhamsted School, whose reputation for academic excellence has not always been as secure as it is today. Within the local community there were those who were determined to spread educational opportunity more widely and their champion was the idealist Augustus Smith. He was a man of considerable wealth and influence who was born in the town and had grown up on

his family's impressive estate at Ashlyns Hall. It was at a meeting held on 25th March 1833 that the Vestry finally decided to give their full support to Augustus Smith's resolution that "a good parish school should be established, where boys and girls should be taught reading, writing, arithmetic and useful work".

One year later Berkhamsted's first elementary school had been built at the corner of Park View Road, on the site of the town's derelict workhouse. When founded in 1834 it was known as the British or Chalk School and was open to children of all denominations, provided they also attended a local Sunday School. In addition to the Rector, Curate and other parish officers, the Ministers of the Baptist, Congregationalist and Quaker communities were all represented on the school committee. However, only three years into the life of the new school, a serious rift developed between the non-conformists and those representing the Church of England on the committee. As a result of these disagreements the Rector of St Peter's Church, the Rev. John Crofts, began to campaign for a separate Church of England school and, given his prominent position in the local community, he was well placed to gain substantial backing for this initiative. The

The Board School at the time of the Coronation of Edward VII, 1902.

Rector could count on the full support of the Countess of Bridgewater, who helped finance the venture and also provided the land he required. In addition to financial contributions forthcoming from other members of the local gentry and from the town's shopkeepers and businessmen, two awards of one hundred pounds were received from the Treasury and from King William IV. An additional donation of one hundred pounds was also made by Queen Victoria, shortly after her accession to the throne. The sum of money eventually collected totalled £1,403 and this was sufficient to build some classrooms on land provided behind the Court House. A small schoolmaster's house was also constructed next to this historic building. When the new National School opened its doors on 16th July 1838, it was an immediate success admitting 238 children in its first year of operation.

Although two schools had now been established in the town, there was no guarantee that the majority of the children registered would attend regularly. In addition to any loss of income caused by the release of their children, another disincentive was that parents also had to provide what was then termed 'the school pence'. This was a weekly fee of between one and three pence, paid by every pupil as a contribution towards the running costs of the school. However it was possible for the very poorest families to apply to the Board of Guardians for exemption from these fees. This situation remained until 1870, when an important Education Act gave local authorities the right to make a child's basic education compulsory. This key legislation was soon reinforced by the Elementary Education Act of 1876, making employers liable to a stiff fine of £2 for employing a child under the age of nine. However this act still did not forbid the practice of such young children working outside of school hours, in the holidays or at harvest time.

Rapid population growth in the second half of the nineteenth century, combined with the effects of national legislation, meant that both local schools had to expand. Records reveal that in 1875, no less than 453 children were already enrolled at the National School and another 292 were attending the first 'Chalk School' at Park View which, following the Education Act of 1870, had become known as the Board School. In addition to a new building opened by the church authorities at Gossoms End in 1844, it had also become necessary to build a Church of England infant school in Chapel Street. The Board School was extended in 1871 and a separate department provided for the infants in 1894. Overcrowding continued to be acute at the National School and there was simply no room left to expand behind the Court House. Fortunately this problem was relieved by the generosity of leading landowner, Mrs. Lionel Lucas of Kingshill, who provided the school with a brand new site to the rear of Prince Edward Street. It was now possible for the Church Guardians to press ahead with plans to provide the first of two Victoria Schools, which were to be built to commemorate the Queen's Diamond Jubilee in 1897.

The foundation stone for the first school was laid by Thomas Halsey, MP for West Hertfordshire, on 13th July 1897. Building work was completed in time for the boys from the National School to be transferred to the new Victoria School in 1898. The first Headmaster, Mr. George 'Cabbage' Green was assisted by a staff which included a nurse and four teachers. In 1903 sufficient new classrooms and accommodation were added around the school hall to enable the creation of the Victoria Girls School and it was now possible for boys and girls to be taught separately on the same site in Prince Edward Street. Single sex education continued at Victoria School until after the Second World War. Many former pupils of the school during the war years will have fond

memories of Mr. Edward Popple, a kindly but strict headmaster who spent fifty years teaching at Victoria School. He eventually retired in December 1946, after 36 years as Headmaster. During his time in the town, he was also a leading member of the local community, at one time serving as Chairman of the Urban District Council and Clerk to both Salter's Charity and the Bridgewater Trust. He was also Chairman of the History Society and Library Committee, as well as President of the Arts and Crafts Society.

Under a re-organisation conducted in October 1945, one section of the buildings at Victoria became a mixed junior school, with the remainder acting as a secondary modern department. The truth was that this successful church school had once again outgrown itself and it was with some reluctance that the managers of Victoria School finally relinquished their hopes of building a new Church of England secondary school for the town. A co-operative agreement was then established with the County Council, whereby Victoria Secondary School was closed in 1951, with all its pupils aged 11 or over being transferred to Ashlyns School. This new policy allowed Victoria School to concentrate on the more realistic role of becoming a mixed

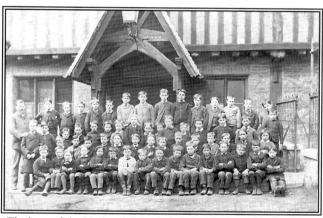

The boys of the National School photographed outside the Court House, circa 1880.

The laying of the foundation stone for Victoria School, 1897.

Victoria School, 1985.

Victoria School football team in 1938, with Headmaster Edward Popple (extreme right)

junior and infant school. At the other end of the town, Hertfordshire County Council had since taken control of the old Board School in 1948, from which time it became known as Park View School. Mr A. 'Robbie' Robinson was Headmaster at Park View School for a record thirty years until its closure in 1971.

Given the massive post-war building boom, spearheaded by the construction of the Durrants and Westfield council estates during the 1950's, Hertfordshire County Council, as the local education authority, had an obligation to significantly increase educational provision in Berkhamsted. Its acquisition of the impressive buildings of Ashlyns School in 1955 meant that it already had a large secondary school in place and this allowed the authority to concentrate on expanding its capacity by building three new modern junior schools. The first of these, Westfield School, opened in 1962 and was followed by Greenway School in 1966. This second new school shared its site with the St Thomas More RC JMI School, which had opened in January 1966 and was built as a voluntary aided Roman Catholic School to serve Berkhamsted and Tring. Swing Gate Lane School followed, opening in January 1967, and although the intention was that Westfield School would make the aged buildings of Park View School redundant, the demand for school places was such that it was not possible to close down this old elementary school until 1971. Park View then became the temporary home for the local police force and the school buildings were not finally demolished until 1984. A major re-organisation of state schooling took place in the town in 1970, when it was decided to adopt a three-tier system of education in Berkhamsted. At this point the now historic buildings of Victoria School became a voluntary aided first school for children aged from five to nine, along with four other first schools that were created at Westfield, Greenways, St Thomas More and Swing Gate. Three new purpose-built middle schools were then constructed to cater for pupils aged 9-13. The Augustus Smith Middle School in Swing Gate Lane was the first of these to open in 1970; this was followed by the Thomas Bourne Middle School, which opened in Durrants Lane in 1971, and finally the Bridgewater School, which was built off Bridle Way in Billett Lane and opened in 1972. Subsequently the Thomas Bourne and Augustus Smith Schools were amalgamated in 1988, to form the Thomas Coram School on the Augustus Smith site. The redundant buildings of the Thomas Bourne School were then purchased by the Egerton Rothesay School.

Egerton Rothesay School

This independent school began life in a large Victorian house in Berkhamsted High Street. It was originally a small preparatory school called Rothesay, founded by Miss Whitaker in 1922. The school subsequently moved to another substantial detached property in Shrublands Road and here Miss Margaret Sauer was Headmistress from 1945-64. An exciting chapter in the life of the school began in 1981 when John and Heather Adkins purchased Rothesay School from Miss Rhoda Ford. Three years later the Adkins also took the opportunity to purchase the town's other principal preparatory school, Egerton School in Charles Street, which had been founded in 1950. Ambitious plans were now being drawn up for the newly merged Egerton Rothesay and these were realised when the school managed to acquire the redundant buildings of the former state middle school, Thomas Bourne, in Durrants Lane. With this additional accommodation, it was possible to extend the school's educational range up to GCSE level, with the lower school operating at Charles Street and a Middle and Upper School based in Durrants Lane. The new Egerton Rothesay School was officially opened by the Prime Minister, the Rt. Hon. Mrs Margaret Thatcher M.P. in September 1988. From a pupil roll of 92 in 1981, the school now has over 600 students and has recently established a sixth form catering for a wide range of A level studies.

Bourne School

The Thomas Bourne Middle School which opened in 1971, owed its name to one of Berkhamsted's great social benefactors, Thomas Bourne (1656-1729). He was a very wealthy and successful man who in 1728 bequeathed the sum of £8,000 to build and endow a local charity school. Given this remarkable act of generosity, it is surprising to learn that Thomas Bourne did not live in the town. Although he spent most of his time working in London, he travelled frequently to Berkhamsted to visit his married sister. In 1735 some £700 of his bequest was used to build the first Bourne School, which featured classrooms on either side of a stone corridor and was originally built to cater for only twenty boys and ten girls. Separate accommodation for both the schoolmaster and mistress was also included within this first building. The original classrooms of the Bourne School faced onto the High Street and were in regular use for the next hundred years. The first schoolmaster and mistress, Edward and Elizabeth Eastmead, took up their duties in 1737. Free uniforms were supplied to all pupils, whose parents also received a

The buildings of the Bourne School in 1897, when used by the Berkhamsted School for Girls.

Rothsay Preparatory School and Kindergarten, 1983.

Bourne School scholar in traditional dress.

maintenance grant in the region of one shilling per child, as school funds allowed. The Bourne School's distinctive dress code of blue coats, corduroy breeches and blue caps with red tassels (for boys) and blue cloth dresses with aprons and straw hats (for girls) was applied strictly in accordance with the wishes of the school's founder, Thomas Bourne. The wearing of the traditional uniforms he designed continued until 1871. In keeping with the chauvinistic thinking of the day, Bourne had also directed that the boys were to be taught "to read English, write and cast accounts", whilst the girls were only to be "perfected in reading English" and then set to task learning "more womanly duties". It was not until 1761 that the girls were also taught to write and, even then, this instruction was only given in their last year at school. With its day to day finances secure and a shortage of educational provision in the town, the Bourne School was assured of success.

In 1853 public subscriptions were invited for the provision of a new classroom/school hall to be built in the garden behind the school. More than half the cost of this extension work was generously provided by General John Finch of Berkhamsted Place. He later increased his commitment to the Bourne School by personally financing the entire cost of repairing the original fabric of the building, which by now had become rather dilapidated. However less than twenty years later, the national legislation introduced by the Education Act of 1870 signalled the end for the charity schools and in 1875 all the Bourne School children were transferred to the National School. A new scheme for administering the remains of the Bourne Charity funds was now required and in 1880 special £5 Bourne scholarships were introduced for a limited number of pupils attending church schools in Berkhamsted and Potten End. Although the outdated eighteenth century uniforms had now been discarded, the Bourne Scholars attending local schools continued to wear the distinctive bonnets and caps until 1914. The vacant Bourne School buildings became the first home for the Berkhamsted School for Girls in 1888. Their Governing Body extended the school hall in 1893, prior to moving to their new school buildings at Kings Road in 1902. By 1949 the trustees of the Bourne Bequest, which was now over 200 years old, had stopped appointing scholars in Church of England schools and instead began awarding grants and exhibitions to local students attending secondary and higher education.

Ashlyns School

The story of Ashlyns School begins in London during the first half of the eighteenth century and features a retired sea captain by the name of Thomas Coram. The poverty and squalor then rife in the Capital appalled Captain Coram, who was particularly concerned for the welfare of the countless number of orphans and abandoned babies who were the inevitable victims of such widespread social deprivation. He was determined to reduce the suffering of these innocents and was successful in gaining a royal charter to support his efforts. On 17th October 1739, sixty children were admitted to temporary premises and in 1742 work began on a purpose built Foundling Hospital in Lambs Conduit Fields, Bloomsbury. The charter that had now been awarded to Captain Coram stipulated that no child could be turned away, but with new born babies literally being left in baskets at the hospital's gates every day, his resources were severely stretched. By 1752 he already had over six hundred youngsters in his care and Parliament responded to this crisis by awarding the Foundling Hospital an annual income of £10,000. Following their admission the very youngest children were first sent out to specially selected foster mothers in the country, who raised them until they were five years old and then returned them to the Hospital School to be educated. The impressive scale of Thomas Coram's achievement soon made the Foundling Hospital a fashionable cause and one of the better known charitable institutions of its time. Famous artists such as William Hogarth, Thomas Gainsborough and Joshua Reynolds were all eager to present paintings to the Governors. The school was renowned for its Chapel services, which attracted large audiences who were moved by the singing of the orphan children. With its musical traditions, the leading composer of the day, George Frederick Handel, took an interest in the school and was a frequent visitor and benefactor. In 1753 he presented an organ to the school chapel and also decided that the inaugural performance of 'The Messiah' in London should take place at Thomas Coram's Foundling Hospital.

The original Foundling Hospital survived until 1926 when the valuable central London site it occupied was sold for ten million pounds. The Hospital Foundation purchased the Ashlyns estate in 1929 and the Governors positioned boundary posts, some of which still remain, to mark the full extent of the new land they had acquired. It was then necessary for the school to be transferred to temporary accommodation in Redhill, Surrey, for several years until the impressive buildings we now know as Ashlyns School were built at Berkhamsted between 1933 and 1935. In September 1935 this new Foundling Hospital School was ready to admit up to 400 children, aged between five and fifteen. An elegant, but formal plan of mock Georgian style buildings, with an imposing chapel as its central feature, still makes it one of the most architecturally distinctive state schools in the Country. The school site, together with its extensive grounds, had been purchased from the estate of the nearby mansion at Ashlyns Hall. The role of the institution changed in January 1951, when it became a secondary modern school for the town of Berkhamsted. The school now catered for local children, aged eleven years and over, in addition to Coram foundling students. In 1955 Hertfordshire County Council purchased all the buildings, together with the forty acre site, from the Thomas Coram Foundation in order to create Ashlyns School. The foundling boarders had already been phased out in 1951 and what was now redundant domestic accommodation was converted into new classrooms, large science laboratories, workshops, a domestic science block and arts/crafts areas. Handel's organ, which had been installed in the school's Chapel, was removed to a London church in 1955, although the wooden staircase in the front hall was left to serve as a reminder of the school's heritage. This had been an original fitting, brought out to Berkhamsted from the Foundling Hospital, as are the columns which are still along the main drive, providing an architectural link to the days of Thomas Coram.

As Ashlyns School expanded a grammar stream was added and under new Headmaster, Mr. J. H. Babington G.C., who was appointed from September 1955, Ashlyns enjoyed high academic standards, becoming the first bi-lateral school in Hertfordshire. Mr. Babington's successor, Mr. A. N. Johnson, oversaw the process by which Ashlyns became the town's senior school in a new three-tier middle school system which was introduced to Berkhamsted in 1972. The name of the school's founder was perpetuated in 1988, when two of Berkhamsted's original middle schools, Thomas Bourne and Augustus Smith (both of which had already been named in memory of local champions of education) were amalgamated to become the Thomas Coram Middle School in Swing Gate Lane. More recently, another important structural change occurred at Ashlyns in April 1995, when the Governors decided to break free from local authority control and opt for grant maintained status.

The impressive frontage of Ashlyns School in 1935.

Prince Arthur of Connaught attends the inauguration ceremony at the Foundling Hospital School, July 1935.

Pupils in the school library at Ashlyns in 1949.

Foundling School pupils in front of the School Chapel in 1935.

Rear of the Kings Road campus, circa 1912.

Berkhamsted School for Girls

The Rev. Edward Bartrum, appointed Headmaster of Berkhamsted Boys School in 1863, had great plans to revitalise what was then the rather shaky reputation of this historic institution and had little inclination to devote any of his time or resources to the business of educating the girls of the town. However a local shopkeeper Henry Nash, supported by the influential John Evans (later Sir John Evans) was determined to press the issue. Partly encouraged by the legislative safeguards provided by the Endowed Schools Act of 1869, they were eventually successful in securing an agreement to finance a local girls school. In 1887, under the Chairmanship of John Evans, the Governors of the newly formed girls school acquired the lease of the empty Bourne School building in the High Street. With the security of a £200 bank loan, the Berkhamsted Girls Grammar School was formally opened by the Countess of Brownlow on 11th May 1888. The school began its life with only 14 pupils, under the care of the first Headmistress, Miss C. Disney. Academic standards were high and the number of girls enrolled grew steadily; reaching 36 pupils in 1891 and 64 pupils by 1892. During Miss Disney's tenure the school hall was enlarged in 1893, with extra classrooms and a laboratory built in the gardens of the former

Bourne charity school. At this time the girls also had the use of tennis courts in the town and a swimming bath at the local waterworks.

When Beatrice Louise Harris succeeded Miss Disney in 1897 there were 80 pupils at the girls school, but the ambitious new Headmistress was determined that larger accommodation, with better facilities, was now necessary if the school was to make the substantial progress she desired. The Governors followed her lead, proposing that the Boys School should acquire a suitable site and then lease it back to the Girls School. As a result of this plan, an impressive new building, initially capable of offering schooling to 150 girls, was provided in Kings Road. The new school was opened in 1902 with great ceremony by Viscount Peel, a former Speaker of the House of Commons. Until 1932 the school's boarders lived on the upper floor of the new Kings Road building. Miss Harris was a great believer in physical exercise forming an important part of the girls' education and two portable classrooms were transferred from the old Bourne School and combined to become a gymnasium. A games mistress was appointed and by the early 1900's the school was already running tennis, hockey and lacrosse teams. The girls school was now beginning to flourish under Miss Harris' direction and in 1915 a new wing was added. The new accommodation included six additional classrooms, the Hall, a science laboratory, a domestic science room and a music department. These new facilities were officially opened on 15th June 1915 by Mrs. Winston Churchill who, as Clementine Hosier, had formerly been a pupil at the school. When versatile teacher Miss Sowels was promoted to take over the Headship from Miss Harris in 1917, the success of the school under her predecessor was demonstrated by the fact that there were now 240 pupils enjoying first class education at Berkhamsted Girls Grammar School.

The immediate post-war period was a difficult time for most independent schools, but the Headmistress, Miss Sowels, was supported in her management of the school by a newly elected Chairman of Governors, Major General Sir Charles Hadden of Rossway. Sir Charles adopted a policy which aimed to significantly increase the number of boarders and began acquiring suitable property in the town. St David's was purchased as the school sanatorium and Beeches was used as a junior house for the day girls and boarders. Sir Charles also provided the school with a new hockey field, prior to his untimely death in

October 1924. Following the resignation of Miss Sowels, Miss Charlotte Finlayson Mackenzie was appointed Headmistress in 1929. Sir Charles' widow, Lady Hadden, continued her husband's tradition of supporting the school by offering funds to equip a new kindergarten at the Beeches. A major achievement by the new Chair of Governors, Brigadier General R. M. Ford, was the opening of the long promised swimming pool in 1931. At this time the Boys School was experiencing a drop in the numbers of boarders, so the Girls School took the opportunity to buy one of their properties in the High Street called London House. This was re-named School House and was in use by September 1933. Disney Lodge was built in the grounds of the Beeches in 1935 to provide attractive accommodation for the new Headmistress. The Girls School continued to expand and during her tenure Miss Mackenzie was responsible for securing the additional properties of Loxwood, Milton House, Alderley and Four Oaks, as well as overseeing the construction of a new library, dining hall and hard tennis courts. By the time that Miss Mackenzie retired in 1949, the number of girls at the school had risen to 440.

The new Headmistress Miss Barbara Russell,

Berkhamsted School for Girls Tennis Team, 1901.

Three former headmistresses of Berkhamsted School for Girls (l-r) Miss C. F. Mackenzie, Miss B. Russell, Miss M. R. Bateman.

Netball practice, 1995.

Classroom studies, 1995.

appointed in 1950, brought with her a fresh approach and launched an appeal to provide another wing, which she planned would incorporate new classrooms for the teaching of cookery, needlework, geography and biology. Her initiative proved successful and the new buildings had been completed by September 1957. Their new facilities were fully operational and ready for inspection by Her Majesty, Queen Elizabeth the Queen Mother, who visited the school on 13th June 1958. During Miss Russell's time important improvements were also made to the boarders' accommodation. Beeches, Four Oaks and Loxwood were all enlarged, with the refurbished Four Oaks being re-christened Churchill, after the school's famous former pupil. Appropriately Loxwood was also re-named Russell's, as a mark of respect for this hard working and fully committed Headmistress who retired in 1971. The nine years spent by her successor, Miss Mary Rose Bateman, were dominated by disruptive and protracted negotiations concerning a possible merger with the Berkhamsted Boys School. Once the prospect of this re-organisation had temporarily receded, her successor Miss Valerie Shepherd, appointed in 1980, was able to present a fresh action plan to Governors. As a result, a new sixth form building was provided in January 1983 and was named the Nash Building, in memory of one of the school's original founders. Space vacated at the Kings Road building was then used to create two new classrooms and a new general science laboratory. With the school's centenary approaching, an appeal was launched to build the impressive new Centenary Hall which opened on time in 1988. Co-educational development with Berkhamsted Boys School began in September 1994, with the establishment of a joint sixth form and in 1996 the Berkhamsted Girls Grammar School finally agreed to merge with the Boys School to form the Berkhamsted Collegiate School. The combined strength of these two leading independent schools now offer an unparalleled range of educational opportunity under the leadership of Principal Dr. Priscilla Chadwick. Dr. Chadwick issupported by her two Vice Principals, Dr. D. J. Nelson and Dr. H. Brook.

Berkhamsted School

The founder of Berkhamsted School was John Incent, a prominent member of the sixteenth century Berkhamsted community. His father, Robert Incent, served as Secretary to Cicely Duchess of York during her time at Berkhamsted Castle. John Incent was made Dean of St Paul's Cathedral in 1540 and, one year after this prestigious appointment, he was successful in gaining a licence from the King to fund a school in Berkhamsted, which was not to exceed 144 boys on its pupil roll. John Incent had been elected President of the local Brotherhood of St John the Baptist in 1523 and had long since persuaded his fellow trustees that it would be beneficial to use the considerable endowments, no longer required by the disbanded monastic hospital, to support educational development in the town. Having gained royal approval, he was able to press ahead and the school building he long envisaged was finally completed in 1544, one year before his death. An impressive and attractive structure, built in brick and freestone, it drew praise from the noted seventeenth century antiquarian William Camden, who declared on a visit to the town that "this fine old school building was the only structure in Berkhamsted worth a second glance!"

The school's first Headmaster Richard Reeve was a leading academic of the day, but held strict Protestant views and because of his beliefs was dismissed on the orders of Queen Mary in 1555. After this unfortunate start, Berkhamsted School enjoyed an early period of growth and prosperity under two subsequent Headmasters, William Saltmarsh (1561-99) and his successor Thomas Hunt (1599-1635). Pupil numbers had now reached around one hundred, with some Berkhamsted scholars achieving academic distinction. The first Berkhamsted 'old boy' to enjoy some celebrity was Henry Atkins, who left the school to train in medicine and succeeded in being elected President of the Royal College of Physicians in 1606. During his distinguished career he was appointed in turn Court Physician to Elizabeth I, James I and Charles I. He died a wealthy man, leaving the sum of £200 to the poor of Berkhamsted. There is no doubt that the following period, dominated by the Civil Wars and the ravages of the Plague, witnessed a considerable deterioration in the infrastructure of the school. Although a degree of revival seems to have taken place under Newboult (1668-85) and Wren (1685-91), during the protracted Headship of John Theed (1691-1734) frequent complaints were made about the quality of education then being offered at Berkhamsted School. The

Teaching staff at Berkhamsted School for Boys circa 1910, with the Rev. Thomas Charles Fry (front row centre) and C. H. Greene to his immediate right.

situation was deteriorating rapidly and in the 1760's the school only had a handful of pupils left.

The school was rescued from this perilous situation by the Rev. John Dupré (1789-1805) whose experienced leadership ensured that a wide curriculum was taught and, during his tenure, pupil numbers again rose to over one hundred. However the Rev. Dupré promptly undid all his good work by handing over the school to his dissolute son Thomas in 1805. This twenty-two year old had no intention of taking his responsibilities seriously and at first refused to teach the boys anything but Latin and Greek. He eventually abandoned all pretence at Headship and by 1815 was living in Lincolnshire, having appointed various members of his family nominally as Usher, in order that stipends could still be collected. This scandalous situation was allowed to continue until 1841, when the repeated representations made to the Court of Chancery by Augustus Smith, and other leading members of the local community, finally forced the resignation of Thomas Dupré. In order to prevent any re-occurrence of such difficulties, a new scheme of administration was immediately introduced to the school. The positions of Master and Usher were stripped of their ultimate

authority and these post holders were instead made members of a new Governing Body of eleven, which together had responsibility for the proper organisation and finance of the school. Forewarned by Thomas Dupré's poor example, it was also made compulsory for senior masters to live at the school. When Berkhamsted School officially re-opened in August 1842, forty-three boys had been enrolled and seven were boarders. Augustus Smith had encouraged the appointment of the Rev. Edward John Wilcocks who, together with the new Usher George Scott, spent the next thirteen years thoroughly re-organising the school.

With secure foundations now in place, the school's next Headmaster, Dr. Bartrum (1864-87) was able to press on with his ambitions to establish Berkhamsted School as a leading independent boarding school. An excellent administrator and rather colourful character, it was under his determined reign that the school, for the first time, exceeded Dean Incent's original target of 144 pupils. Dr. Bartrum was also a keen sportsman and a firm believer in physical exercise, who subsequently encouraged his Governors to lease ten acres of ground from Lord Brownlow of Ashridge, so that Kitcheners Field could be used as a school sports ground. The school also acquired an interest in the field between the canal and the railway, where a cricket ground was shared with the town and a pavilion built in 1885. Under Dr. Bartrum's tenure Founders Day was celebrated for the first time on 23rd July 1885. This initiative proved highly successful, with a service in the parish church being followed by a cricket match against the 'old boys' and then a well attended dinner at the Kings Arms. When Dr. Bartrum retired in 1887, he was succeeded by the Rev. Thomas Charles Fry (1887-1910) a highly committed and successful Headteacher, who initiated various schemes of improvement which gradually created the school we know today. First he doubled the width of the west wing, providing more dormitories and this released space in School House for new classrooms, a library and a music room. A new junior department was provided and, at his own expense, Dr. Fry then bought Overton House, together with some land where he built a new senior boarding house called St Johns. Not content with this, he also launched a school chapel and gymnasium fund in 1889 and managed to secure a County Council grant to help him build a new 'Science School'. Although a temporary chapel and gymnasium were opened in 1890, the project dearest to his heart was the building of a permanent school chapel. At a Governors meeting held in April 1894, he offered to erect this place of worship at his own expense, despite the estimated cost of £2000. Once again, the School Board did not refuse his generosity. The foundation stone was laid three months later and the new building dedicated on 27th June 1895. This impressive chapel, whose design was inspired by the Venetian Church of Santa Maria dei Miracoli, today stands as a fitting monument to the man who was arguably the school's most successful Headmaster. As a testament to the achievements of Dr. Fry's Headship, a special one day holiday was held on 27th June 1905 to celebrate the school's roll reaching 400 pupils for the first time. To his great satisfaction, work had also begun on Dr. Fry's last great project, Deans' Hall, when he left the school to become Dean of Lincoln in 1910.

It fell to Dr. Fry's successor, Charles Henry Greene (1910-27) to oversee the completion of Deans' Hall, the building of the school's first sanatorium and the acquisition of extensive new playing fields at the top of Chesham Road. The advent of the First World War heralded a distressing and difficult period in the life of the school and, of the 1145 'old boys' who served in the Great War, 184 were killed and another 117 were wounded. However under the steady leadership of C. H. Greene the school was at least able to recover from the financial hardships it had endured and in 1926 managed to secure a loan for the demolition of the old mill and its adjacent buildings in Mill Street. This cleared the way for a fresh phase of development, which began in 1926 with the construction of an impressive Music School, together with new 'fives courts'. In Charles Greene's last term, Edward Greene offered the school a gift of the land, subsequently named Greene Field, in memory of his brother's contribution as Headmaster. The area is now the site of the school's all-weather tennis courts, close to Lower Kings Road. Here by the railway, is a new development of flats which have been named Greenes Court in honour of the Greene family. Graham Greene, who studied at the school under his father, grew up to become the most famous old Berkhamstedian of them all. With his major novels, such as Our Man in Havana, Brighton Rock, The Third Man and The Power and The Glory, he firmly established himself as the foremost British writer of his generation. Another famous literary 'old boy' was Algernon Methuen (1856-1924) who enjoyed great success founding a leading publishing house. His widow subsequently gave the school the sum of £10,000 in his memory, which allowed the Governors to establish some entrance scholarships and leading bursaries to Oxford. Two of Graham Greene's brothers, who were also educated at Berkhamsted, achieved their own share of distinction with Sir Hugh Greene eventually becoming Director General of the BBC and Dr. Raymond Greene practising medicine as a leading Harley Street specialist.

C. H. Greene was succeeded as Headmaster by Mr. H. L. O. Flecker (1927-31) and then by Mr. C. M. Cox (1931-45) who was a former pupil of the school. The fondly remembered Cuthbert Cox managed to successfully steer the school through the hardships of the Second World War, before handing over control to Mr. C. R. Evers who used the immediate post-war period to begin the construction of Wingrave. Following the Butler Education Act of 1944, an important structural change took place when Berkhamsted School switched from being a 'direct grant' to a fully independent school. Major developments then began again under the tenure of the next Headmaster, Basil Hugh Garnons Williams (1953-72) who was soon overseeing the construction of an impressive range of brand new school buildings in Mill Street. Known as Newcroft, these were designed principally for the teaching of science and were officially opened by Her

View of the quadrangle and school chapel at Berkhamsted School for Boys, 1912.

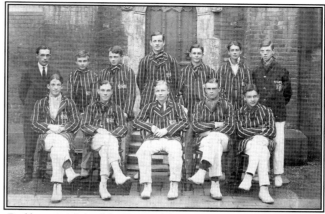

Berkhamsted School for Boys cricket team in the 1912/13 season, with coach Isaac Evans (back row left).

Berkhamsted Boys School Rugby XV, wearing their colours and caps, 1929.

The old School House at Berkhamsted School, 1965.

Majesty, Queen Elizabeth the Queen Mother, when she visited the school on 13th June 1958. In 1962 one of the school's governors Col. A. L. Wilson OBE MC donated the sum of £10,000 to help provide a new headmaster's house. Built in part of the old School House garden, which had fomerly been a graveyard for the Baptist Chapel in Water Lane, Wilson House took two years to plan and eventually cost £16,400. Another significant step forward in school facilities was triggered by a substantial donation from former 'old boy', the millionaire Sir Jules Thorn, who had made his fortune in the electrical industry. This allowed for the demolition of one of the town's former public houses, The Fish, together with some adjoining old cottages purchased by the school in 1959. Space was now available for the construction of the modern classrooms of the Thorn block and the foundation stone was laid in February 1970. Two years later a modern medical centre and sanatorium was also built for the school on the site of the former 'sunken cottages' in Castle Street.

From the days of Dr. Bartrum in 1864, the story of Berkhamsted School has been one of determined expansion and progress. For over one hundred years the Governing Body has been steadily acquiring property and assets around the town, financing building work and opening up new facilities, in order to increase the range and quality of education offered. It fell to the thirtieth and last Headmaster of Berkhamsted Boys School, the Rev. Keith Wilkinson (1989-96) to oversee the beginnings of co-educational development with the Berkhamsted Girls Grammar School. This process began in September 1994, at sixth form level, with the establishment of Ashby House for the girls. The recent full merger with the Girls Grammar School, to create the new Berkhamsted Collegiate School in 1996, is another important step forward in an ambitious process of expansion. There are currently three hundred pupils in a flourishing co-educational sixth form and, between the ages of eleven and sixteen, a further three hundred and fifty boys (on Castle Campus) and two hundred and fifty girls (on Kings Campus) who are taught in single sex groups. In addition there are another four hundred pupils (aged three to eleven) who attend the Junior/Preparatory School, which became fully co-educational in 1998. Under the direction of Principal Dr. Priscilla Chadwick and her two Vice Principals, Dr. D. J. Nelson and Dr. H. Brook, the Berkhamsted Collegiate School now looks superbly well equipped to meet the challenges of the future.

Police Service

By the middle of the eighteenth century the local area, with its main road into London and the presence of so many fine houses and estates, offered abundant potential for criminal activity. Against such a backdrop, unpaid parish constables, appointed annually by the Parish Vestry, struggled to maintain law and order in towns like Berkhamsted. In order to protect their own assets and help reduce levels of crime, the wealthier members of the local community banded together to form the Great Berkhamsted and Northchurch Property Association. Together the members of the association undertook to share the cost of advertising, apprehending and prosecuting persons who had committed offences against members. Substantial rewards were also offered to those who were prepared to help bring to justice highwaymen, horse thieves and cattle maimers, burglars, poachers and others who damaged members' property by felling trees or stealing crops. At its inaugural meeting, held on 23rd June 1794, John Page, Innkeeper of the Kings Arms and High Constable of Berkhamsted, was elected first treasurer of the Association - a post he held until 1836.

The origins of Berkhamsted's police station can be traced back to 1764 when Mr. T. H. Noyes was instructed to find a suitable place to establish a small prison or 'bridewell' in the town. He managed to secure a small row of dilapidated tenements on the corner of Kings Road (then called Cocks Lane) that were speedily converted into a prison at a total cost of £250. The first keeper of this prison, George Hoar, received a salary of £20 per year for managing what was then small and very unpleasant accommodation. The men's prison measured only 16½ ft. by 10½ ft. and the women's room was of a similar size. The prisoners were let out once a day into a yard which measured only 25 ft. by 14 ft. and had to survive on rations of one pound of bread a day with water. For the more troublesome inmates there was also a dungeon, dug into the ground, which was described as "the most dreadful hole without air or light".

During the early part of the nineteenth century two rate payers, rather than one, were being appointed to serve as Parish Constables in the town and by 1839 the County Police Act had been adopted throughout Hertfordshire. This re-structuring of policing prompted improvements at Berkhamsted and in 1843 a programme of alterations was carried out to the old Bridewell, converting it into a police station still capable of detaining prisoners on remand. The local police force was now directly responsible to the Justices of the Peace and its cost was met by the introduction of a local three pence rate. In 1851 George MacKay was appointed Superintendent of the Hertfordshire Rural Police Force and by 1882 the town's resident police force consisted of an Inspector, supported by three other officers. In 1894 the old police station, together with adjacent shop accommodation, was demolished to enable the construction of a far more substantial building. At this point, part of the corner site was also sacrificed to enable a widening of Kings Road, which by this time had become part of a busy thoroughfare to Chesham. The pattern of policing in Berkhamsted during the first half of the twentieth century proceeded relatively undisturbed, with the exception of the wartime years. During both major conflicts the majority of peace-time policemen signed up to join the armed forces and there was therefore a need for special constables to be appointed temporarily to keep law and order at home. These were mainly older men who also played an important wartime role, patrolling the streets during air raids and guarding key installations such as gas works and water reservoirs. During the second world war groups of special constables were also posted on regular patrols across Berkhamsted Common, to guard against the threat of German paratroopers landing at night.

The traditional 'bobby on the beat' style of policing was eventually adapted when a Unit Beat system was first introduced to Berkhamsted in 1967. The three local officers on foot patrol could now use their radios to call on the Unit Beat vehicle for support. In 1971 the Home Office approved the re-building of Berkhamsted Police Station at an estimated cost of £100,000. The old Victorian police station was demolished and during construction work in 1972, the local police force was accommodated in the old classrooms which formerly belonged to Park View School. Today's modern police station is staffed by a team which includes one Inspector, one Sergeant and eight police constables. At the present time, the police station in Berkhamsted houses the Dacorum Traffic Unit and is also the operating base for one of the County's Dog Sections, which comprises four German Shepherds and two specialist dogs. The officer currently in charge of policing Berkhamsted and Tring is Inspector Dixon-Gough, who first began his career as a police constable at Berkhamsted in 1972.

Early view of the original Police Station in the 1860's.

Berkhamsted Police Station, newly built at the corner of Kings Road in 1894.

Local bobby in attendance in Berkhamsted High Street at the time of Queen Victoria's Diamond Jubilee in 1897.

Berkhamsted's wartime Police Force circa 1941.

P.C. Andrew Cooke, Sergeant David Dumbleton and P.C. Jeffrey Ellis at the rear of Berkhamsted Police Station, 1998.

Fire Service

Some four hundred years ago, when most buildings were predominately of timber construction with thatched roofs, the threat of fire was a very serious and regular hazard. The church warden's accounts reveal that Berkhamsted had its own set of fire-fighting gear as long ago as 1648. However such equipment then consisted of no more than a set of ladders, leather buckets and fire hooks. Until the introduction of steam driven water pumps, towards the end of the eighteenth century, this was always going to be insufficient to deal with serious conflagrations, such as the fire which completely destroyed the town's old market house in 1854. From 1682 it had been possible for individual property owners to reduce their risk by taking out private fire insurance, which allowed them to display a branded metal plate on their building. This ensured that they would receive priority attention in the event of a blaze and the only remaining firemark in Berkhamsted can still be seen on the front of Brown & Merry estate agents at Nos.128-130 High Street. In 1749 twenty-four leather buckets were provided for the town's own brigade and in 1788 a new manual pump fire engine was purchased for £58 15s. Unable to finance their own facilities in smaller towns like Berkhamsted, leading fire insurance companies such as the Sun, Phoenix and Royal Exchange contributed £21 towards the cost of this new engine. Despite this commercial support, the statutory responsibility for the provision of some form of local fire service remained with the Parish Vestry authorities in Berkhamsted until 1898.

Local firemen then wore distinctive uniforms; members of the Berkhamsted brigade wore white smocks with their brown leather belts and billycock hats. In contrast their opposite numbers at Hemel Hempstead wore red coats and caps. Although it may now seem incongruous, the town's fire engine was at first kept in the Parish Church of St Peter, where it was housed in a small chamber in the south-west corner of the building. The inner walls of this small 'engine room' were later demolished when it was incorporated into the south aisle, during Butterfield's restoration of the church in 1870/71. A major fire occurred at Cooper's Upper Works in 1903 and it took six horse-drawn engines to control the blaze. For many years the town's first horse-drawn engine was kept in the yard of the Goat Inn until a new engine, with steam-driven water pump, was bought by local land owners. This was presented by Lord Brownlow to the Urban District Council in August 1907. By this time Berkhamsted had its own fire station in buildings which are now part of the council yard off Clarence Road. It was here that this new sturdy horse-drawn engine, christened 'Alice', remained in service throughout the 1920's. Local garage owner, Mr. George Callaghan, was given the annual contract of regularly providing teams of horses, sufficient for Alice to attend all fires and also perform six drills throughout the year.

One of the town's most serious fires occurred at Kepston's Pulley Works in 1929, the year that the first motorised fire-fighting vehicle was introduced to Berkhamsted. This was a Dennis fire engine which carried a central ladder with firemen seated on benches either side. The advent of the Second World War, with its prolonged bombing campaigns, prompted the creation of the National Fire Service, under whose auspices many trucks and vans were hastily converted to cover for the shortage of purpose-built fire engines. Immediately before the war, a tall hose tower had been built at the fire station behind the Civic Centre. The town's main air raid warning siren was fixed to the tower and continued to alert fire fighters for many years after the hostilities ceased in 1944. Prior to this, local firemen had been called out to action by a steam hooter which had been installed by local ironmongers Wood & Son at the Waterworks in 1904.

The National Fire Service was disbanded in 1948 and respnsibility for fire-fighting was transferred to Hertfordshire County Council. During the 1950's and early 1960's much improved Commer fire engines came into service and a modern fire station was built for the town, off Castle Street in 1969. The redundant hose tower behind the Civic Centre was eventually demolished in 1979 and the old fire station's remaining buildings have since been converted into an impressive conservation store for the Dacorum Heritage Trust. Berkhamsted Fire Station in Castle Street is currently staffed by a retained crew, led by Station Commander Peter Halsey. The station's existing vehicle is a Dennis water tender, with 45 ft. ladder, which together with its crew of six can carry 400 gallons of water. When attending a fire, it is also capable of pumping 500 gallons of water per minute. This engine and crew, who can call on back-up from the main station at Hemel Hempstead when necessary, still covers a wide area around Berkhamsted including Northchurch, Potten End, Little Gaddesden, Nettleden and Ringshall.

'Alice', Berkhamsted's first steam driven fire engine, is presented to the Urban District Council by Lord Brownlow in August 1907.

The Berkhamsted Fire Brigade, photographed at Potten End with their Dennis fire engine, in the 1930's.

Retained fire fighters at Berkhamsted's modern fire station in Castle Street, 1998.

Berkhamsted firemen attending to a major fire at the Durrant's furniture factory at Gossoms End, 1962.

Wartime Berkhamsted

First World War

As the possibility of international conflict grew more likely in 1940, few could have foreseen the scale of carnage and futility awaiting them in the trenches of France and Belgium. Consequently, on the outbreak of the First World War, there was a rush of local volunteers to serve in the London Territorial Force and the levels of patriotism then ran so high that the initial call for 30,000 volunteers was satisfied within one week in August 1914. The war was a few weeks old when the first detachment of Northumberland Fusiliers arrived in Berkhamsted to begin their training. The Court House and various school rooms were made available to offer the Company some makeshift accommodation and the soldiers were permitted to conduct their exercises in Berkhamsted Park and on Butts Meadow. After being billeted in Berkhamsted for only a few weeks, in excess of 3000 fighting men, who belonged to the Third New Army, then left the town to continue their training at Halton.

Prior to the departure of the Fusiliers, the first of the troops that were to make the town their own during the war began to arrive. These were the men of the Inns of Court Officer Training Corps, thousands of whom were to be trained to the peak of fighting readiness in the countryside around Berkhamsted. Many of these commissioned officers were later to lose their lives fighting in France, fully living up to their Corps' proud nickname of the 'Devil's Own'. On 28th September 1914, four infantry companies of the Inns of Court O.T.C. began setting up their tents in Berkhamsted Park, whilst the cavalry established a base at the old Locke & Smith brewery buildings in Water Lane. Two huge marquees were also erected in the castle grounds for a musketry school. During 1915 the ranks of the Inns of Court steadily increased until the number of men billeted in Berkhamsted had reached 2,500 recruits. The soldiers' church parades became a weekly event in the town and the Rector of St Peter's Parish Church, the Rev. Hart-Davis, rose to the challenge by regularly addressing the massed ranks of troops who far outnumbered the size of his normal peace-time congregation.

Almost half way through the War, on 1st August 1916, King George V paid a morale boosting visit to Berkhamsted to see the Inns of Court O.T.C. training at first hand. On arrival he visited their parade ground in the Park, where he watched demonstrations of drill practice, sword exercises and bayonet fighting. The King then travelled up to the Common where he was able to observe several companies practising trench fighting and bombing and inspect other soldiers engaged in wood fighting at Frithsden Beeches. Although the troops' base had been established much closer to the town, Lord Brownlow had placed the entire Ashridge estate at the disposal of Lieutenant Colonel Errington and his men. The countryside around the town, with its vast stretches of open common fringed by dense woodland, offered a superbly varied terrain for the soldiers to practise all the necessary elements of early twentieth century warfare. Full scale battalion exercises were at first held twice, and then later once a week, with over thirteen thousand yards of trenches being excavated on the Common. Lord Brownlow's private waiting room at Berkhamsted railway station became the Quartermaster's office and stores and Lady Brownlow allowed parts of the mansion house at Ashridge to be used as a military hospital. Ashridge became the first of forty Emergency Medical Stations (EMS hospitals) set up in Hertfordshire during the First World War and Voluntary Aid Detachments (VAD's) of the local Red Cross helped staff this important facility. The Inns of Court also established their own smaller hospital, first at Barncroft and then at Beeches, which was closer to the town centre and now belongs to the Collegiate School. The large sheds of Key's timber yard, close the canal by Castle Street, proved to be ideal accommodation for the Inns of Court mess rooms and were capable of catering for up to 900 soldiers at a time. The Officers' and Sergeants' mess were also here, whilst the Court House in Back Lane was used as an Orderly Room.

By the end of the War a total of over 12,000 troops had at one time been garrisoned for training in Berkhamsted. With the sudden influx of so many soldiers, local shops and restaurants enjoyed something of a boom in business. Despite the number of local men who had volunteered to fight, the population of garrison towns like Berkhamsted actually increased during the period of the conflict. Although air warfare did not present the same level of hazard as in the Second World War, night-time enemy Zeppelin raids still posed a threat to the towns in the south-east of England. The biggest raid of the War took place on 2nd September 1916 when fourteen airships crossed the Norfolk coast, with a view to raiding London from the north-west. One of these Zeppelins (the L32) actually passed

The troops of the Inns of Court march along Lower Kings Road, 1915.

over Tring and the north of Berkhamsted Common, before dropping bombs on Hertford and Ware. One year later, at 11.00 p.m. on 19th October, another airship (the L45) passed directly over the town, as it followed the railway line into London. This Zeppelin was more successful, eventually dropping some of her bombs on Piccadilly Circus, killing seven and injuring eighteen people. Far away from the battlefields of France, the nation also suffered the consequences of enemy submarine action and in February 1917 an unrestricted campaign was launched against our merchant vessel fleet. This was a significant blow because, at the outbreak of the War, Britain was heavily dependant on foreign imports for its food supply. The need to increase food production at home became of paramount importance and in 1917 the Prime Minister, Lloyd George, appointed a National Food Controller. With a shortage of men to tend the land, hundreds of German prisoners were set to work on local farms. Because most peace-time policemen had enrolled as regular soldiers, there was also a real need for Special Constables to help with the policing effort in the Berkhamsted area. These officials played an important war-time role patrolling the streets during air raids and guarding key installations, such as the railway and power supplies.

Nationally organised saving campaigns, which included the Tank Week held from 4th March 1918, helped raise the funds necessary for the never ending supply of equipment and ammunition required to continue the intense conflict with Germany. The town of Berkhamsted excelled itself by raising over three quarters of a million pounds towards the war effort. Although the cost of the protracted struggle placed a terrible burden upon everyone, the will of the nation proved sufficiently strong to secure victory, with news of the Armistice eventually reaching Berkhamsted at mid-day on 11th September 1918. The rest of the day became a national holiday; the bands of the Inns of Court paraded in Berkhamsted High Street and, as an act of celebration, a great bonfire was lit in Kitcheners Field. The rather stark obelisk, which stands at the top of New Road on Berkhamsted Common, still reminds us that the price of victory was a terrible loss of life. Of the twelve thousand men who received their first training in trench warfare in the local countryside, two thousand were never to return home to their families. Berkhamsted's own war memorial, originally sited at the top of Water Lane and now relocated close to St Peter's Church, remembers the names of 144 local men who also made the ultimate sacrifice for their Country.

The massed ranks of the Inns of Court parade in Kitcheners field, 1916.

General Bethune and Lieutenant Colonel Errington inspect the troops at Kitcheners Field, August 1916.

Inns of Court Officer Cadet Battalion, 1914.

An informal view of officers relaxing on the Common, circa 1915.

One of the Inns of Court administrative headquarters at Barncroft, circa 1915.

Tents of the Inns of Court O.T.C. Camp in Berkhamsted Park, 1915.

Inns of Court Camp at Ashridge, 1914.

Troops enjoying their rations, circa 1915.

Soldiers marching past the O.T.C. Camp at Ashridge, 1914.

Inns of Court soldiers practice bayonet skills in Berkhamsted, circa 1915.

First World War troops being cared for at Ashridge, circa 1918.

Special Constables in the grounds of Berkhamsted Castle, circa 1917.

Mock up of a tank outside the Town Hall to promote War Loans Week in March 1918.

An early view of Berkhamsted War Memorial in its original position, close to the corner of Water Lane.

Second World War

After only twenty years of peace, at 11.15 a.m. on 3rd September 1939, the Prime Minister Neville Chamberlain declared that we were again at war with Germany. Legislation, in the form of the Military Training Bill, had already been put in place in May 1939 to ensure the registration for military service of all young men, aged 20 or 21, who were of British nationality. As the conflict gathered momentum this criteria was soon extended to all British males between 18 and 41 years of age. Once again thousands of troops were billeted in the Berkhamsted area, with many platoons using the Ashridge estate as a base from which to complete training and make the final preparations for warfare. In 1940, following Dunkirk, troops from the British Expeditionary Force and the 51st Highland Division were stationed at Ashridge and, during the later stages of the War, Dutch, Polish and American troops all trained in the district. The Polish and Dutch army personnel were based near Ringshall, whilst a detachment of the XIth Dragoon Guards camped at Hudnall. Local conscripts from the town itself joined the Hertfordshire and Bedfordshire Regiment, whose soldiers took part in a variety of actions around the globe fighting in Europe, North Africa, the Middle East and Malaya. For example men from the Herts. and Beds. were famously involved in the Anzio landings, fought to resist the Japanese in Singapore and also helped in the capture of Monte Cassino.

On the Home Front petrol very quickly became scarce and food rationing was also introduced on 8th January 1940, when bacon/ham and butter were both rationed to four ounces a week and the weekly allowance for sugar was set at twelve ounces. The 'Dig For Victory' campaign encouraged everyone to use parts of their own garden to grow vegetables and by May 1941, over one thousand allotments had been established in Berkhamsted, with parts of Berkhamsted and Hudnall Commons also being used to help boost local food production. As air warfare in particular gathered momentum, the armed forces need for metal intensified. Gates, fencing and implements were all urgently recycled and in 1941 even the iron railings of St Peter's Church were lost to the war effort. People were also encouraged to hand in pots and pans for melting down, particularly if they were made of aluminium which could be used to make and repair aircraft. Encouraged by the Admiralty, warship weeks were organised by the National War Savings Committee to support the naval campaign. Berkhamsted, Potten End and Little Gaddesden were together given the target of raising £175,000 to provide a new

submarine hull. This sum was comfortably exceeded by over £40,000 and the town's adopted vessel was completed in April 1942 as HM Submarine P44. On 31st January 1943 it was finally given its adopted name of HM Submarine United and saw action with the 10th Submarine Flotilla, which operated in the eastern Mediterranean from a base in Malta. During an eventful sixteenth month tour of service it undertook twenty patrols, sinking one Italian U boat and badly damaging another. It was also successful in destroying one salvage ship, three supply schooners and over twenty thousand tons of supply shipping. Later in the War, on the afternoon of 9th November 1943, the crew of HMS United were given a rapturous welcome when they visited the town which had supported them. At an official ceremony, the ship's Commander Lieutenant J. C. Y. Roxborough DSO, DSC, presented the people of Berkhamsted with a shield, bearing the crest of HMS United and a replica of the submarine's Jolly Roger. This flag was later installed at the local Sea Cadet Headquarters between 1949-52, but sadly its current whereabouts is not known.

A major feature of life on the Home Front was the struggle to cope with the hazards of German aircraft flying over the town on the way to bombing raids in London. Berkhamsted was only five minutes flying time from the Capital and, with the main railway line as a clear guiding feature, it lay directly on the route used by the

The crew of HM Submarine United on service in the Mediterranean, 1942-43.

C.P.O. J. R. Wickens and First Lieutenant John Wingate on the bridge of the P.44 (HMS United) in 1942.

Berkhamsted's wartime auxiliary fire brigade, circa 1942.

Northchurch Platoon of the Home Guard, 1943.

Luftwaffe as they turned to attack. A great deal of planning and organisation therefore went into minimising the damage caused by enemy action, establishing procedures to help protect the civilian population in the event of bombs being released on the local area. The local branch of the Red Cross were organised into Voluntary Aid Detachments and as early as April 1939, Berkhamsted had 34 trained men prepared in first-aid parties, with a further 14 women and 75 men ready to be stationed at first-aid posts. Black-out had been introduced on 1st September 1939 and by the beginning of October the Air Raid Precautions (A.R.P.) Control Centre at Berkhamsted Town Hall was being manned 24 hours a day. This local centre was staffed by a controller supported by four operators, two map plotters and a team of messengers. Elaborate fire watching schemes were also set up around the town to help reduce bomb damage and, at the start of the War, there were 76 local men training as volunteer firemen in Berkhamsted. In preparation for air attacks, many trenches were dug out in the open, to help people who might be caught out in the streets during a bombing raid. At Berkhamsted sufficient trenches were provided to cater for up to 10% of the population. A shelter was built in the garden of Victoria School for the school children and a further

substantial splinter-proof bomb shelter was built close to Butts Meadow at a cost of £396. In order to limit the damage caused by incendiary bombs every home in the town was also given at least one sandbag. Early in the conflict, there was considerable concern about the possibility of gas attacks and local people were encouraged to make one room in their house gas-proof, using wet blankets and brown paper. To help with the preparations, school boys from Victoria School and Berkhamsted School were also employed, assembling gas masks in Kings Hall.

With the threat of imminent German invasion, orders were issued on 16th May 1940 that battalions of the Local Defence Volunteers (L.D.V.) were to be organised and made effective immediately. Berkhamsted fell within an area covered by the 7th Battalion, commanded by Captain G. M. Brown from headquarters in Tring High Street. The local company of the Berkhamsted L.D.V., 17 Coy, was soon in place and held its first muster on 18th May 1940 in Butts Meadow. L.D.V. observation posts were set up and amongst the responsibilities of the new ranks were the regulation of petrol use and the manning of security road blocks. By September 1940 the L.D.V. forces had become known nationally as the Home Guard and all men aged between 18 and 51, not already involved in Civil Defence, could now be compelled to serve in areas where numbers were low. However if men were enrolled in both the Home Guard and the A.R.P., the standing instruction was that the A.R.P. was to be given priority, unless the enemy were already in the vicinity. A local Invasion Committee was formed and in December 1941 a full scale invasion practice simulated fierce fighting around Tring and Berkhamsted, with the Berkhamsted Home Guard being made responsible for defence.

With the onslaught of the Blitz in June 1940, the evening skies above the town were often busy with enemy aircraft. The worst period for local bombing took place between September and October 1940, with bombs falling somewhere in the district virtually every day. However most of these were the result of unloading, rather than targeted strikes and thankfully the vast majority of German explosives fell on open ground. In one of the worst incidents, a house in Shootersway was badly damaged and the railway bridge at Sunnyside was completely destroyed by a high explosive bomb in the Summer of 1941. Bombs also fell in Kings Road, where a water main was breached, resulting in a period of water rationing

for the town. In Berkhamsted casualties were mercifully light; one person was killed, with five people being seriously injured and only one other slightly injured by enemy action. Although the hazards of wartime life in the town were real enough, it is worth noting that the area was considered to be sufficiently safe for some of the major statues from London to be transferred for storage in the grounds of Berkhamsted Castle. Here these irreplaceable objects clearly stood a far better chance of survival, than attempting to withstand the perils of the wholesale Blitz on the streets of the Capital. Men of the 17th Company of the Royal Observer Corps. manned the local observer post F.3, which was situated on the high point of Berkhamsted Common, overlooking the castle and the town from the north. Teams of observers, working in shifts, were kept fully occupied monitoring the movement of enemy aircraft. At first they operated from only a small sand-bagged dug-out, which was later replaced by an elevated brick-built platform. Much later in the War, following the D Day invasion on 6th June 1944, there was a new but short-lived menace in the skies above south-east England. This was Hitler's insidious V1, an unmarked flying bomb whose buzzing flight above signalled terror below. Happily none of these fearsome

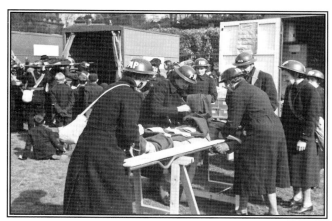

First aid parties conduct training exercises in Butts Meadow.

V.A.D. first aid party ready for inspection in Butts Meadow.

The additional pre-fabricated ward buildings erected in the grounds of Ashridge during the Second World War.

Expectant mothers being cared for at Ashridge, circa 1940.

incendiaries managed to cause any casualties in the Dacorum area, although one doodle-bug did fall on Toms Hill, near Aldbury.

Another feature of life on the Home Front was the presence, at various stages throughout the War, of many hundreds of evacuees in the town. As early as January 1939 local authorities had been asked to conduct surveys of available accommodation in the communities for which they were responsible. It was calculated that Berkhamsted had a total of 4,690 surplus rooms, with offers of accommodation which totalled 3,283. By August 1939 the Government had decided to evacuate schoolchildren, together with all expectant mothers from London within one week of their confinement. On 1st September 1939 the first of 1,900 evacuees began arriving in Berkhamsted. Most were residents of the London County Council area, who travelled by train from suburbs like Willesden, Acton, Chiswick and Hampstead. With German forces initially fully committed elsewhere, this first wave of evacuations from London proved to be unnecessary. This period became known on the Home Front as the 'Phoney War' and by Christmas 1939 over 80% of mothers and infants who earlier fled the Capital had returned home. However the second programme of evacuations certainly proved very necessary and was prompted by the start of the London Blitz in 1940. Berkhamsted School, Ashlyns and the Girls School were all asked to provide some accommodation for the children, many of whom did not return to their homes until late 1943. The Girls School gave shelter to 300 girls from South Hampstead High School and, in order to increase safety for boarders, shelters equipped with bunks were dug in the school grounds. With the numbers of youngsters in the town now so high, the Government encouraged the use of a double shift system, whereby local children could attend school in the morning and groups of evacuees were taught in the same buildings in the afternoon. The third and final phase of evacuations took place towards the end of the conflict, between June and September 1944, when Hitler's V1 flying bombs made a brief but terrifying appearance in the skies above London. Throughout the entire period from 1939-45, the Women's Voluntary Service played a leading role supporting the war effort at home. The Women's Royal Voluntary Service (W.R.V.S.) were particularly involved in helping to receive and support the various waves of evacuees arriving in the town. At Berkhamsted the local group operated from a base at the Civic Centre, under the leadership of Lady Haslam. As the conflict

continued into 1943, all women aged under 40 were now expected to make some kind of contribution. By June 1944 the Women's Land Army had over 80,000 members nationally, some of whom were helping to tend the fields of local farms. Towards the end of the War some German and Italian prisoners of war were also used to increase home food production and there was a local hostel for them at Northchurch, on the site of what is now Stoneys Close. In addition to the thousands of troops camped out on its estate, the buildings of Ashridge House also played a significant role, having been commandeered on the outbreak of war as an emergency hospital. A large operating room was established at Ashridge, which became the scene of over 12,000 operations carried out during the next six years. The Orangery was completed gutted for use as a nurses' home and large huts were built on the lawns to the front of the house, in order to increase the hospital's accommodation. The main hall served as a reception centre and the first patients to be received were 500 wounded soldiers, who had been rescued during the Dunkirk Landings in May 1940. However the majority of the 20,000 patients treated at Ashridge were civilians, who had been transferred out to the countryside away from the hazards of central London. Some three thousand babies were born at Ashridge between 1940-46 and at one time two wards were occupied by German prisoners of war, who were survivors of submarine warfare. The last patients to be treated at Ashridge emergency hospital were our own prisoners of war, most of whom returned home suffering from malnutrition. General de Gaulle, who was then leader of the French Free Forces, spent a year in exile at Berkhamsted, living at a house called Rodinghead, near Ashridge. During his stay, which extended from the Autumn of 1941 until the Autumn of 1942, the General regularly attended Mass at the old Catholic Church in Park View Road.

In the months immediately prior to the D Day invasion, there was a significant build up of troops and equipment in the countryside around Berkhamsted. In addition to training exercises, some of the soldiers' time was spent waterproofing fleets of vehicles, which were kept under cover in the woods of Ashridge and under the trees along New Road at Berkhamsted. This impressive array of vehicles was to be used in the allied force's 'final push' into Europe and consisted of Humber scout cars, dingoes and the huge American USAF Staghound armoured cars, weighing thirteen tons each. Field Marshal Montgomery arrived at Ashridge on 24th

February 1944, together with General Eisenhower and the Allied Commander in Chief, Air Chief Marshall Tedder, to inspect progress and make sure final preparations were well in hand. The troops' departure for Millwall docks, finally took place at 3.30 a.m. on 3rd June 1944. Having travelled across the English Channel they landed, together with the other allied forces, on Juno beach in Normandy on 9th June 1944.

Following the outstanding success of the D Day landings on 6th June 1944, the prospect of Germany invading Britain effectively disappeared. On the morning of Sunday, 17th September the sky over Berkhamsted darkened with a large concentration of aircraft flying low and towing huge gliders on their way to Arnhem. With the end of the war now in sight, black out regulations were relaxed and a stand down of the Home Guard began on 1st November 1944. There was also a similar scaling down of A.R.P. activities and a reduction in the number of hours required from the volunteer fireman and fire watchers. On 2nd May 1945 the Civil Defence Organisation officially ceased to be needed for the purposes of war. A news flash broadcast by the B.B.C. at 7.45 p.m. on Monday 7th May proclaimed that Victory in Europe had been

achieved. Later that same evening the 9 o'clock news announced a two day national holiday to celebrate and V.E. Day on Tuesday 8th May was a joyous day, featuring street parties, dancing and revelries which lasted well into the night. In the centre of Berkhamsted, the piano was brought out of the town hall to provide some accompaniment to all the merriment and a huge Nazi flag was unceremoniously laid out on the main road for everyone to trample upon. The following day a large open air service of thanksgiving was held outside the Civic Centre and the Chairman of the Urban District Council, addressing the crowds, quoted directly from a congratulatory telegram he had sent to Winston Churchill - it concluded with the stirring words: "together we pray that we build a better Britain and a better Berkhamsted". Three months later, following the Japanese surrender, Victory over Japan (V.J. Day) saw a fresh round of celebrations which took place on 16th August 1945. The town's War Memorial was then located close to the entrance of Water Lane, in front of the Court Cafe. In 1952 this memorial was re-positioned close to the main west door of St Peter's Church and the names of local men who lost their lives, fighting in the Second World War, were added at this point.

Colonel Haslam and General de Gaulle at Potten End in 1942.

General de Gaulle taking the salute at the Home Guard march past in Potten End, 1941.

General Eisenhower reviews the XIth Hussars at Ashridge 1944.

The Story of Northchurch

For most of its life Northchurch has been a small agricultural community, with a working population of mainly farm labourers or small holders. To this day the village respects its rural traditions and, despite the busy main road, remains unspoilt by the presence of any substantial factories or workshops. In Victorian times local men seeking industrial experience walked to work in the large timber yards and sawmills of Berkhamsted. At the beginning of the nineteenth century the women and children of Northchurch stayed at home to plait straw in their parlours, with some also working as domestic servants in one of several large houses built close to this hamlet. Situated adjacent to an extensive area of common land, on the edge of the Ashridge estate, Northchurch has always been fiercely protective of its own unique heritage. Thus far it has been successful in preventing the growing urban influence of Berkhamsted from swamping its identity. In fact the village has the architectural proof to lay claim that it is an earlier settlement than its now larger and more powerful neighbour. The Parish Church of St Mary is certainly one of the oldest churches in Hertfordshire, being only one of four in the county which has surviving Saxon elements within its structure. In contrast the Parish Church of St Peter in Berkhamsted dates from no earlier than 1222 and it was following its construction that the village became known as Northchurch. This is because it was now situated to the north of the new Church of St. Peter, a parish specially created for the larger community then developing around the Norman castle of Berkhamsted.

A tour of the village will reveal much of the social history of Northchurch, evident in the old sites and historic buildings which still line the main road. At the southern end of the High Street, opposite The Meads, is the Victorian house Northchurch Place, dated 1871. Its near neighbour Lime Tree House was originally built as a gardener's cottage for one of the local estates. This premises then became Stoney Farm Dairy Shop, before it was taken over by the Berkhamsted Co-operative Society. By the time the property was known as Lime Tree House it housed an antique and silversmith business, before changing its speciality to become the piano showroom we know today. In the 1930's a Mr. Humphrey ran a shoe repairs business from the property next door to Lime Tree House. The imposing Baptist Chapel which also stands on the High Street, first opened on 30th May 1900 and was the gift of J. Marnham Esq. J.P. of Boxmoor.

There was a flourishing Baptist community at Northchurch and this new building replaced an earlier chapel in Bell Lane which had been built in 1840, but could no longer cope with the growing congregation. Next to the newly built chapel stood a barn which housed a blacksmith's forge and was attached to No.69 High Street. The corner of Bell Lane used to be dominated by the Bell Lane stores, but all that remains of the former seventeenth century structure is the massive central chimney. In the 1850's wooden bowls were made in a workshop at Bell Lane and the cottage at No.7 was home to the local straw plait school, where Mrs Wimbush taught up to sixty children at a time! Although the original Baptist Chapel in Bell Lane is long gone, the small graveyard remains. The site opposite the old chapel building formerly belonged to the Northchurch Technical Institute, which was originally based in a barn in Durrants Farm. From 1892 it offered some of the first evening classes to be held in Hertfordshire. Originally funded by a grant from tax on whisky, the Institute provided a varied range of classes included subjects as diverse as arithmetic, dressmaking, and car maintenance. At the peak of its operations the Northchurch Technical Institute could boast up to 80 students.

There are still some interesting flint and brick cottages on the other corner of Bell Lane and a little further along is the Anchorage at No.83 High Street. This fine nineteenth century property, with its distinctive tall chimneys, at one time had orchards running up behind the house as far as Alma Road. Earlier writers have commented that it is likely, although not proven, that both the Anchorage and the corner of Bell Lane are the sites of two earlier Northchurch inns, The Bell and The Anchor. Whilst no records of The Bell Inn have yet been traced, a Northchurch inn called The Anchor is mentioned in a law suit which followed the enclosure of Berkhamsted Common in 1866. Earlier in the census of 1851, the Anchor was listed as being occupied by publican William Saunders. The Pheasant used to stand on the corner of Alma Road, Seymour Road and Duncombe Road. However this public house, which belonged to Foster's brewery based at the Swan Inn in Berkhamsted, became a private house in 1922. At the bottom of Duncombe Road (formerly known as Thorne's yard) the George and Dragon still offers refreshment today. This old coaching inn at No.87 High Street was first known as The Swan, when listed in 1772. By 1840 it was owned by Isaac Winter, who also kept the

Approaching Northchurch, 1892.

Northchurch village centre, circa 1910.

Northchurch Baptist Church, 1985.

Bell Lane Stores, 1971.

Northchurch Post Office, 1982.

The George and Dragon, 1982.

Crooked Billet. In 1851 the inn is recorded simply as The George, which was then being kept by a widow Martha Manton, assisted by her daughter. Architecturally the George and Dragon is an interesting building which shows fragments of a late sixteenth century house, joined by an eighteenth century structure with bay windows. In the 1850's a brazier's and blacksmith's shop were attached to this public house and the village stocks stood opposite. The inn's yard was also regularly converted into a fairground at the time of the Statute Fair, which was organised for the hiring of farming and domestic labour. Beyond the George and Dragon is Northchurch Terrace, built in 1896, and Sheila's dress shop which was formerly an off-licence, haberdashery and second-hand clothes store run by Mrs. Arabella Weedon.

At the heart of Northchurch, almost opposite New Road, is the village's old main post office and general store site. Although now a private house, from the turn of the century this also used to be a high class grocery and provisions shop, run for many years by the East family. Close to the old post office, there was a run of three half-timbered sixteenth century buildings which occupied the site now taken by the modern flats of Tudor Orchard. The largest of these was

Willow Cottage, home to the village laundry. Opposite, on the corner of New Road, are offices which formerly belonged to the Berkhamsted Rural District Council. These were built following the demolition of an earlier general store and post office, run by Mrs. Haywood. Beyond these offices, now called Castle House, was a small shoemaker's shop at No.14 High Street and the village butcher. This butcher shop, which started life on the other side of the High Street, originally had its own slaughter house to the rear. It was run for over one hundred years by members of the Ashby family, before becoming Cook's butcher's shop. On the corner of Darrs Lane is Exhims, a property which can be dated back to 1616 when it was owned by Thomas Exham. It formerly had an attractive conservatory where Mr. J. F. Alcock grew orchids and its coachhouse and stable block (now garages) can still be seen to the rear of the building. A little further north, directly opposite Darrs Lane, is Rosemary Cottage which was previously known as Norris's Farm. This attractive building dates from the late sixteenth/early seventeenth century and is timber framed with gabled dormers. It was here in a large barn that Mr. Page employed local women to make straw cases for wine bottles. Rather curiously he later used the premises to establish the Hertfordshire Tobacco Works, which was advertising 'top quality shag' for 3s 3d in 1875. A little further north is the Old Grey Mare which, along with the George and Dragon, is the only other surviving public house in Northchurch. However it is no longer the original Old Grey Mare, which in 1851 was kept by widower Samuel Bedford, who was then 80 years old. The re-built Inn now stands further back from the main road, opposite the former site of Northchurch Hall. The grounds of this old mansion house, just south of Home Farm, provided the land for the construction of the Park Estate and it was the development of these meadows which first fuelled the post-war expansion of Northchurch's housing stock. The original Old Grey Mare Inn was demolished between the two world wars and the present public house built to the rear of the site. It was here by the Springwood Estate, close to the River Bulbourne, that the remains of a Roman villa were first uncovered in the 1920's and then completely excavated in 1973.

New Road is also worthy of specific mention because, one hundred years ago, it was virtually a hamlet in its own right. The course of New Road was determined by an important old trackway up to the Common, which led on through the Ashridge estate towards Dunstable. The road was built, entirely at his own expense, by Earl Brownlow circa 1865 and quickly became a second principal route into the village. Beyond the rear of St Mary's School, on land which was formerly the New Road playground, were the Church Rooms. These became an important venue and were used for most of the main social events in the village. Further up New Road, but before the river, there was also a local Men's Club. However most of the buildings were on the opposite side of the road. The property at No.2, on the corner of the High Street, was home to the village policeman until after the First World War. In Victorian times a bedroom at No.6 New Road provided a village reading room and at the rear of Nos. 6 and 7 was a brick-built wash house, which was later used as the first headquarters of the Northchurch Boy Scouts. Between the cottages at No. 7 and 8 was Bunn and Green Builders Yard and the property at No.8 (now demolished) used to house a greengrocer's business run by Mr. Clarke. A former beer house eventually became The Compasses public house at No.12, where there was also stabling available for canal barge horses. The name of this former village pub, demolished in the early 1960's, is remembered by the modern Compass Point housing development

Exhims, 1971.

London House Stores and the Compasses Inn (left) in New Road, circa 1958.

Woodside Cottage, formerly the local pest house, photographed in 1967.

Rosemary Cottage.

which opened here in 1984. On this same site was a grocery/provisions store, called London House, which also sold an exciting range of sweets to local youngsters. Beyond this shop there used to be a run of eleven 'two up two down' slate roof cottages, each of which had its own outside wash house and lavatory to the rear. Close to the River Bulbourne there were a further three cottages, at right angles, parallel to the water course. Well tended allotments still occupy ground on the other side of the old river bed, whilst additional allotment sites were once available further up the road, beyond the railway. On the 'S' bend is Woodside Cottage, which was formerly the village Pest House. New Road then leads up to the Common, with the fields of Northchurch and Hill Farms beyond.

Rock & Co. engraving of Northchurch St Mary, 1793.

Parish Church of St Mary

The surviving south and west walls of St Mary's Church date from the Saxon period and were originally part of a smaller, much simpler church. This first structure only consisted of a small chancel and nave, with a separate chamber to provide living accommodation for the priest. A more elaborate cruciform shape for the church was created in the early thirteenth century, when the present chancel and transepts were built and a low tower also added along the lines of the old chancel. However the present tower of St Mary's was constructed on strengthened arches in the fifteenth century, when the transepts were virtually re-built. The traditional cruciform shape of the church was then retained until 1881, when one of the original Saxon walls was removed to allow for the addition of the north aisle. Vestries were also built on the north side of the chancel and the south porch was then added. Most of the walls of St Mary's are built with flint although the tower, which contains a peal of eight bells, is stone faced. This attractive church has many interesting features which are worthy of mention. Some of its windows are very early and the chancel lancet dates from the thirteenth

century, although its glass is modern. St Mary's also has a finely carved fifteenth century Flemish chest and an outstanding eighteenth century Spanish painting of the Madonna and Child, which is displayed in the reredos in the north transept. Another early relic is the fascinating stone coffin, currently in the south transept, which historians have speculated belonged to a crusading knight. In addition to the brass commemorating Peter the Wild Boy, the church is also home to several other interesting memorials. The most substantial memorial at St. Mary's is a stone monument on the south wall which remembers John Edlyn of Norcott Hill, whose family were leading benefactors and did so much to protect the common rights of the people of Northchurch. Additional memorials on the walls of the church remember other local notables such as Sarah Cragie, daughter of Alexander Mason of Woodcock Hill, who died in 1822, John Loxley and Elizabeth Smart Loxley of Norcott, the Rev. William Duncombe, only son of William Duncombe of Lagley (1818-1880) and Charles Stanton Hadden of Rossway who died on 5th February 1905. Various charitable bequests to the local parish are also recorded on the wall of the south transept and the oldest of these was given by Edmund Young in 1622. In the north wall the beautiful memorial window to those who died in the First World War features St. Michael the Archangel and St George the Martyr. The charming stained glass window in the south transept is in memory of Peter Noel Loxley of Norcott Court. As a member of Winston Churchill's staff, Peter Loxley died during the Second World War when his aircraft disappeared on its journey to the Yalta conference. The window depicts a local scene, featuring the tower of St Mary's, which was designed by Hugh Easton who was also responsible for the famous Battle of Britain window in Westminster Abbey. Close to the altar is a memorial brass to John Hobart Culme-Seymour Baronet, who rather exceptionally was Rector of the Parish for fifty years (1830-1880). The chancel of St Mary's was restored in his memory by his widow and children in 1882. Another fondly remembered priest was the Rev. R. H. Pope (1909-31) whose family provided a new altar and furnishings. The white ensign which hangs close to the font was presented by Prince Charles in 1971. This replaced a previous white ensign provided by His Royal Highness Edward, Prince of Wales, when he visited to dedicate the War Memorial in the churchyard on 6th March 1920. To this day the Prince of Wales is Patron to the Living of Northchurch St Mary and the appointment of Rector remains in his gift.

Rural view of Northchurch from the canal, circa 1960.

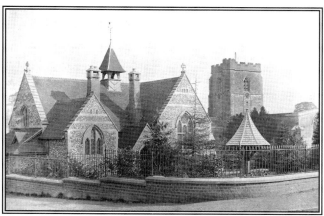

St Mary's School, Northchurch, circa 1900.

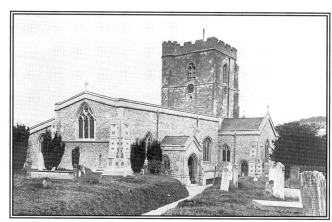

Parish Church of Northchurch St Mary, circa 1908.

Girls of Northchurch School, 1911.

Almshouses at Northchurch, 1988.

Peter the Wild Boy

This unique character will be forever linked to the history of Northchurch, where he is buried in a simple grave near the porch of the parish church. Inside St Mary's Church his memorial on the south wall still excites the curiosity of visitors, many of whom come to Northchurch specifically to learn more about the fascinating story of this eighteenth century 'noble savage'.

Romanticised nineteenth century drawing of Peter the Wild Boy

It is thought that Peter was about twelve years old when in 1725 he was discovered by a local farmer in a field near Hannover in Germany. He was then a wild, brown-skinned, semi-naked boy with no power of speech, who could only grunt and was fond of resting on his knees and elbows in an animal fashion. His strange and untamed demeanour naturally created speculation that he could have been abandoned in the woods and raised by wild animals. At first he delighted the royal court of George I to whom he was presented. They kept the 'wild boy' as something of a pet or curiosity that could be relied upon to provide unusual entertainment and Peter was considered a sufficient attraction to be brought back to England by Caroline of Anspach (1683-1737) who was later to become Queen to George II. However, despite the determined attentions of a tutor to the royal court, Dr. Arbuthnot, it proved impossible to train the 'wild boy' to become more civilised and his novelty value soon wore thin. As a result he was dispensed with and handed over to one of the Queen's bedchamber attendants, Mrs. Tichbourne. With the assistance of an annual maintenance grant of £35, she soon found a good home for Peter with a yeoman farmer called James Fenn of Haxters End Farm in Bourne End. No doubt life on the farm suited the 'wild boy' far better than the polite strictures of the royal court, but he was still something of a liability and would often disappear into the woods for days at a time. On one occasion he wandered as far as Norfolk and, because of this, a specially inscribed leather collar was made for him to help ensure his safe return to the farm at Bourne End. This collar still survives today and is currently in the keeping of the archivist at Berkhamsted School. Leading scientists of the day continued to study Peter's habits and try to understand him. His principal strengths were his agility and stamina; shoes were a pet aversion and he always insisted on remaining bare-footed. His preferred food was raw vegetables, acorns and green twigs and when given treats, such as large nuts and raw onions, he would beat his chest with his fists to express his pleasure. Although he was rarely violent or disturbed in his behaviour, if threatened or teased he was quite likely to bite his tormentors. Peter the Wild Boy was only 5ft. 3ins. tall and, as he grew older, he became tamer in his habits. When Farmer James Fenn died, Peter was transferred to Broadway Farm where he died peacefully on 22nd February 1785, at the estimated age of seventy-two. At this time Broadway was included within the parish of Northchurch, which explains why the 'wild boy' was buried in the grounds of St Mary's Church. Peter's unusual story however lives on and continues to excite the imagination. Many years after his death Charles Dickens included references to him in two of his major works: Edwin Drood and Martin Chuzzlewit. A novel called 'Peter the Wild Boy' was also written by C. M. Tennant and published in 1930.

Peter the Wild Boy as an old man.

Church House

The picturesque half-timbered Church House and cottages, dating from the sixteenth century, are the best known buildings in Northchurch. Often photographed, these almshouses are the oldest surviving structures in the village with a frontage onto the main road. The main architectural feature of Church House is its oversailing first floor, which only adds to its aged appearance. Back in 1590 the property was granted to Sir Edward Stanley, having previously been in the tenure of a character called Axtell. This could well have been Henry Axtell, a wealthy man who rather strangely starved himself to death and was buried at Northchurch in 1625. By 1654 the house was subject to a trust deed, issued by John Edlyn of Norcott Hill, which confirmed its purpose as "a habitation for the aged and poor". An almshouse ever since, Church House was extensively restored in 1966. Rectory Cottage still survives at No.82 High Street, but the substantial old Rectory of St Mary's, which stood on land immediately behind the almshouses, was demolished in 1957. The extensive grounds of the old property were then used for the local housing development known as The Meads.

St Mary's School

This Church of England school was built for the children of Northchurch in 1864, during the ministry of Sir John Hobart Culme Seymour, Rector of St Mary's from 1830-1880. The land for the school site had been provided by Earl Brownlow of Ashridge in a trust deed which is dated 30th March 1863. The project's construction costs were principally supported by an endowment of £4,500 given by Phillip Van de Wall. He was a prosperous industrialist whose will was executed by a law practice in Cheapside, London which counted John Loxley of Norcott Court amongst its solicitors. In order to improve the school's prospects of receiving on-going government funding, Earl Brownlow transferred the land to the Rector and Churchwarden of St Mary's Church and the school thereby became a Voluntary Aided Church School. Built in the heart of the community, close to the Parish Church, this flint and brick structure is an excellent example of a typical Victorian school. St Mary's started life as a mixed school but, as numbers grew, the boys were transferred to another building, almost opposite the old infant school in Gossoms End. However by 1917 the boys were again allowed to attend their old village school and their former classrooms became a woodwork centre for all the local schools. With its own excellent junior school, Northchurch also became something of a pioneer in adult education, when it was one of the first villages in the county to offer technical and continuation classes. These began in 1892 with carpentry lessons in a barn in Durrants Farm, in addition to other classes held at the village school. Local interest was so great that a separate Northchurch Technical Institute was established, which eventually had its own brick-built building in Bell Lane. Until piped water arrived in Northchurch, the old village well used to be in the upper part of what is now the top playground between the High Street and New Road. As recently as the early 1950's, pupils could stay at St Mary's School until they were fourteen years old, although some children left when they were eleven in order to take up scholarships at the grammar schools in Berkhamsted. From 1955 St Mary's became a junior school feeding Ashlyns Secondary School and subsequently a first school only, when a three tier system of middle school education was introduced in 1970.

Marlin Chapel

Situated in a field off Shootersway, near Marlin Chapel Farm, are the ruins of an old chapel of ease which date from the thirteenth century. The local place name 'Marlin' is a likely corruption of the biblical 'Magdalene' and the crumbling remains of Marlin Chapel represent the most significant surviving ruin in the parish of Northchurch. Historians are confident that the building was once the domestic chapel serving the manor of Maudeleynes, which was held by Laurence de Broc towards the end of the reign of Henry II (1133-89). In 1616 this manor was listed as comprising only 110 acres and by the next century, although it had grown, it had been split into two separate estates. In 1778 some 119 acres of Marlin Farm, then let to Henry Thomas, was sold for £1280. A further 122 acres of the neighbouring Marlin Chapel Farm, let to Richard Wood, realised a sale price of £1000, when both farms were sold at an auction held at the Kings Arms in Berkhamsted High Street. The current Marlin Chapel Farm is a much more recent structure built on the old manorial site in 1897. The deep moat which still surrounds the property is a clear indication that the former manor house was of considerable importance and once home to a powerful man. When intact, the chapel itself was nearly 60 ft. long and 19 ft. wide, with walls of worked Totternhoe stone and flint that were 3 ft. thick. It is possible that the chapel's role as a religious building could have lasted some four hundred years until the beginning of the eighteenth century, by which time it was being used as a malt house for the farmstead.

Norcott

In the same way that the manor of Maudeleynes, was eventually split into the two estates of Marlin Farm and Marlin Chapel Farm, the northern manor of Norcott, which fringed the Ashridge estate, was also divided into Norcott Hill and Norcott Court. It is thought that the original manor house stood on the site occupied by Norcott Hill Farm, whilst what became the more significant estate of Norcott Court was established lower down the valley at the beginning of the seventeenth century. William Edlyn is listed as resident at Norcott Hill in 1637 and he was to prove a public spirited man who provided endowments to support the village almshouses. William Edlyn also fought to prevent the enclosure of some 300 acres of Berkhamsted Common by the Crown in 1640. As a result of a similar raid which tore down fences and railings, he was arrested and imprisoned. Because this particular dispute was with the Crown his actions risked the severest censure but, together with several other Northchurch men, William Edlyn was fortunate to be simply cautioned not to offend again.

Norcott Court was built over one hundred years ago by John Loxley and replaced a much smaller structure, which dated from the early 1600's when the manor was first split. Respecting the traditions established by the Edlyns at Norcott Hill, the Loxley family of Norcott Court were also closely associated with the village of Northchurch and became great benefactors to the parish. In 1864 John Loxley provided funds to help build the village school and a memorial in the village church also acknowledges public endowments given by Elizabeth Loxley. A stained glass window in St Mary's is devoted to a later generation of the Loxley family, recalling the sacrifice made by Peter Loxley who died serving his country in the Second World War. Norcott Court is the former family home of John Andrew Davidson, the 2nd Viscount Davidson, who served as Government Chief Whip in the House of Lords (1986-91). His father John Colin Campbell Davidson also enjoyed a prestigious political career. He held the office of Chancellor of the Duchy of Lancaster 1923-24 and again in 1931-37, whilst serving as member of parliament for the district of Hemel Hempstead. His wife, Lady Joan Davidson, who succeeded him in the local constituency, was particularly well known for her active involvement in the community. She was a popular figure in the village and was eventually created Baroness Northchurch.

Norcott Hill, 1997.

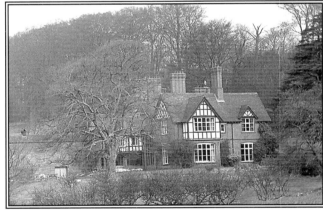

Norcott Court, 1967.

Marlin Chapel Farm in 1899.

Dropshort, 1965.

Frontage of Woodcock Hill in 1905.

Rear of Woodcock Hill, 1905.

Lagley House, 1962

Edgeworth House, 1971.

Dropshort Cottages

At the northern end of the village, opposite the cricket ground, are two distinctive and rather curious looking eighteenth century cottages. They were built by Mr. Smart, then resident at Norcott Court, so that he could await the arrival of the stagecoach on the main road in relative comfort. Dropshort was built specifically to serve as the waiting room; whilst Dropshort Cottage housed one of his estate workers. Mr. Smart was then able to employ the wife of his estate worker to keep the waiting room clean and tidy in readiness for his visits. The curious triangular piece of land opposite the house, which is sandwiched between the cricket pitch and the recreation ground, is often referred to by locals as the village pound for stray animals and was once the site of an old well.

Northchurch Hall

This red bricked three storey house, which was of early nineteenth century origin, was originally a rather gaunt structure, although it was later extended to provide impressive accommodation. Known as Northchurch House in its earlier days, this large property stood back, overlooking the main road, not far from the corner at Darrs Lane. In its hey-day, prior to the turn of the century, this estate comprised 143 acres and also included a Model Farm. Some of the staff employed at the great house then lived in a row of small half-timbered cottages (demolished circa 1960) which stood on the opposite side of the High Street. The most impressive feature of the house was its grand entrance hall, with enormous fireplace and open staircase which led to no less than eleven bedrooms. For many years the Hall was home to the Barnett family, who generously welcomed local villagers to garden parties and horticultural shows held every year in its handsome grounds. The Barnett family employed a cook and five maids, as well as six other outdoor staff to attend to the stables and extensive gardens, which included tennis and croquet lawns. During the Second World War, when the property was owned by Lady Lemon, the house and outbuildings were used extensively by the Local Defence Volunteers and also acted as a base for the St Johns Ambulance Brigade. Following the conflict, the Hall was in a sad state of repair and the cost of upkeep of such a large mansion was becoming prohibitive. Consequently there was little choice but to demolish the grand old house and its estate was sold to provide badly needed housing land for the village. The extensive Park Estate, together with its shopping parade, has since been developed on the former grounds of Northchurch Hall.

Woodcock Hill

The estate of Woodcock Hill is first mentioned in a survey dated 1607. Although a nineteenth century house still survives, it is well hidden behind a series of boundary walls and trees which offer almost total seclusion. The house enjoys an excellent position at the top of Durrants Lane, which provides spectacular views across the valley. In 1840, when the house was purchased by Mr. J. Field for £2775, the price included a coachhouse, stabling, farm buildings, gardens and orchard. There was also 25 acres of fine pasture land which ran for some distance below Shootersway, between Durrants Lane and Bell Lane. The new owner of this estate had the privilege of his own pew at the Parish Church of St Mary and the house itself offered rather elegant accommodation. This included an entrance hall and dining room, a library and drawing room with a decoratively painted ceiling, a separate servants hall, kitchen and scullery, together with numerous master bedrooms and servants quarters. Woodcock Hill soon came into the ownership of Mr. Frank Moore who lavished money on his new purchase, re-building the house in 1848 and eventually extending the estate to 245 acres. Some of the land he acquired included the fields lower down the valley, which have since become the Durrants and Westfield housing estates. He also built the two lodge houses at the top and bottom of Durrants Lane, which remained a private gated drive until 1914. The lodge house at the top of Durrants Lane was badly damaged by the blast from an aerial mine which exploded on the other side of Shootersway Lane during the Second World War. In 1854 Mr. Moore presented a set of silver for the celebration of Holy Communion at the Parish Church of St Mary. Now a leading land owner, he became something of a local squire employing a large staff on his estate. He was very involved in local affairs and served for a period as Chairman of the Board of Governors at Berkhamsted School. When Woodcock Hill was finally sold in 1905 by Mr. A. McNeill Streatfield Moore it boasted thirteen bedrooms. By 1910 the propery had become home to Mrs. McVitie, whose family were connected to the world famous McVitie & Price cake and biscuit manufacturers. The history of Woodcock Hill took an interesting turn in 1940, when it was acquired to serve as a nunnery for the Carmelite sisters. The large drawing room was converted into a chapel until 1951, when the nuns moved back to Presteigne in Wales. Since this period Woodcock Hill has been shared by three different families. Beneath the old house there are still extensive cellars and an old well which is 200 ft. deep.

Edgeworth

The remodelled property of Edgeworth was constructed in 1767, a date which can still be found carved on one of its chimneys. However the site is much earlier than this and the house which survives today was built on the remains of a sixteenth century structure. At its north western end, the mansion still has Elizabethan bricks within its foundations. Prior to 1911 the house was called The Limes and owes its current name to an Irishman, Richard Lovell Edgeworth, who chose to live there in 1776. Mr. Edgeworth was married four times and fathered a total of nineteen children. His eldest daughter, Maria, grew up to become a very successful novelist. From the Edgeworths the property passed to Mr. Walter Hutchinson who lived at the house between 1784 and 1795. It was then sold to Walter Moore, after whom the house was acquired by the Duncombes, who also owned Lagley House opposite. Edgeworth was considerably altered and extended during the nineteenth century, when a west wing was added. The property then passed to a Mr. Spencer L. Holland in 1902, after which it changed hands several times. The old stables block was lost when part of the frontage of the estate was sacrificed for road widening on the main A41 road in 1937. In 1951 Edgeworth became home to Mr. & Mrs. E. J. Talbot Ponsonby.

Lagley

There are records of a local place name called Lagley Field which date back to 1607 and the original property at Lagley then stood very close to the main road. In 1832 Mr. W. A. Duncombe built an impressive mansion behind the remains of this much earlier house. The new Lagley was a highly distinctive building, featuring yellow stock bricks, a large slate roof and a stone stepped porch to a front door, which was adorned by Greek Doric fluted pilasters and columns. W. A. Duncombe's initials, together with the date of construction, also appeared on the facade of this new house. From this time Lagley had its own stables and coachhouse, with staff accommodation above. In the first half of this century the property was home to Mrs. E. Douglas. During the 1930's Lagley hosted the local scout fetes until Mrs. Douglas died in 1940. The house was taken over by the Army until the end of the War, when it became home to Colonel and Mrs. Johnston. Lagley House was then acquired by the District Council, who at first converted it into flats, before demolishing the property in order to build a development of council-run flats and bungalows for senior citizens, which still bear its name.

Literary Berkhamsted

In common with its outstanding religious and educational traditions, there can be no denying that Berkhamsted has an exceptional literary heritage. This can best be illustrated by taking a closer look at a number of eminent authors, all of whom have definite links with the town. It is particularly noticeable that the incidence of successful writers associated with Berkhamsted gathers momentum during the late Victorian era, when families belonging to the emerging professional and middle classes became increasingly attracted to the town. By this time Berkhamsted's excellent transport links, combined with its proximity to London and the ready availability of good quality schooling, had made it a highly desirable place in which to live or be educated. Nevertheless, prior to this 'golden period', which spawned many more writers and journalists than we have space to mention, the beginnings of the town's literary lineage can be traced back to the Middle Ages.

Geoffrey Chaucer c.1343-1400

One of the most often quoted and certainly the earliest literary connection with the town is perhaps one of the most tenuous. However the name of Geoffrey Chaucer, who wrote the Canterbury Tales between 1387-1392 and is generally considered to be the greatest English poet of the Middle Ages, does feature in the recorded history of Berkhamsted. In 1389, during the reign of Richard II, he is listed as holding the office of Clerk of Works at Berkhamsted Castle, although there is no surviving evidence to indicate that he spent much time in the town. Despite doubts concerning the frequency of his visits, leading academics are confident that the eminent local physician, John of Gaddesden, who served as Court Physician to Edward III, was the model for Chaucer's rather spiteful portrait of the 'Doctor of Physic' in the Canterbury Tales.

William Cowper 1731-1800

The poet William Cowper was born in Berkhamsted, where his father the Rev. John Cowper served as Rector of St Peter's Parish Church 1722-56 and he later described his childhood, spent at the Rectory, as a "blissful time". William may well have inherited some of his poetic gift from his mother, Anne Donne, who was a direct descendent of the nation's foremost metaphysical poet John Donne (1572-1631). Despite a mental collapse in 1763, Cowper was nursed to recovery by his companion Mary Unwin and went on to write some of the defining poetry of the late eighteenth century. His simple and direct style, combined with subject matter chiefly devoted to nature and the human condition, marked the point when English poetry began to move away from the concerns of neo-classicism to romanticism. A substantial volume of William Cowper's poetry was published in 1782 and one of his last great poems was the depressing but powerful 'Castaway' written in 1794. Many people may not realise that his poetic phrasing was responsible for adding several stock phrases to the English language. It was Cowper who, for example, first penned: "Variety is the spice of life", "I am the monarch of all I survey" and "God moves in mysterious ways". Although he is far from a fashionable poet in the late twentieth century, it would be difficult to exaggerate the celebrity and affection he enjoyed in his day. Robert Southey's subsequent 'Life of Cowper', published in 1833-7, confidently declared that "Berkhamsted will be better known in after ages as the birthplace of Cowper, than for its connection with so many historical personages who figured in the tragedies of old".

William Cowper.

Maria Edgeworth 1767-1849

When she was nine years old her father, the eccentric Irish landowner Richard Lovell Edgeworth, brought the family to live at a house then called 'The Limes', which still stands on the main road near Northchurch. The eldest daughter in a family of nineteen, Maria Edgeworth became one of England's most successful female novelists with the publication of her highly popular novels of Irish life. 'Castle Rackrent' was published 1800, 'Absentee' in 1812 and 'Ormonde' in 1817. Her work had a definite influence on her friend Walter Scott who was then writing the 'Waverley' novels and Jane Austen also appreciated her achievements, sending her an early copy of 'Emma' shortly before its publication in 1816. At the beginning of the twentieth century the house where Maria grew up was re-named Edgeworth in respect of its significant literary connection.

William Longman 1813-77

Although not an author in his own right, William Longman still fits our literary criteria. His father, Thomas Norton Longman III, was the outstanding publisher of his day who was fortunate to be able include the works of Southey, Walter Scott and Wordsworth on his list. William Longman moved from Chorleywood to live at Ashlyns Hall in 1859 and continued his father's success by acquiring the rights to the works of John Stuart Mill. He also published Roget's Thesaurus and then launched T.B. Macauley's authoritative series the 'History of England'. This soon became the most profitable publishing initiative of its time, when over 13,000 copies of the first two volumes were sold in twelve weeks. Only three months after the publication of Volumes III and IV in December 1855, Longman was able to pay Macauley what was then the most famous cheque in the history of publishing. This was for £20,000 and over the next thirty years 140,000 copies of T.B. Macauley's great work were sold in Britain alone. William Longman's last great coup was to successfully negotiate the rights to the first two novels of Anthony Trollope's Barchester Chronicles.

J. M. Barrie 1860-1937

The celebrated Scottish playwright and novelist, James Matthew Barrie, enjoyed an outstanding period of success which began in 1902, when two of his best plays 'Quality Street' and 'Admirable Crichton' were both performed on the London stage. This breakthrough was followed by the enduring triumph of 'Peter Pan' only two years later and it was during this exciting time that J.M. Barrie was a frequent visitor to Egerton House in Berkhamsted. This substantial house was then home to Arthur Llewellyn Davis, whose sons the playwright had befriended when they lived in London at Kensington Park Gardens. Two of the five boys, one of whom was called Peter, had provided the inspiration for his seminal tale of the youngster who refused to grow up and this magical story of fairies, pirates and a treasure island was especially created to entertain the Llewellyn Davis children. When Peter Pan first opened at the Duke of York Theatre in 1904, all five boys were taken regularly to the rehearsals. The following Christmas, when one of the boys was too ill to attend, Barrie decided to take some of the scenery and the entire cast to give a special performance at Egerton House. However in 1907 tragedy struck this happy family when Arthur Llewellyn Davis died of cancer, only for his wife to die three years later. The five boys were then left in Barrie's care, a responsibility he carried out diligently until his own death in 1937. J. M. Barrie was knighted in 1913.

W. W. Jacobs 1863-1943

This noted humorist and short story writer lived in Chesham Road in a large house called Beechcroft which has since been demolished. Often seen walking around the town, he was also a regular patron of the Court Theatre where he particularly enjoyed watching the latest film releases. William Wymark Jacobs, a friend and contemporary of P. G. Wodehouse, was the author of no less than twenty volumes of his own short stories. His first collection was 'May Cargoes', published 1896, others included 'Skippers Wooing' published in 1897, 'Light Freights' in 1901 and 'Sea Whispers' in 1906. W. W. Jacobs is most commonly remembered for his macabre short story 'The Monkey's Paw'.

Dr. George Macauley Trevelyan 1876-1962

G. M. Trevelyan, who was the best known historian during the first half of the twentieth century, brought his family to live in Berkhamsted in 1918, acquiring a substantial property in Kings Road, opposite the Girls School sports ground. The publication of 'England Under the Stuarts' in 1904 had confirmed his reputation as a scholarly but popular writer. Trevelyan also became an acknowledged expert on Italian history, when he wrote three outstanding books on Garibaldi published between 1907 and 1911. His 'History of England', published in 1926, became a best-seller and he was appointed Regius Professor of Modern History at Cambridge University in 1927. Today Trevelyan's nostalgic study 'English Social History', published in 1944, remains his best known work. His family provided several other literary connections; his wife, Janet Penrose, was the daughter of the famous writer Mrs Humphrey Ward (1851-1920) who Tolstoy once described as "the world's greatest living novelist" and Trevelyan's own daughter, Mary Moorman, also made her mark, becoming a leading authority on the poet Wordsworth.

H. E. Todd 1908-88

Herbert Eatton Todd was a well-known resident of the town who lived in Brownlow Road. He was the author of over twenty Bobby Brewster stories, written for children, the first of which was published in 1949. The hero of these popular tales was a small mischievous boy, with a round face, blue eyes and a nose like a button, which 'Bertie' Todd readily admitted was a part of himself. H. E. Todd was also a broadcaster, lecturer and regular story teller with magical appeal. His tales of Bobby Brewster have an enduring quality and have since been translated into many languages.

Graham Greene 1904-95

Arguably the finest writer of his generation and one of the most widely read novelists of the twentieth century, Graham Greene is undoubtedly the town's favourite literary son. He was educated at Berkhamsted School, where his father C. H. Greene was headmaster, and later admitted in his autobiography 'A Sort of Life', published in 1971 that "if I had known it, the whole future must have lain all the time along these Berkhamsted streets." Following studies at Balliol College, Oxford, a key event in his life was his conversion to Catholicism in 1926. Graham Greene wrote for the Times and was appointed literary editor of the Spectator in 1940; also working for the Foreign Office during the War in Sierra Leone 1941/3. His first novel 'The Man Within', published in 1929, was a historical thriller deploying many themes such as pursuit, guilt, treachery and failure which were to become the hallmark of his fiction. He enjoyed his first popular success with 'Stamboul Train' published in 1932 and major novels followed. His first explicitly Catholic novel was 'Brighton Rock' published in 1938, which explored principal concerns pursued in some of his subsequent novels: 'Power and Glory' (1940) 'Heart of the Matter' (1948) and 'Quiet American' (1955). One of his last novels 'The Human Factor', published in 1978, was partly set in the town. This was soon made into a film, released in 1979, which was directed by Otto Preminger and starred Nicol

Sir Hugh Carleton Greene, with Graham Greene (centre) and Ken Sherwood at the Berkhamsted Citizens Association meeting, held in the Kings Hall, August 1974.

Williamson in the principal role as secret service agent Maurice Castle. Amongst the many accolades received during his lifetime, Graham Greene was made Companion of Honour in 1966 and Chevalier de la Lègion d'Honneur in 1969. More recently in October 1997 the Graham Greene Birthplace Trust was established, specifically to promote and celebrate this distinguished writer's connections with Berkhamsted. The new Trust has already successfully launched several initiatives, principal amongst which was a five day festival, organised in the town between 29th September and 3rd October 1998. The feature event celebrated the anniversary of the author's birthday on Friday, 2nd October.

Claud Cockburn 1904-1981

Claud Cockburn was a pupil at Berkhamsted School, where he was a contemporary of Graham Greene, who was later to describe him, along with G. K. Chesterton, as "one of the two greatest journalists of the twentieth century". Cockburn completed his education at Keble College, Oxford, and then worked as Correspondent of the Times in New York and Washington between 1929-32. He undertook the role of Diplomatic and Foreign Correspondent for the Daily Worker 1935-46 and, from around 1953, the majority of his writing was produced for magazines such as Punch, New Statesman, and Private Eye. Claud Cockburn wrote several books including 'Beat the Devil', published in 1952, 'Nine Bald Men' (1956) and 'Aspects of History' (1957); several volumes of his autobiography were also published between 1955-61.

Peter Quennell 1905-1993

Peter Quennell was born in Berkhamsted and, in common with Graham Greene, educated at Berkhamsted School and Balliol College, Oxford. Quennell's early reputation as a talented poet launched him on a literary path and an early collection of his work 'Poems' was published in 1926. As his career developed, biographical

Berkhamsted School, the breeding ground for many of Berkhamsted's finest writers.

Broadcaster and author, Gerald Priestland.

Richard Mabey, 1998.

writing tended to predominate and a major study of Byron was first published 1934-5, with works on Ruskin and Hogarth following in 1949 and 1955 respectively. He also wrote biographies of Shakespeare in 1963 and Alexander Pope in 1968. Peter Quennell founded the journal 'History Today', which he edited from 1951-1979, and an autobiography 'Marble Foot' was published in 1976. His parents were C. H. B. and Marjory Quennell, authors of several series of educational books, principal amongst which was 'A History of Everyday Things in England', first published by Batsford in 1918.

Gerald Priestland 1927-1991
This popular writer and broadcaster was born in Ravens Lane, close to the factory then owned by his uncle Sir Richard Cooper. The Priestland family soon moved to a larger property called 'Meadow Cottage' in Gravel Path and eventually settled in a house built for them in Potten End. Gerald Priestland was educated at Charterhouse and New College, Oxford. At the age of 26, he became the youngest ever Foreign Correspondent for the BBC, earning prestigious postings to India, the Middle East and the United States. After something of a spiritual re-awakening, following a nervous breakdown, he

subsequently became the Corporation's most successful religious affairs correspondent and his radio programmes such as 'Yours Faithfully' and 'Priestland's Progress' soon became national institutions. 'Something Understood', a first volume of autobiography published in 1986, devotes considerable attention to his early life in Berkhamsted.

Richard Mabey
This successful author and broadcaster, who was educated at Berkhamsted School and St Catherine's College, Oxford, still lives in the town. Now one of the nation's best known natural history writers, Richard Mabey has produced a number of highly acclaimed titles on the flora of the English countryside. An early success was the best-seller and often re-printed 'Food For Free', first published in 1972. This was followed by other key titles such as 'Unofficial Countryside' (1973) 'Plants with a Purpose' (1977) 'Common Ground' (1980) and 'Frampton Flora' (1985). Richard Mabey has also written an award-winning biography of the naturalist Gilbert White, which won the Whitbread Biography Prize in 1986, and his definitive 'Flora Britannica', published in 1996, became an impressive bestseller in the Christmas of that year.

Social Life

Berkhamsted Mechanics Institute

Historically there were many social groups attached to the Church such as savings clubs, Mothers Union, bell ringers, needle and craftwork societies, nursing association etc. However with the honourable exception of the Berkhamsted and Northchurch Property Association (see p.124), the Mechanics Institute was the town's oldest independent society. Founder members were Mr. R. Norris of Lower Mill, together with shopkeeper and local champion of education, Henry Nash. In 1845 the Society's inaugural lectures on the 'Philosophy of the Human Mind' were held in the school room of the National School. The Institute's first reading room opened in a house belonging to Mr. Plaitrier, the printer, which later became part of Ward's large drapers shop in the High Street. Subsequently the reading room moved to No.21 Castle Street, prior to this property becoming the Gardeners Arms. For a time it was also housed in a room in Nash's Yard, which stood on the site now occupied by the Civic Centre. By the time the Town Hall opened in 1860, the Mechanics Institute had already become sufficiently well established in the town that a reading room was designed into the facilities offered by this magnificent new public building. With the benefit of such excellent accommodation the Institute soon expanded its activities, arranging an impressive programme of lectures which attracted regular audiences in excess of three hundred. In order to encourage local artists and craftsmen, the Mechanics Institute also organised a grand annual exhibition at the Town Hall, where substantial prizes and medals were awarded for the best work. In 1890 extension work at the Town Hall provided the Institute with its own billiards and snooker room. However the most important and long lasting benefit of this organisation, which was an unswerving champion of "education for all", was the creation of a programme of evening classes in subjects as diverse as chemistry, woodwork, elocution and shorthand. These classes began back in 1847 and ensured that Berkhamsted was offering some form of adult education long before most other towns in Hertfordshire. The term Mechanics was dropped from the Institute's title in 1930 and the Berkhamsted Institute was finally wound up in April 1993. Today its valuable tradition is reinforced by the continuing presence in the High Street of the Adult Studies Centre, which is now run by West Herts College.

Berkhamsted Town Hall, home of the Mechanics Institute, seen here in 1860 prior to the construction of Lower Kings Road.

Street party on the Swing Gate estate to celebrate the Coronation of Queen Elizabeth in June 1953.

Staff from the Mantle Furniture Factory on a works outing to Southend, circa 1950.

Berkhamsted Town Football Club

Competitive football in the district began with the formation of the West Herts League in 1891 and two local teams were founder members. Berkhamsted School and Berkhamsted Sunnyside both played in that first season, but by 1895 the Sunnyside team had disbanded and Berkhamsted Town F.C. was formed. In only the club's second season they won an impressive treble, becoming league champions in 1896/97 and were also victorious in the St Mary's Cup and the Apsley Charity Cup. In these early days leagues were small and by the 1898/99 season Berkhamsted Town F. C. was competing in the Herts County League as well as the West Herts League. However a collapse in form meant that by 1906 the club could no longer continue and a reformed Sunnyside then enjoyed a short period as the town's senior footballing side. Following a pattern that we see repeated in many other towns and villages around the county, the current club was reformed in 1919 by ex-servicemen returning from the First World War. At first the local team was called the Berkhamsted Comrades and they played on the town's cricket ground in Lower Kings Road. This name was dropped in 1922 when Berkhamsted Town F.C. gained admission to Division Two of the Spartan League. In 1925 Berkhamsted Town finished fourth and their player R. Devlin finished the season as the league's top scorer, netting 40 goals in 25 matches. By the 1932/33 season a star had emerged in the team in the shape of a local lad named Frank Broome who, as a seventeen year old, scored 53 goals in that one season. Inevitably his exploits soon attracted the attention of larger clubs and in 1934 he turned professional with Aston Villa; no transfer fee was involved but Berkhamsted Town later received a donation of the princely sum of £25. Frank Broome soon became a regular scorer in the First Division and in 1946 was transferred to Derby County for £5000. During a long career he also played with Tommy Lawton at Notts. County and won seven England caps. He scored on his England debut in May 1938, during the team's famous away win in Berlin, which was played before Hitler's lieutenants, Rudolf Hess and Josef Goebbels.

Berkhamsted Town continued to be successful after the War, reaching the final of the Herts. Senior Cup for the first time in the 1946/47 season. Amateur football was then a popular attraction and on Easter Monday 1947 the club played in front of a record crowd of 2000, when they defeated Apsley in an important league match. Eager for further development, in 1951 the club became a founder member of the Delphian League. This gave the team the opportunity to play against much stronger opposition, competing with teams like Aylesbury, Bishop Stortford, Dagenham and Slough. The club's greatest triumph in its history took place at the end of the 1952/3 season, when they won the Herts Senior Cup with a 4-2 victory over St Albans. Maurice Cook, who scored in this famous victory, went on to enjoy a successful professional career playing for Watford and also Fulham, where two of his illustrious team-mates were Johnny Haynes and Jimmy Hill. However several years later the club's fortunes slumped and between 1957 and 1961 they finished bottom of the league in four consecutive seasons. A poor financial situation meant that the club had little option but to withdraw from what was then the Athenian League and transfer to the Spartan League in 1966. Less than ten years later the club's fortunes had revived and it won the Herts Charity Shield outright for the first time in 1974. In the 1974/75 season the first team managed to finish in the top six, earning a place in the league's premier division, when it merged with the Metropolitan London League. Berkhamsted Town then enjoyed a wonderfully successful season in 1979/80 winning the London Spartan League Championship, the Herts Charity Shield and the St Mary's Cup. Important developments took place in 1983, when the club's Lower Kings Road ground was sold and a series of flats built on the old pitch. The base for the football club then moved across the canal-side meadow to the old cricket pavilion at Broadwater, where new dressing rooms and a stand were built. The impressive new facilities, complete with floodlights, earned the club an immediate return to the more prestigious Athenian League. However this league was almost immediately replaced by an additional division of the Isthmian League in 1984. First team trophies won then included the Herts Charity Shield and the Wallspan Floodlit Cup in 1984/85. In 1991/92 Berkhamsted Town F.C. again secured the Herts Charity Shield and finished fourth to earn a place in the de-regulated Division Two. In 1993 the club was successful in gaining promotion to Division One of the Diadora League, where they continue to play today.

Berkhamsted Football Club, winners of the Apsley Charity Cup, 1903-4.

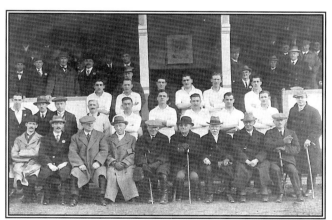

Opening of the grandstand at Berkhamsted Town Football Club in the 1920's.

Berkhamsted Town F.C. first team 1974-5 season.

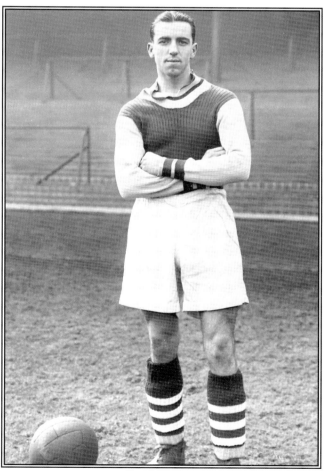

Frank Broome.

Members of the Berkhamsted Golf Club pose in front of their wooden pavilion in the castle grounds, circa 1890.

Ladies of Berkhamsted Golf Club. 1905.

Playing up towards the car park from what is now the ninth tee, in 1909.

The clubhouse and car park at Berkhamsted Golf Club, 1962.

Berkhamsted Golf Club's new clubhouse, photographed in 1998.

Berkhamsted Golf Club

Berkhamsted Golf Club owes its origins to a keen young golfer and local schoolmaster, G.H. Gowring, who first learnt to play the game at the Royal Eastbourne Golf Club before moving to the town to teach at Berkhamsted School. Together with fellow masters, the Rev. T.C. Fry and C.H. Greene, he founded Berkhamsted Golf Club on 12th December 1890. As the Club's first honorary secretary and treasurer, it was Gowring's job to secure Lord Brownlow's permission to play on the Common. By the time that the Golf Club held its first Annual General Meeting at Berkhamsted Town Hall in November 1891, it already had a paid up membership of forty, which included four ladies. The first rather modest nine hole course exploited the width of Broad Walk, beside Frithsden Copse, and was soon attracting a playing membership of around one hundred. For a couple of years the Club changed its approach, hiring fields in Berkhamsted Park and erecting a wooden clubhouse near the Castle. However in 1896 Gowring returned the Club to its original objective of developing a quality course on the Common. The clubhouse was moved back to Ashridge and Willie Park (the younger), winner of the Open Championship in 1889, was engaged to advise the committee on the development of what was still only a nine hole course. In 1899, the offer from Lord Brownlow of the lease of an eighth of an acre of orchard, opposite the first tee, allowed for the construction of a permanent clubhouse. A debenture fund was created to raise the necessary finance and by 1901 a brick-built structure had been completed. The first eighteen hole course, designed by J.C. Gilbert, was ready for play in 1909 and by 1912 the Club had reached its original membership ceiling of 250 men and 100 ladies. This limit was extended to 300 and 130 respectively and a new policy was adopted, which aimed to ensure that local applicants received priority.

The Club was fortunate to survive the privations of the First World War, living off its financial reserves together with contributions from the Inns of Court officers, who were training on the Common. With the death of Lord Brownlow in 1921, parts of the Ashridge estate became available and in 1923 club member Edwin Williams of Goreside was able to purchase 489 acres of Berkhamsted Common. Together with another leading club member, Mr. T.H. Blackwell of Haresfoot, he then set up the Berkhamsted Golf Club Trustee Company which could hold the land for the permanent benefit of the Club. This was a key moment in the history of golf in Berkhamsted, when playing rights across the Common where assured in perpetuity. The current eighteen hole golf course was created in 1927 and still enjoys the distinction of being one of the few leading competitive golf courses in the Country which has no sand bunkers. During the 1930's the Club, on its own initiative, entered into an agreement with the local councils and the Citizens Association to allow local people a legal right to enjoy "air and exercise" over this part of the Common. This concession was granted with the proviso that "no one should in any way interfere with members' enjoyment of their golf" and this public-spirited tradition of free access to the course continues to this day. The Second World War and the immediate post-war period was a difficult time for the Club, given a sharp drop in membership and the damage caused by fleets of tanks and other heavy vehicles that exercised at Ashridge, churning up large tracts of the course. It was not really until the 1950's that Berkhamsted Golf Club began to restore its fortunes to become the prestigious venue that we know today.

One of the Club's first trophies was the Ladysmith Gold Medal, first awarded in 1900, and so named after the defence of Ladysmith which was led by Baden Powell during the Boer War. With ladies' membership an intrinsic element of the Club, mixed foursomes has always been an important competition at Berkhamsted and the trophy, which was first offered in 1925, is still played for today. However by far the most significant competition held at Berkhamsted every year is the Berkhamsted Trophy, which has long since become the traditional curtain raiser to the English amateur golf season. Previous winners of this competition have provided the golf club with treasured links to some of the sport's household names. Peter Townsend won the Trophy in 1966 and Sandy Lyle triumphed at Berkhamsted in 1977. Both these exceptional golfers went on to play Walker Cup and Ryder Cup golf for their Country, with Scotsman Sandy Lyle later achieving golfing immortality with his seven iron-approach shot from the bunker on the final hole at Augusta, which made him Masters Champion in 1988. A significant name to all the regular members at Berkhamsted is Basil Proudfoot, the Club's resident professional, appointed in 1962. He has recently completed an outstanding 36 years of service at Berkhamsted. Despite planning restrictions, which meant that the changing rooms and a utilities area had to be constructed underground, an impressive new clubhouse opened at Berkhamsted Golf Club in July 1993. Unlike its predecessor it offers an excellent view across the golf course.

Berkhamsted Cricket Club

Earliest records of competitive cricket date back to two derby fixtures against Tring; one played at Tring Park and the other on Berkhamsted Common in 1835. In the 1860's several notable games took place at Haresfoot, then the home of Col. R.A. Smith-Dorrien, and by 1870 organised cricket was being played regularly on Butts Meadow. The first official fixture list of the Berkhamsted Cricket Club dates back to 1875, when cricket was played on the four and a half acre field just off Lower Kings Road, between the canal and the railway. At this time Lord Brownlow owned the land and in 1880 an arrangement was made whereby Berkhamsted School, who had previously been playing cricket in the Castle grounds, could share this field with the town's cricket club. However by 1915 the Boys School no longer needed the facility, having acquired impressive new playing fields at the top of Chesham Road. Following the First World War the local football club also began playing their fixtures on Lord Brownlow's land and were eventually joined by the Berkhamsted Hockey Club. In order to co-ordinate the activities of the various teams at Lower Kings Road, a local Sports Ground Association was formed, which was eventually able to purchase the fields. This Association, whose purpose was to promote the development of sport for the people of Berkhamsted, is still in existence today. In 1923 the West Indies touring side paid a visit to Berkhamsted Cricket Club and the occasion was so successful that they returned to play again in 1928 and 1933. The New Zealand test side also visited in 1927 and an All India side played a match at Berkhamsted in 1932. In these days the Cowley brothers, together with childrens' author, Bertie Todd as wicketkeeper and several masters from the Boys School, ensured that there was quite a strong team. After the Second World War, farmer Alec Bell proved to be an astute captain, the Waller brothers were strong players and Norman Warren became a regular mainstay of the first team. Derek Morgan, who later became captain of Derbyshire, also made occasional appearances for the Berkhamsted First Eleven during this period.

League cricket did not really take a proper hold in southern England until the end of the 1960's. Prior to this, Berkhamsted competed against a range of major clubs throughout Hertfordshire and Buckinghamshire; some clubs from Bedfordshire and North London were also entertained. By this time Brian Collins had arrived at the Club and, with his fierce fast deliveries, he soon developed to become the County's outstanding seam bowler for two over decades. The Hertfordshire Competition began in 1968 and was almost immediately won by Berkhamsted in 1969 and again in 1971. Amongst other key players, the Club's most successful captain, Colin Meager, was supported in this winning streak by Barry Keeling, a formidable opening bat with Steve Dunford and Colin Buckle opening the bowling and Dennis Atkins behind the stumps. Other talented players to play for Berkhamsted were John Neal, who was a fine all rounder and skipper of Hertfordshire, as well as Geoff Tolchard who went on to play first class cricket for Leicestershire.

Berkhamsted also became the first winners of the newly formed Hertfordshire League in 1974, with the team newly strengthened by the bowling of Jon Griffin, the batting of John Mocotta and the all round skills of John Smith. Brian Collins was Captain of the team in its centenary year in 1975, when Dennis Atkins was Chairman of the Club. However by 1983 the Sports Ground Association had sold half the cricket ground to property developers, who built the Broadwater flats on what had been the town's football pitch. Berkhamsted Town F.C. moved over to establish an impressive new football ground on the former cricket field; also taking over the old cricket pavilion. As a replacement, the Sports Ground Association developed a ten acre plot at the bottom of Castle Hill, which became a new home for the town's Cricket Club. This area, known as Kitcheners Field, provides sufficient space for two professionally laid cricket squares and now hosts games played by four elevens on both Saturdays and Sundays during the cricket season. In 1993 the Hertfordshire Cricket League was formed, being an amalgamation of the Bryan Herts League and the Farren Herts League. This league currently offers a total of eight different divisions and involves no less than 160 different teams. The Berkhamsted Cricket Club has to date made little serious impression on this competition, although the First Team has enjoyed more success locally, winning the Gazette Cup on ten different occasions. The future of the Club now lies in the playing strengths of its Colt sides (for boys aged 9-17) which have developed very well in recent years. In 1997 the U.15's were County winners and the U.13's were runners-up in their Division. Another feature of Berkhamsted Cricket Club is the appearance of members of the Middlesex team to play pro-am matches at Kitcheners Field. Current leading lights such as Fraser, Tufnell, Embery and Ramprakash have all sampled the delights of playing cricket in the summer sunshine at Berkhamsted.

The original cricket field in Lower Kings Road, circa 1906.

The West Indian touring team visits Berkhamsted in 1928.

Berkhamsted Cricket Club 1st XI 1996, showing former Captains Colin Meager and Brian Collins (both front row right)

Berkhamsted Cricket Club, Gazette Cup winners 1993.

Berkhamsted Lawn Tennis and Squash Rackets Club

Records still exist which confirm that the original Berkhamsted Lawn Tennis and Croquet Club dates back to at least 1899, although the precise date when the first courts were laid on the re-claimed reed beds between the canal and the railway is not known. During the 1920's a separate Hard Courts Tennis Club was established which used two shale courts, immediately adjacent to the main club, rented from the Sports Ground Association. A Berkhamsted Directory, dated 1929, informs us that "the club adjoins the cricket club and consists of one croquet ground, six grass tennis courts and two hard tennis courts. The club has over 120 members and owns the freehold of the ground". By the time that a later edition of the directory was issued in 1934, a bowling green had replaced the croquet lawn and the club membership had risen to 150 members. The Hard Courts Club expanded until it had three courts and was eventually amalgamated with the neighbouring Lawn Tennis Club in 1966. Although the rather charming original Lawn Tennis Clubhouse was retained, a spacious modern clubhouse, which instead overlooked the main courts from the north, was constructed in 1970. Behind this new building the first of four squash

courts were built and in 1976 a thriving new Squash Club was merged with its parent organisation to form the Berkhamsted Lawn Tennis and Squash Racket Club that we know today. During the winter of 1977/78 an impressive new fifth squash court was added, with a glass back and viewing area. The Tennis Club's original grass and shale courts have gradually been converted into a variety of all-weather surfaces and nine of the club's twelve courts now have floodlights. The club encourages international contacts and the tennis section has links with a club in West Germany, whilst the squash club is twinned with a club in South Africa. The Berkhamsted Lawn Tennis and Squash Rackets Club has a total membership of 880 and, at the time of writing, an impressive new brick-built clubhouse has been built to replace the wood and glass pavilion provided in 1970. The tennis club has recently developed several highly promising youngsters and the professional coach is also heavily involved with local schools to promote an interest in the sport. Similarly the squash section of the club continues to thrive and currently has both the under nineteen and under fourteen County Champions amongst its members. Only this year (1998) it has been awarded the Squash Club of the Year by the Herts Squash Rackets Association.

Berkhamsted's public swimming pool, shortly after opening in 1923.

The new clubhouse at Berkhamsted Tennis and Squash Rackets Club, 1998.

Berkhamsted Red Cross

The presence of the Red Cross in Berkhamsted dates back to 1913 and its first members were soon put to the test with the outbreak of the First World War in 1914. Throughout the conflict local Red Cross personnel were involved running mobile van units for first-aid and also undertook air raid precaution duties, working in shifts around the clock. When Ashridge became an Emergency Medical Station (E.M.S.) Hospital, the Red Cross provided a Voluntary Aid Detachment (V.A.D.) to help with the nursing requirement, under the direction of Commandant Mrs. Ruth Bond. In 1936 a Junior Cadet Force was established in the town and during the Second World War the local Red Cross were again heavily involved in nursing at Ashridge. This time they also played an important role manning Red Cross ambulances and staffing special first-aid posts in and around Berkhamsted. The Brigade helped prepare for two royal visits in 1959, when the Duke of Edinburgh visited both Ashlyns and Berkhamsted School for Girls in connection with his award scheme. A detachment of the local V.A.D. also formed the guard of honour when the Queen Mother visited West Herts Hospital in that same year. More recently, local members remained on alert during the Gulf War in 1991 and were ready to assist, if necessary, at R.A.F. Halton and Bassingbourn, near Royston. The current work of the Red Cross is very much focused on running training courses for the general public and also providing first-aid cover at major sports and public events. The Berkhamsted Centre of the British Red Cross, which is now based at the old chapel in Park View Road, offers a medical loan service for home care, three mornings a week. A team of specially trained hand-care workers also regularly visit the Elderly Care Unit at Gossoms Ryde. Given such a flourishing local organisation, it was no surprise that the Red Cross shop, which opened at Berkhamsted in 1994, was the first of its kind in Hertfordshire.

Womens Institute

The Northchurch Womens Institute, which preceded the Berkhamsted branch by 47 years, was formed in 1920 and this makes it one of the oldest groups in Hertfordshire. In 1922 some members took part in the Berkhamsted Pageant, dancing a minuet in the Castle grounds. The local group was soon very active, hosting a variety of social events, such as whist drives and dances. By 1934 they had raised a considerable sum of money towards the cost of building a village hall. However, for reasons outside of the group's control, it was not possible to bring this particular project to fruition until 1965. The money raised by the Northchurch ladies was invested until then, when it represented some seven per cent of the total building cost of the new hall. As an important contribution to the war effort, the local W.I. operated the Northchurch Fruit Preservation Centre, making vast quantities of jam and canned fruit for the Ministry of Food; members also knitted copiously for the armed forces. Since then the Northchurch W.I. became well known for the variety of crafts practised by its members, which has included lampshade and glove making, smocking and chair caning. In the 1980's the group made a special patchwork quilt, which was eventually auctioned and sent to Canada. Over the years the Northchurch W.I. has met in a variety of venues around the village, but now holds its regular monthly meetings at the social centre in Bell Lane.

In contrast, the Berkhamsted branch of the Womens Institute was not formed until 1967. However, with an initial enrolment of almost one hundred members, interest was so great that a waiting list had to be formed. The first meetings of the local W.I. were held in the Town Hall, although the Gable Hall has since become the normal venue for the regular evening meetings, which are held every month. The organisation aims to make a contribution to both the education and social life of women in Berkhamsted and provides a varied and exciting programme of events to help achieve this objective. For many years some members have helped out on a voluntary basis at the local Day Centre for elderly and handicapped people in Manor Street. Today the Institute remains very involved in a diverse range of community activities; helping to plant trees, supporting the church, clearing litter and visiting the sick in hospital. A new initiative took place on 7th April 1989, with the additional formation of the Berkhamsted Castle W.I. specifically as an afternoon group. Regular meetings, with a speaker, are now held once a month at the Court House and current membership of this branch is in the region of forty ladies.

Berkhamsted Citizens Association

The Berkhamsted Citizens Association held its first meeting in the grounds of Berkhamsted Castle in 1924 and at this time there were already seventy members. Throughout its lifetime the association has always been firmly 'apolitical' and in its own words: "takes no sides, its sole aim being to represent the interests of the citizen". It sees itself as an enabler, offering local people a platform for discussion and an opportunity to air their concerns on important topics of local interest. In keeping with this role, between 1925 and 1974, the association established a tradition of well attended annual meetings, whereby candidates for election to the Urban District Council were able to address the townspeople and be available to answer their questions. A key part of the Citizens Association's workload has always focused upon protecting the local environment. In this respect committee members have always worked closely with the National Trust, the Golf Club and other major landowners in the town. The association's members remain particularly active today, ensuring that all local footpaths and rights of way are kept open. The Berkhamsted Citizens Association first published its own footpath map in 1938, which has subsequently been re-published in several later editions and has since sold many thousands of copies. For the past 25 years, the association has been especially concerned with the character of new development, both public and private, and its members meticulously inspect local planning applications every week, on an organised basis.

From its inception, the Citizens Association has every year hosted a series of lectures and public meetings on matters of local interest and the pre-war committee were also quite involved in fund raising. For example in 1930 the association successfully launched an appeal to re-furbish the Sayer Almshouses in the High Street. A later appeal in 1953 raised sufficient funds to enable the commission of a large wooden town sign, which was then presented to the Town Council to commemorate the Coronation. This impressive and symbolic gift (see photo on the front flyleaf) still stands in the High Street on the pavement outside the Civic Centre. Certainly for the last 50 years, the thorny issue of High Street traffic and parking have occupied much of the association's attention and it continually pressed the Ministry of Transport to provide the A41 by-pass which finally materialised in 1993. The association also takes an interest in the quality of transport services and regularly lobbies for improvements to the local bus and train services. It also helps keep a watchful eye on the local stretch of the Grand Union Canal, which it is keen to protect as one of the town's key amenities. Historically, education has been another focus for the association which, for example, arranged a major public meeting in 1955 to discuss Hertfordshire County Council's proposal to establish a bi-lateral grammar/secondary modern school at Ashlyns. Later in 1967 a similar meeting was held to discuss the implications of a three tier system of middle school education in Berkhamsted.

Looking back over the last 70 years, it is obvious that a clear benefit of the Citizens Association has been the drive and enthusiasm of its members involved in a series of important initiatives in the town. For example several members were involved in the institution of a local Flower Show in 1933 and in 1949 the association sponsored the public meeting which led directly to the formation of the Berkhamsted and District Local History Society. The Berkhamsted Citizens Association also played a leading role in helping to found the Chiltern Society in 1950 and in 1968 helped encourage the establishment of a local volunteer group called the 'Guardians of the Countryside', whose aim is to help protect Ashridge and other countryside areas from the threat of litter and rubbish. Following concerns expressed at the Annual General Meeting and a special meeting convened in May 1975, the association officially lent its support to the Town Hall Rescue and Action Group. The association was also keen to support a twinning arrangement for Berkhamsted with the French town of Beaune on the Côte d'Or. The first exchange of schoolchildren took place in 1975 and this led to the formation of the Beaune Society in 1976. One of the outstanding local events organised by the Citizens Association occurred in August 1974, when the novelist Graham Greene and his brother, Sir Hugh Greene, attended a special meeting of the association, held in the Town Hall, to reminisce about their schooldays in Berkhamsted. Twenty years later, this unique occasion proved to be the catalyst for another local initiative. This was the creation of the Graham Greene Birthplace Trust on 2nd October 1997. This new group has already organised a special five day festival which was successfully launched on 29th September 1998. Quite apart from its invaluable role as a watchdog, the Berkhamsted Citizens Association also manages to make a social contribution by organising a regular programme of meetings, visits and rambles.

Berkhamsted Amateur Operatic and Dramatic Society

The Berkhamsted Amateur Operatic and Dramatic Society owe their origins to a meeting held at the Kiku No Chaya Tea Rooms in Lower Kings Road in 1926. Here seventeen members founded a society which was sufficiently well organised in its first year to present a production of the musical 'Iolanthe' at the Court Theatre in December. The farce, 'Lord Richard in the Pantry', became the society's first play when it was performed in 1927 and this established a pattern whereby one play and one musical was presented each season. However the advent of the Second World War meant that the 1938 productions of 'Storm in a Teacup' and 'Iolanthe' were to be the last until 1946. Normal service was resumed in 1947, with a production of 'Yeoman of the Guard', and the populist tradition continued until the society decided to tackle Smetana's 'The Bartered Bride' in 1952. More ambitious work followed this success, with a performance of the concert version of 'Carmen' in 1954, starring June Bailey in the title role. The following year the B.A.O.D.S. presented Vaughan Williams' opera 'Hugh Drover' and were honoured when the composer himself attended the final performance. Few town's amateur dramatic societies could have been so fortunate as to have regular access to such an impressive venue as the Court Theatre. In 1934 this theatre was thoroughly refurbished by Shipman & King and its seating capacity enlarged from 625 to 1,000. In 1939 Mr. John Humphreys and his wife Elvira founded the Court Repertory Co. which brought West End stars out from London to act in the town. For its principal role as a cinema, the Court Theatre was also provided with a magnificent illuminated organ, which was mounted on a special console with a lift. The loss of the Court Theatre, which eventually closed at

Easter 1960, was undoubtedly a blow to the B.A.O.D.S., but the enthusiasm of the society's members ensured that positive momentum was maintained. During the late 1950's and early 1960's American musicals were very much the flavour of the time and the society responded by producing shows like 'Annie Get Your Gun' in 1958 and 'South Pacific' in 1963. With a membership of over 150, it was now necessary to alternate the choruses in musicals so that everyone had the opportunity to perform. A popular innovation was the introduction of an Old Time Music Hall in 1967. This certainly helped to swell the coffers and, in what was then something of a hey-day for the B.A.O.D.S., total audiences for some of their musical productions regularly topped 2,000. Not that the dramatic arm of the society was without ambitions of its own and in 1970 the principal play performed was the challenging 'Day in the Death of Joe Egg' by Peter Nichols. Directed by David Overton, the cast included a nine year old Sarah Brightman in the title role as a spastic child. The society was delighted to arrange a special Gala Performance on New Years Eve 1983 to celebrate the re-opening of the enlarged main hall at the Civic Centre, which has since become its principal venue. Today the Berkhamsted Amateur Operatic

The Berkhamsted Amateur Operatic and Dramatic Society's performance of HMS Pinafore at the Court Theatre in 1950.

and Dramatic Society still has a strong nucleus of performers and is also fortunate to have its own workshop/studio in Middle Road where a large wardrobe of costumes, together with equipment and scenery can be stored. At the time of writing its most recent production was a successful revival of 'My Fair Lady' in November 1998.

Berkhamsted Art Society

The Berkhamsted Art Society was formed in 1929, when thirty-three mainly amateur artists banded together in order to "further the interests of the artists of the district". In these early days an annual exhibition was held every spring at the old Sessions Hall in the Town Hall which lasted for three to four days. As membership increased so did facilities offered to members and there were soon two exhibitions held every year in the spring and the winter. By the 1950's membership had grown to over one hundred and today the society caters not only for painters, but also those interested in pottery, sculpture and wood carving. Between June and September monthly meetings take place in the Civic Centre and often feature demonstrations in various media. Drawing classes are regularly held in the Court House and sketching trips are also arranged during the summer months. Currently two major

exhibitions are held in May and December and each run for a week in the main hall of the Civic Centre. Every member of the Society can submit up to four pieces for each exhibition and a regular display of over four hundred varied works of art pay testament to the continuing health of this important local society.

Berkhamsted Choral Society

The enthusiasm of Miss Kathleen Talbot was largely responsible for the formation of what was then called the Wayfarers Choral Society in 1930. The Headmistress of Berkhamsted School for Girls, Miss Mackenzie, allowed the new society to hold its first practices in the school premises. A notable early performance was 'In Windsor Forest' by Vaughan Williams and in these early days the Wayfarers also regularly took part in Music Festivals organised in Mid and West Herts. This Berkhamsted choir won several cups and was sufficiently well recognised to be asked to provide four members to sing in a special chorus at the Royal Albert Hall. Conducted by Sir Walford Davies, this grand concert was held on 24th May 1934 in the presence of King George V. Miss Dorothy Coates took over the conductorship in 1949 and the society continued to enjoy a rich vein of success winning cups and

Display produced by the Berkhamsted Archaeological Society for the 'Bygone Berkhamsted' Exhibition in September 1972.

The National Youth Jazz Orchestra performs for Berkhamsted Jazz on the stage of the Civic Centre, 1998.

Northchurch W.I. patchwork group in the Summer of 1982.

Members of the Berkhamsted and District History Society working at the Dacorum Heritage Trust store, 1998.

certificates, as well as gaining the Grand Aggregate Shield on the last occasion it was awarded in the district. During this period the choir also combined with the Berkhamsted School for Girls Glee Club to perform larger works such as The Messiah, Elijah and Brahms Requiem. When Robin Oldham became conductor in 1956, Dorothy Coates continued as rehearsal accompanist and the scope of the choir's concert repertoire was considerably extended. In addition to singing in various festivals, the society then aimed to provide two or three public concerts a year. More recently an orchestra, usually the Hatfield Philharmonic, has been engaged to support more ambitious pieces, which are sometimes co-productions involving singers from other choirs. The society achieved a total membership of around eighty by the time that its name was officially changed from the Wayfarers to the Berkhamsted Choral Society in 1982. These days the choir normally performs either at St Peter's Church or at the Collegiate School. In June 1995, when Robin Oldham retired after forty years as conductor, the choir performed a major concert of English music to celebrate his outstanding contribution. Irene Tate, who had been his rehearsal pianist for almost twenty years, retired with Mr. Oldham and this left the society suddenly without two of its leading stalwarts. However in April 1997 Graham Willi became the new conductor and brought with him some new members, who were part of a group he had formed called the New Purcell Singers. Their arrival has since rejuvenated the Berkhamsted Choral Society, which now looks set fair to produce a range of excellent work for many years to come.

Berkhamsted Music Society

The Berkhamsted Music Society, which is fortunate to have the renowned composer and conductor Anthony Hopkins CBE as its President, was founded in November 1954. Its first President was another notable local resident, the pianist Benno Moiseiwitsch, and over the years the Society has been outstandingly successful hosting concerts by performers who have since become household names. An illustrious list of those who have appeared for the Berkhamsted Music Society include Leon Gossens, Donald Swann of the celebrated duo of Flanders and Swann, a young Leslie Garret, the baritone Brian Rayner Cook and the World Leider prize winner, the bass baritone Neil Davies. The society's concerts are normally held at the Civic Centre or the Collegiate School. Recently there has been a policy of encouraging younger artists and consequently, for the past few years, the society has opened its season with a performance by the latest Young Musician of the Year. Well known ensembles who have also performed for the society include the Emperor String Quartet, the Nash Ensemble, the Coull Quartet and the Allegro String Quartet. Currently the Berkhamsted Music Society has an enthusiastic membership of around 240 and organises an average of four coach trips every year to major concert venues in London.

Berkhamsted Film Society

This flourishing local society presented its first season in the winter of 1967/68. A small group of enthusiasts banded together to hire 16mm film, direct from the distributors, which were then shown in the Catholic Hall. Members of the Society then paid a modest annual subscription of around thirty shillings which entitled them to view all the films shown in a season, which generally ran from September to April. In 1972, under the Chairmanship of Jeff Edwards, the Berkhamsted Film Society won the Film Society of The Year Award and was delighted to be presented with a brand new 16mm projector by the Rank Organisation.

Flushed with success the Society was soon able to buy another projector and no longer had to hire projection equipment. In 1973 the Film Society was operating from the Kings Hall, but by 1977 films were presented at the Civic Centre. Today the Berkhamsted Film Society continues to show 16mm film and, in this supposed 'video age', it is heartening to know that in the 1996/97 season a record annual membership level of 298 local movie buffs was achieved.

Berkhamsted and District Local History Society

At a public meeting held by the Berkhamsted Citizens Association in 1949, it was recognised that little was then being done to protect and preserve items related to Berkhamsted's historic past. The concerns expressed at this meeting led directly to the inauguration of the Berkhamsted and District Local History Society in January 1950.

The first President of the society was Miss B. W. Russell, the Headmistress of Berkhamsted School for Girls and Mr. E. Popple, former Headmaster of Victoria School, was elected as Chairman. Leading local historian Mr. P. C. Birtchnell was appointed Secretary, an office which he retained until his death thirty-six years later. The principal aim of the society is to encourage and promote an active interest in all matters of historic enquiry, within a local area which covers the parishes of Berkhamsted St Peter, Northchurch St Mary and Nettleden with Potten End. Since its foundation forty-eight years ago the Society has worked steadily to build up what is now an impressive treasury of maps, photographs, books and other documentation, relating to Berkhamsted and the surrounding area. Its members have also conducted surveys of some of the older surviving buildings in the town and collected many artefacts linked to the social or industrial history of Berkhamsted. Today the Society is fortunate to be able to store the bulk of its collection in the Dacorum Heritage Trust's conservation store, which is located in the town's former fire station buildings, behind the Civic Centre. With an existing membership of approximately one hundred, the Society currently organises a programme of monthly meetings in a season which extends from September to March. These are normally held at the Civic Centre and usually feature an illustrated talk on a topic of local interest.

Berkhamsted and District Archaeological Society

As the post-war boom in housing and road construction gathered pace during the 1960's and 70's, it was almost inevitable that exciting archaeological finds, long hidden in the local countryside, would be revealed. The first such significant example was the discovery of a substantial Roman villa in Gadebridge Park, which was excavated by David Neal between 1963-68. No doubt inspired by possibilities which had now become tangible, several members of the Berkhamsted and District Local History Society decided to form a separate archaeological society, whose purpose would be to record and where possible preserve any local archaeological evidence which came to light. With the support of Gareth Davies, then Curator of Verulamium Museum, the inaugural meeting of the Berkhamsted and District Archaeological Society was held in January 1972 and the Society's first elected Chairman was the Egyptologist, Frank Filce Leek F.S.A. Most of the early members had little or no experience of practical archaeology, but received tuition from

David Neal and attended extra-mural courses run by the University of Oxford. The membership's new found skills were soon put to the test, when they assisted in the excavation of some Belgic cremation burials and shaft furnaces used for the production of iron, revealed by construction work for Bridgewater School in 1972. The Society has also contributed to work on three important Roman villas, found at Gorehambury and Northchurch in 1973, under the direction of Dr. David Neal, and at Kings Langley in 1981, under the direction of Dr. Angela Wardle and Denis Miles. Members have also worked on sites at Berkhamsted Place, Little Gaddesden and Flamstead, as well as undertaking a nine year excavation at the Cow Roast, which is now acknowledged as being an important Romano British settlement. The Society is now in its 27th year and continues to flourish, under the leadership of its present Chairman, Peter Clayton F.S.A., who is himself a noted author and Egyptologist. Currently the Society has an active membership of around fifty, together with another twenty or so individuals who regularly attend the series of illustrated talks and lectures organised every year. The Berkhamsted and District Archaeological Society also organises an annual excursion to visit a site of historic interest and continues to meet once a month in the Newcroft Block of Berkhamsted Collegiate School.

Cowper Society

The Cowper Society, which grew out of the Parochial Church Council of St Peter's Church, was founded in 1976. The Society's objective is to extend the cultural, dramatic and musical life of the church in the town and, in so doing, it helps to emphasize the church as a key focal point in the community. Public talks, readings and presentations, organised by the Cowper Society, are held in the Town Hall or Court House, whilst musical or dramatic works are normally performed in the church itself. In the past the Society has presented 'Berkhamsted At War' and a study of the town's architecture entitled 'The Making of Berkhamsted'; it has also organised productions of John Aubrey's 'Brief Lives' and 'Jesus Christ Superstar'. Under the auspices of the Society, May Day Madrigals are sung at dawn every year from the church tower by the Chiltern Chamber Choir. One of its more recent productions, 'Glimpses of Ashridge', entertained a packed audience at the Town Hall in 1997 and was repeated in November 1998. Currently an important project for the Cowper Society is the commissioning of a new engraved glass window for the nave of St Peter's Church. The design of this window will celebrate 'Inspiration', which derives from the beauty of the natural environment around Berkhamsted; from the church and community life, and from the writings of the celebrated eighteenth century poet after whom the society is named.

Berkhamsted Jazz

Until this Society was formed in 1979, jazz music was performed only fitfully in Berkhamsted, with occasional concerts held in the Kings Arms or the Crown public house. The Society's founding concert took place at the Court House and featured local composer and jazz pianist Michael Garrick, together with vocalist Norman Winstone and local guitar enthusiast Tony Male. Since 1980 Berkhamsted Jazz Society has been very active hosting over two hundred concerts, the majority of which have been held at the Civic Centre. There has also been the occasional excursion to St Peter's Church for a jazz mass and the Hall at the Collegiate School was more recently used on Saturday, 13th November 1993 to perform 'A Wing and a Prayer'. This ambitious concert featured, amongst others, a jazz group and soloists performing work based around the theme of the USAF Air Base, which was established at Bovingdon during the Second World War. In their time most of the Country's leading jazz musicians and singers have performed for the Berkhamsted Jazz Society, which has a well deserved reputation for hosting some of the best live jazz performances in the United Kingdom. The word 'society' has since been dropped from the organisation's name, which is now known simply as Berkhamsted Jazz.

Berkhamsted Arts Trust

The activities of most of the art and culturally based societies in Berkhamsted are now co-ordinated by the Berkhamsted Arts Trust, which was established in 1961. Since that time the Trust has been active assisting its member organisations, helping to promote their various activities. The Berkhamsted Arts Trust has also enjoyed some success of its own, organising several notable events. Recent achievements for the Arts Trust have been the joint promotion, with the Dacorum Arts Trust, of the presentation 'Music in my Life' by Richard Baker in October 1997 and its co-operation with the Dacorum Heritage Trust to facilitate the public display of the 'Bayeux Tapestry Finale' at the 'Images of Dacorum Heritage' Exhibition, which was held at the Berkhamsted Civic Centre in October 1998.

The early churches of Berkhamsted played a leading role in organising social activities. Here an impressive number of local families gather together on a Baptist Church outing to the Bridgewater Monument, circa 1910.

Chronology

1066	William the Conqueror accepts Saxon surrender at Berkhamsted Castle
1086	Two working mills in Berkhamsted are listed in the Domesday Book
1104	Chancellor Randolph rebuilds Berkhamsted Castle
1156	Henry II awards tax exemption charter to the merchants of Berkhamsted
1213	Hospitals of St John the Baptist and St John the Evangelist founded
1216	Berkhamsted Castle besieged by Prince Louis of France
1222	Consecration of St Peter's Parish Church
1286	Dedication of Ashridge Monastery
1333	Berkhamsted returns its own Member of Parliament
1356	The Black Prince imprisons King John of France in Berkhamsted Castle
1381	Peasants Revolt produces local unrest
1483	Berkhamsted holds important Market Charter awarded by Edward IV
1495	Berkhamsted Castle is deserted by the Royal Court
1516	Berkhamsted's medieval hospitals disbanded
1539	Dissolution of Ashridge Monastery
1539	Market Charter awarded to the rival town of Hemel Hempstead
1544	Berkhamsted School opens
1554	Princess Elizabeth arrested at Ashridge on the orders of Queen Mary
1580	Berkhamsted Place built by Sir Edward Carey
1583	Market House built in the High Street
1618	Charter awarded to the town by James I
1640	William Edlyn fights to stop enclosure of Berkhamsted Common
1662	King Charles II withdraws the Charter of Incorporation from Berkhamsted
1684	Sayer Almshouses built
1696	Salter's Workhouse established in the High Street
1722	First Baptist Chapel opens in Water Lane
1731	William Cowper born in Berkhamsted
1737	Bourne School opens
1739	Captain Coram begins his charitable work in London
1747	Francis Henry Egerton inherits Ashridge as 3rd Duke of Bridgewater
1762	Formation of Sparrows Herne Turnpike Trust
1777	Henry Lane launches his nursery business
1785	Death of Peter the Wild Boy
1798	Grand Junction Canal reaches Berkhamsted
1801	Population of Berkhamsted is 1690
1804	Augustus Smith born at Ashlyns Hall
1808	Building work begins at Ashridge House
1826	Ironworker James Wood begins trading in the town
1831	New workhouse built on the corner of what is now Kitsbury Road
1834	Berkhamsted's first elementary school is built
1837	London to Birmingham Railway is completed
1838	National School opens
1840	Job East establishes his first timber yard
1843	William Cooper has arrived in Berkhamsted
1845	Foundation of the Mechanics Institute
1847	Berkhamsted Gas Company formed
1853	Pilkington Manor estate sold by Frederick Miller
1854	Market House destroyed by fire
1860	Town Hall opens
1860	Lord Brownlow obtains the Manor of Berkhamsted
1863	Charles Stanton Hadden purchases Rossway
1864	Berkhamsted Waterworks Company established
1864	St Mary's School is built in Northchurch
1865	Baptist Chapel opens on the corner of Ravens Lane
1866	Enclosure of Berkhamsted Common thwarted by Augustus Smith
1867	Primitive Methodist Church opens in the High Street
1867	Congregational Church is built on the corner of Chapel Street
1868	Sale of Kitsbury Farm for housing development
1872	Rural Sanitary Authority created

1875	New railway station provided for Berkhamsted
1877	West Herts Infirmary opens at Hemel Hempstead
1885	Lower Kings Road built by public subscription
1888	First part of Kingshill estate sold for housing development
1888	Berkhamsted Girls Grammar School opens
1894	Rural Sanitary Authority becomes Rural District Council
1894	Berkhamsted Police Station built
1895	Dedication of the Chapel at Berkhamsted School
1898	Berkhamsted Urban District Council takes up office
1898	High level sewer provided in the town
1898	Victoria School opens
1898	National Telephone Company installs local telephone lines
1901	Population of Berkhamsted is 5140
1909	Consecration of the Church of St Michael and All Angels at Sunnyside
1910	Deans' Hall is completed at Berkhamsted School
1916	King George V inspects Inns of Court soldiers training at Berkhamsted
1917	Court Theatre opens
1918	Armistice ends First World War
1920	Motorised bus services introduced by Aylesbury Bus Company
1922	Sale of Ashridge estate following the death of Lord Brownlow in 1921
1926	Upper Mill is demolished
1927	Remains of Roman building discovered at Frithsden Beeches
1928	Council house building begins at Swing Gate Lane and Gossoms End
1929	Serious fire destroys former Locke & Smith brewery buildings
1929	Domestic electricity installation now available
1935	Foundling Hospital School built at Berkhamsted
1935	Prince of Wales visits Berkhamsted Schools and the Castle
1937	Egerton House demolished
1938	Civic Centre built
1943	Crew of HMS United visit the town
1944	Troops depart Ashridge to take part in D Day landings
1948	Council house building begins on Durrants Estate
1950	Foundation of Berkhamsted and District Local History Society
1952	War Memorial moved to St Peters Churchyard
1955	Hertfordshire County Council opens Ashlyns school
1958	M1 motorway is complete
1960	Court Theatre closes
1962	Hard winter freezes up the canal
1966	Fully electrified train services introduced
1967	Demolition of Berkhamsted Place
1967	Church of the Sacred Heart opened by Cardinal Heenan
1969	Modern fire station built in Castle Street
1970	Middle School education introduced to Berkhamsted
1972	Excavations at the Cow Roast reveal an early Roman settlement
1972	Modern Police Station is built on the corner of Kings Road
1973	Excavation of Roman villa at Northchurch
1973	Rex Cinema closes
1974	Dacorum District Council created in local government re-organisation
1974	Congregational Church is demolished
1976	Town Council gains right to elect a Mayor
1976	Construction work begins on the Chiltern Park housing estate
1981	Population of Berkhamsted is 15,549
1981	Berkhamsted Town Hall Trust established
1986	M25 orbital motorway is completed
1991	Neolithic finds made during construction work for A41 by-pass
1993	A41 by-pass completed
1996	Local independent schools merge to form Berkhamsted Collegiate School
1997	Agr-Evo UK finally closes former Cooper plant
1997	Graham Greene Birthplace Trust established

Bibliography

BALLS, C.H.A. H.M. Submarine United (P.44) 1942/43
Pub. 1987

BELL, V. Little Gaddesden
Pub. 1949

BERKHAMSTED PAROCHIAL REVIEW
All Vols. 1872 - Current

Berkhamsted School for Girls 1888-1938
Pub. 1938

BIRTCHNELL, P.C. A Short History of Berkhamsted
First Pub. 1960. Revised and enlarged 1972
ISBN: 1871372003

BIRTCHNELL, P.C. Bygone Berkhamsted
Pub. 1975 ISBN: 0900804149

BOURNE, T.C. London and Birmingham Railway
Pub. 1839

BRANCH-JOHNSTON, W. Hertfordshire Inns:
Vol 2 - West Herts Pub. 1963

BRANCH -JOHNSTON, W. Industrial Archaeology of
Hertfordshire
Pub. 1970 ISBN: 0715247756

BRANIGAN, K. Archaeology of the Chilterns
Pub. 1994 ISBN: 0951634518

COBB, Rev. J. W. History and Antiquities of
Berkhamsted

COCKMAN, E.G. Railways of Hertfordshire
2nd Ed. Pub. 1983 ISBN: 0901354112

Concise History of the Free Grammar School
Pub. 1842

COULT, D. A Prospect of Ashridge
Pub. 1980 ISBN: 0850333601

CUSSANS, T.E.   History of Hertfordshire
Orig. Pub. 1870/1. Reprinted in three vols 1972

DACORUM HERITAGE TRUST   Dacorum at War
Pub. 1995 ISBN: 0951094424

DACORUM HERITAGE TRUST
Agriculture in Dacorum
Pub. 1990

GARDNER, H. (Comp.) Berkhamsted Citizens
Association:
A Diamond Jubilee History 1924-84
Pub. 1984

GARDNER, H.W. A Survey of Agriculture in
Hertfordshire
Pub. 1967

GARNONS-WILLIAMS, B.H. Berkhamsted School
For Girls: A Centenary History 1888-1988
Pub.1988

GARNONS-WILLIAMS, B.H. The History of
Berkhamsted School 1541-1972
Pub. 1980

HASSELL, J. A Tour of the Grand Junction Canal in
1819
Pub. 1968

HASTIE, S. & SPAIN,D. A Hertfordshire Valley
Pub. 1996 ISBN: 0952863103

HERTFORDSHIRE ARCHAEOLOGY
All Vols. 1969- Current

HERTFORDSHIRE COUNTRYSIDE
All Vols 1949

HOSIER, B. Hedgehog's Northchurch
Pub. 1994 ISBN: 0952288206

JOLIFFE, G. & JONES, G. Hertfordshire Inns and
Public Houses
Pub. 1995 ISBN: 0901354791

KITCHINSIDE, G. The West Coast Route to Scotland
Pub. 1976 ISBN: 0715372106

LONGMAN, G. A Corner of England's Garden
1600-1850
Pub. 1977

Looking Back: The Story of the Cooper Business
1843-1943
Pub. 1943

MARGERY, I.D. Roman Roads in Britain
3rd. Ed. Pub. 1973 ISBN: 0212970011

NASH, H. Reminiscences of Berkhamsted
Pub. 1890

NORRIS, R.A. The History of Berkhamsted St Peter
Pub. 1923

PEVSNER, N. Hertfordshire. (Buildings of England)
2nd. Ed. Pub. 1977 ISBN: 0140710078

PRIESTLAND, G. Something Understood
Pub. 1986 ISBN: 0233975004

REMFRY, P.M. Berkhamsted Castle 1066-1495
Pub. 1995   ISBN: 189937609

ROBINSON, G. Book of Hemel Hempstead and
Berkhamsted
Pub. 1975   ISBN: 0860230112

ROBINSON, G. Hertfordshire
Pub. 1978 ISBN: 0860230309

SANECKI, K. History of Ashridge
Pub. 1996   ISBN: 1860770207

SENAR, H.   Little Gaddesden and Ashridge
Pub. 1983   ISBN: 0850334608

SHIPMAN, C. & JACKSON, R. Dacorum Within
Living Memory
Pub. 1988   ISBN: 095117737

SIMONS, R.G. Cricket in Hertfordshire
Pub. 1996 ISBN: 0952948508

STOBBS, J. History of the Berkhamsted Golf Club
1890-1990
Pub. 1992

VICTORIA COUNTY HISTORY: Hertfordshire Vol II
Orig. Pub. 1902-25. Reprinted 1971

WHYBROW, G.H. History of Berkhamsted Common
Pub. 1934

WINGATE, J. The Fighting Tenth
Pub. 1991 ISBN: 0850522005

WRIGHT, O.E. Baptists of Berkhamsted
Pub. 1990

INDEX

A41 By-pass...37,164
A41 Trunk Road...24
Adelaide, Countess of Bridgewater...54
Adelbert, Earl Brownlow...54
Adelbert House...84
Alford, Lady Marion...54
All Saints Church...108
Almshouses, Northchurch...139,143
Alsford Timber Yard...46,82
Alsford Totem Pole...30
Amateur Operatic & Dramatic Society...164,165
Amersfort...58,59
Anchor, Inn...138
Archaeological Society...168
Anchorage, Northchurch...138
Art Society...166
Arts Trust...169
Ashlyns Hall...57,116
Ashlyns Housing Estate...72
Ashlyns School...57,113,114,115,116
Ashridge...20, 52-54, 130, 132
Ashridge Golf Club...54
Ashridge Hospital...136,163
Ashridge Management College...54
Ashridge Monastery...17,18
Augustus Smith Middle School...114,116
Authors, local...149
Avica House...98
Axtell, Henry...145
Babington, J.H...116
Back Lane...27,78
Bailey & Sons, jewellers...90
Bailey, stationers...94
Balshaw's Charity...23
Baptist Chapel, Water Lane...84
Baptist Church, Northchurch...138,140
Baptist Church...102,103,169
Barclays Bank...93
Barnett family, Northchurch Hall...147
Barrie, J.M...63,150
Bartrum, Rev. E...121
Bateman, Miss Mary Rose...120
Bayeux Tapestry...3
Bell Lane Stores, Northchurch...138,140
Benskins Brewery...42,87
Berk. & District Archaeological Soc...168
Berk. & District Building Soc...98
Berk. & District Local History Soc.................................164,166,167,168
Berk. & Northchurch Property Assoc...124
Berk. Amateur Operatic & Dram. Soc...164,165
Berkhamsted Art Society...166
Berkhamsted Arts Trust...169
Berkhamsted Castle...11-15, 19,38,135
Berkhamsted Choral Society...166
Berkhamsted Citizens Association...163,164
Berkhamsted Collegiate School...12,120-123
Berkhamsted Common...40,41,135
Berkhamsted Cricket Club...160-161
Berkhamsted Film Society...167
Berkhamsted Football Club...156-157
Berkhamsted Gas Works...28,35,69
Berkhamsted Boys School...84,120-123
Berkhamsted Girls School...118-120
Berkhamsted Golf Club...159-160
Berkhamsted Jazz...169
Berk. Lawn Tennis & Squash Club...161-162
Berkhamsted Market...40
Berkhamsted Music Society...167
Berkhamsted Place...20,41,55,56
Berkhamsted Railway Station...31,33,34,35
Berk. Rural District Council...70
Berkhamsted School...84,120-123
Berkhamsted Steam Laundry...98
Berkhamsted Town Hall...65,66,76,90,154
Berkhamsted Town Hall Trust...66
Berk. Urban District Council, Offices...71
Berkhamsted Waterworks Co...69
Bibliography...172
Billet Lane...98,99

Birtchnell, P.C...2,168
Birtchnell's, outfitters...87,93
Black Ditch...68,70,84
Black Horse, Inn...80
Black Prince...14,17,40
Blackhouse Mead...103
Blackwell, T.H...159
Boat, Inn...28
Bonhommes, College of...17
Boote, Inn...82
Bourne Charity...115
Bourne School...94,111,114,115
Bourne, Thomas...114,115
Boxwell House...64,68,94,96
Brentnall & Cleland, coal merchants...91
Brewing...42
Bridgewater, Duke of...18,27,52
Bridgewater Boats...30
Bridgewater Monument...52,53
Bridgewater Road...73
Bridgewater School...114
British Film Institute...60
British Legion...90
Britwell...50
Broadway Farm...144
Broc, Laurence de...145
Bronze Age settlement...7-8
Broome, Frank...156,157
Brownlow Arms, Inn...42
Brownlow, Earl...20,31,40,54,57,130,159
Bulbourne Factory...91
Bulbourne, River...7
Bull, Inn...79
Burnham's, greengrocers...92,93
Bus services...36
Butler, Reg...56
Butterfield, William...100
Button, grocers...90
Butts Meadow...60,134
Callaghan, garage...78,126
Callard, corn merchant...93
Camilla Terrace...93
Campling, William...107
Canal...26,27-30
Carey, Sir Edward...20,55
Carmelite Sisters...148
Carpenters Arms, Inn...98
Castle House and Chambers...79
Castle Hotel...30,82,84
Castle House, Northchurch...140
Castle Street...82,83
Catholic Church...106-107
Catuvellauni...9
Chadwick, Dr. Priscilla...120
Chaffcutter Arms, Inn...86
Chapel Street Infant School...112
Charles I, King...20,55
Charles II, King...20
Charles, Prince...142
Charles Street...67
Charter of Incorporation...20,22
Chaucer, Geoffrey...15,149
Chesham Brewery...42
Chiltern Park, housing estate...73
Chocolate Box, confectioners...87
Choral Society...166
Chronology...170-171
Church House, Northchurch...139,144,145
Church Lane...20,78
Church Rooms, Northchurch...141
Churchill, Lady Winston...79,119
Cicely, Duchess of York...15,19
Citizens Association...163,164
Civic Centre...71,86,87,126,165
Civil Wars...20
Claridge Court...90
Coachbuilders...93,95,96
Cockburn, Claud...152
Common, Berkhamsted...40,41,57

Common, Enclosure of	57
Compass Point	141
Compasses, Inn	141
Congregational Church	82,104,105
Cook, Maurice	156
Cook's, butcher, Northchurch	140
Cooper, Richard Powell	50,110
Cooper, William	49,102,149
Cooper Technical Bureau	79
Cooper's	49
Cooper McDougall & Robertson	50
Co-operative Society	93
Coram, Thomas	116
Corby, Palmer & Stewart	91
Corporation, Berkhamsted	20
Costin's, boatyard	28
Court House	20,21,128
Court Theatre	75,87,165
Cow Roast	10,25
Cowper, Rev. John	102
Cowper, William	102,169
Cowper Society	168
Cox, C.M.	122
Cricket	160-161
Cripps, bakers	98
Crooked Billet, Inn	28,99
Cross Oak Road	64,67
Crown, Inn	86,88
Crystal Palace, Inn	28,82
Cummerford, Father Vincent	107
Constable Curtis, Captain	61
Constable Curtis, H.G.	61,102
Dacorum District Council	73
Dacorum Heritage Trust	126,168
Darrs Lane	147
Davidson, Lady	146
Deans' Hall	84,122
Dean Incent	121
Dean Incent's House	21,86
Dell & Son, removals	98
Dickman's, chemist	94,96
Disney, Miss C.	118
Dissolution of the Monasteries	17
Dorrien, John	58
Douglas, Mrs E.	148
Drainage	68,70
Dropshort Cottages	146,147
Duncombe, William	142,148
Duncombe Road	138
Dupre, Rev. J.	121
Durrants Farm	138,145
Durrants Housing Estate	72,114
Durrants Lane	148
Dwight, W.	48,110
Dwight's, garage	87
Dwight's Pheasantries	48
East, Cornelius	99
East's Cottages	99
East's Timber Yard	28,44,80,99
Eddy Street	99
Edgeworth	147,148
Edgeworth, Maria	150
Edlyn, John	142
Edlyn family, Norcott Hill	146
Edmund, Earl of Cornwall	17
Education	111-123
Edward I, King	14,17
Edward II, King	14
Edward III, King	14
Edward IV, King	15,19
Egerton, Francis Henry	27,52
Egerton, Thomas	18
Egerton House	63,79,105
Egerton-Rothesay School	114
Eisenhower, General	137
Electricity installation	70
Elizabeth I, Queen	18
Elms	93
Errington, Lt. Col.	128,130
Evangelists	106
Evans, John	118
Evacuees	136
Excelsior Laundry	98
Exhims	140,141
Farming	38
Farriers House	90
Fenn, James	144
Figg, chemist	87
Film Society	167
Finch, General John	56,115
Fiorentina, Italian restaurant	90
Fire service	126-127
Firemark	126
First World War	128
Fish, Inn	84
Five Bells, Inn	87
Food rationing	133
Football	156-157
Foundling Hospital School	116
Fox's, ironmongers	86
Fraine, Daffy de	86
Frithsden Beeches	8
Fry, Rev. T.C.	121,122
Gardeners Arms, Inn	82
Garnons Williams, B.H.	122
Gas Works	69,84
Gaulle, General de	107,136,137
Gaveston, Piers	14
Gem, Cinema	93
Geography, local	7
George V, King	128
George, Inn	93
George & Dragon, Inn, Northchurch	138,140
George & Dragon Temperance Hotel	84
Gibbs Dairy	96
Gibbs, chemist	90
Gilbert's, TV & radio shop	90
Glaxo	50
Goat, Inn	78
Golf	54,159
Gordon Cottage	82
Goss Brushworks	44,96,97
Gossoms Cottage	99
Gossoms End	96,97,98,99
Gossoms End Elderly Care Unit	98
Gossoms End Infant School	45,96,112
Gossoms Lodge	99
Gossoms Ryde	98
Gowring, C.H.	159
Graball Row	75,78,88
Graham Greene Birthplace Trust	164
Grand Junction Canal	28
Grand Union Canal	30
Grapevine, High Street	87
Gravel Path	67
Green, George	113
Greene, C.H.	121,122
Greene, Graham	122,151,152,164
Greene, Hugh	122,151,164
Greenways School	114
Grims Dyke	8
HMS United	133,134
Hadden Paton family, Rossway	58
Hadden, Major General Sir Charles	119
Hall Park Gardens	72
Halsey, Thomas	61,113
Handel, George Frederick	116
Happy Valley	82
Hardy, Father Henry	107
Haresfoot	58,59
Haresfoot School	58
Harris, Miss B.L.	118
Harrowell & Atkins, lawyers	64
Haslam, Lady	136
Hazell, William	65
Hazell's Folly	76,90
Health, public	22,23
Health Service	70
Henry of Berkhamsted	15,100
Henry II, King	14,19
Henry VIII, King	19
High Street, Berkhamsted	24,37,74-77,78-99

Highfield House 62,67
Historical Background....7-10
Hobbs, Pastor Joseph....103,111
Holliday Street....79
Holliday's, cycle shop....81
Home Farm, Northchurch....141
Home Guard....135
Homestead....94,95
Hopkins, Antony....66,167
Hosier, Clementine....119
Hospital, St. John the Baptist....17
Houses and Estates....52-64
Housing Development....66-69, 72
Humphreys, J.....165
Ice Age, effects....7
Incent, John (Dean)....17,21,111,121
Incent, Robert....21
Industrial Development....38-51
Inns of Court OTC....128,129,130,131
International Stores....90
Jacobs, W.W.....150
Jazz....169
Jeykll, Gertrude....58
John I, King....14
Kepston's, pulley works....84,87,126
Key's Timber Yard....28,46,82,128
Khaki Tea Shop....90
Kiku No Chaya, tea shop....90,164
King & Son, coach builders....26,95,96
Kings Arms, Inn....86
King Edward VI, Inn....84,85
King's, printing works....91
Kings Road....93,124,125
Kings Road Evangelical Church....106
Kingshill....60,61,68
Kitcheners Field....41,128,129,130,160
Kitsbury Cycle Works....96
Kitsbury Farm....68
Kitsbury Road....67,96
Lace making....43
Lagley....98,142,147,148
Lamb, Edward....66
Lamb, Inn....94
Lane's Nurseries....46,47,77,95,96
Leatherdale's, stationers....93,98
Lees Mineral Water....79
Lemon, Lady....147
Library, public....86
Lime Tree House....138
Literary Berkhamsted....149-153
Llewellyn Davis, A.....63,150
Lloyds Bank....93
Loader, George....93
Local Defence Volunteers....134
Local History Society....164,166,167,168
Locke & Smith Brewery....42,84
Lockhart, Donald, builders....96
London to Birmingham Railway....31
London House, grocery, Northchurch....142
Longman, William....57,150
Loosley, stationers....89,90
Louis XVIII, King of France....86
Lower Kings Road....68,78,90,91,94,160
Lower Mill....41,42,84
Lower Works, Cooper's....51
Loxley, Peter Noel....142
Loxley family, Norcott Court....146
Lucas, Mrs Lionel....60,113
M25 Motorway....37
McVitie, Mrs....148
Mabey, Richard....153
Manor of Berkhamsted....20
Market, Berkhamsted....20,40
Market House....19,20,40
Marlin Chapel....145
Marlin Chapel Farm....145,146
Matthews, builders yard....82
Mawley, E.....110
Mayo, tabacconists....94
Mechanics Institute....66,154
Meeks Stables....91
Meeting House, Quaker....104
Methodist Church....98,105,106
Mill Street....84,85
Miller, Frederick....49,59
Millfield....61,62
Mills, water....41
Moiseiwitsch, Benno....167
Monastery, Ashridge....17
Monke, Thomas....102
Monks Garden, Ashridge....53
Monks, grey....17
Monks House....96
Moore, Frank....148
Moorman, Mary....151
Morris, watchmaker....92,94
Mortain, Count of....11
Motor Transport....36-37
Mousehole Cottage....99
Murray, Ann....55
Music Society....167
Nash, Henry....82,154
Nash, James, farrier....90
Nash, William....87,105
National Fire Service....126
National School....111,112
National Westminster Bank....93
Neolithic, settlement....7
New Road....141
Newcroft....84,85,122
Norcott Court....142,146
Norcott Hill....146
Norman, influence....11
Norris Terrace....99
Northchurch....138-147
Northchurch Hall....141,147
Northchurch Place....138
Northchurch Technical Institute....138,145
Northchurch Tunnel....30,34
Northchurch Workhouse....23,99
Nugent, Rev. George....22
Old Grey Mare, Inn....141
Old Shep....39
One Bell, Inn....89
Osbourne, David....98
Overton House....86
P.44, HM Submarine....133,134
Page, John....86,124
Park Estate, Northchurch....141
Park Street....98
Park View Road....93
Park View School....94,111,112,125
Pearson, E.J.....109
Pearson, M.A.....62
Peter the Wild Boy....142,144
Peter Pan....60,150
Picture Playhouse, cinema....86
Pightle House....78
Pike's Corner....90
Pilkington Manor....49,59,66,82
Plymouth Brethren....105
Pocock's, blacksmith....28,78,81
Police Service....124,125
Poplars....50
Pope, Rev. R.H.....142
Popple, Edward....113,168
Population, Berkhamsted....65,72
Post Office....86,87,89,90
Post Office, Northchurch....140
Poverty, 17th-19th centuries....22
Primitive Methodist Church....105,106
Prince Edward Street....86,89
Priestland, Gerald....153
Prison....124
Prisoners of War....136
Prospect House....96
Provident Place....79
Public Record Office, Ashridge....54
Public Services....69
Quakers....96,104,106
Quennell, Peter....152
Queens Arms, Inn....78

Ragged Row 23
Railway 26,31-35
Railway Tavern 82
Raven, John 100
Ravens Lane 79,103
Rectory Cottage 145
Red Cross 128,134,135,163
Red House 64
Religious History 16-18,100-110
Reservoirs, near Tring 28
Richard, Earl of Cornwall 14
Richard II, King 15
Rising Sun, Inn 28
Riverside Gardens 99
Road Transport 24-26,36,37
Roberts, fishmonger 93,94
Robinson, A. 114
Robinson, Joseph 64
Rodinghead 136
Roman Catholic Church 106-107
Roman, settlement 9-10
Roman villa, Northchurch 141
Rose & Crown, Inn 42,99
Rosemary Cottage 140,141
Rossway 58,59,64
Rowlands, Dr. Gwyn 96
Rowlands, Dr. J.J. 64
Royal Oak, Inn 92
Royal Observer Corps 135
Rural District Council, Berkhamsted 70
Rural Sanitary Authority 69
Russell, Miss B.W. 119,168
Sacred Heart, Church of 107
St Catherine's Chapel 102
St George's Temperance Hotel 84
St James, Chapel of 16,96
St John the Baptist, Brotherhood of 17
St John's Well 16
St Johns Well Lane 96,98
St Mary's Parish Church, Northchurch 138,142,143
St Mary's School, Northchurch 143,145
St Michael and All Angels, Sunnyside 109,110
St Peter's Parish Church 16,82,84,100,101
St Thomas More R.C. School 107,114
Salter, Edward 93
Saltmarsh, hardware store 90
Salvation Army 90,108,109
Sayer, John 20,55,102
Sayer Almshouses 56,92,93,164
Saxon, settlement 10
Second World War 133
Seymour, John Hobart Culme 142,145
Sharlands, department store 94
Sheep dip, Cooper's 49,51
Shenstone Court 50
Shops and Traders 78-99
Shepherd, Miss Valerie 120
Shrublands Road 73
Siddons, Rev. G.H. 109
Sidney House 93
Sills Timber Yard 46
Smith, Augustus 40,57,111,121
Smith, James 102
Smith-Dorrien family, Haresfoot 58,102
Smith-Dorrien monument 82,84
Smiths, W.H. 87
Social Life 154-169
Soup kitchen 23
Southey & Co., motor engineers 36,87,93
Sparrows Herne Turnpike Trust 24,25,26
Special Constables 132
Sports Ground Association 160
Spring, holy 16,104
Squash 161,162
Squire, William 94,99
Stafford Brush Works 87
Stag, Inn 99
Stage Lane 98
Stagecoach travel 24,25
Stainsby, Rev. W. Chipchase 101,102,108
Star Supply Stores 87,89
Stone Age, settlement 7
Straw Plaiting 43,138
Street Party 155
Stupples Dairy 82,91
Sunday Schools 111
Sunnyside Church 100,109,110
Swing Gate Lane 78
Swing Gate School 114
Swan Inn 86,88
Tank Week 129,132
Tawell, John 64
Telephone services 70
Tennis Club 161,162
Thomas Bourne Middle School 114,116
Thomas Coram Middle School 114,116
Timber Industry 44-46
Timson's, baker 94
Timson's, coalyard 96
Timson's, draper 94
Tobacco Works, Northchurch 140
Todd, H.E. 151,160
Torrington Road 67
Torrington tomb 100
Totem Pole, Alsford's Wharf 46
Town Development 65-73
Town Hall 65,66,89,154,164
Tramway, local 36
Transport 23,24-37
Trevelyan, G.M. 150
Tring Cutting 31,32
Tring Summit 28
Tuckin Cafe 91
Tudor House, Water Lane 87
Tunnel Fields 39,73
Turnpike Trust 24,25
Underhill & Young, garage 36,96,97,98
United Reformed Church 104
Upper Mill 41,42,84
Urban District Council, Berkhamsted 72
Vestry Authority 22
Victoria School 112,113,134
Victory Road 98
Voluntary Aid Detachment 128,134,135
War Memorial 129,132,137
Ward, Mrs. Humphrey 151
Ward Cottage 84
Ward's, draper 92,94
Wartime Berkhamsted 128-137
Watercress 47
Water Lane 75,84
Water tower 69
Waterman, Dr. Charles 96
Warship Weeks 133
Wellcome Foundation 50
Westfield Housing Estate 72,114
Westfield School 114
White Hart, Inn 90
White House 91
Wild Boy, Peter the 142,144
Wilderness 84,85
Wilkinson, Rev. K. 123
William the Conqueror 11
Williams, Edwin 159
Williams, Vaughan 165
Wilson House 84,103,123
Windmill 38
Womens Institute 163,166
Womens Royal Voluntary Service 136
Woodcock Hill 147,148
Woodhouse, Christopher 104
Woods Ironworks 47,95,96
Woods Music Warehouse 79,91
Woodside Cottage, Northchurch 141,142
Workhouse 22,23,93
Workhouse, Northchurch 99
World War I 128
World War II 133
Wyattville, Jeffrey 100
Yew Cottage 82
Youth Club 98
Zeppelin Raid 128

BERKHAMPSTEAD

Gosson's End

Ordnance Survey map of Berkhamstead
dated 1877
Reproduced with the kind permission
of Ordnance Survey

Published on the 10th April 2012, in commemoration of the 50th anniversary of the loss of Stuart Sutcliffe.

Published by Media Junction, 2 Archer Street, Soho, London W1D 7AW, UK

Editors: Giles Cooper, Michael Hall, Pauline Sutcliffe & Diane Vitale

Creative Direction: Giles Cooper, Michael Hall & Adam Robinson

This publication is produced in conjunction with and by kind permission of the Stuart Sutcliffe Estate. All images and photographs are the property of The Stuart Sutcliffe Estate, unless otherwise marked.

Design by Media Junction www.mediajunction.co.uk

Special thanks to Vladislav Ginsburg for permission to reproduce the work of Astrid Kirchherr.

Printed by John Good Limited

ISBN: 978-0-9572262-0-3

Front Cover Image: Untitled 'Red Self-Portrait' by Stuart Sutcliffe c.1960
Photograph (opposite) of Stuart Sutcliffe by Astrid Kirchherr c.1961

Measurements of artworks throughout this publication are given in centimetres or metres, height before width and depth.

www.StuartSutcliffe.org

66

He chose art and love over
being in the greatest rock 'n' roll
band of all time

99

KLAUS VOORMANN

IN CONVERSATION WITH
STUART SUTCLIFFE
HIS LIFE, WORK AND RELEVANCE

STUART SUTCLIFFE
In Conversation with...

Michael Ajerman
Andrew Bick
Kit Craig
Andrew Curtis
Nick Goss
Mark Hampson
Jann Haworth
Idris Khan
Laura Lancaster
Bob Matthews
Bruce McLean
Marilène Oliver
Flora Parrott
Martina Schmid
Steven Scott
Jamie Shovlin
Sergei Sviatchenko
Jessica Voorsanger
Stephen Walter
Uwe Wittwer

and many more...

Conceived by Michael Hall
Edited by Giles Cooper, Michael Hall, Pauline Sutcliffe & Diane Vitale

09 - 10	ACKNOWLEDGEMENTS *by Giles Cooper*
12 - 13	FOREWORD *by Michael Hall*
16 - 33	AN INTRODUCTORY ESSAY *by Pauline Sutcliffe and Diane Vitale*
40 - 45	BACKBEAT *by Iain Softley*
49 - 55	AN ART OF CONVERSATION *by Graeme Gilloch*
60 - 71	HAEMORRHAGE IS AMONG MY FAVOURITE WORDS *by Richard Makin*
76 - 79	RESPONSES TO A LIFE FOREVER FROZEN IN POP MYTHOLOGY *by Fisun Güner*
82 - 135	STUART'S WORK
138 - 179	ARTIST'S RESPONSES TO STUART'S WORK
180 - 181	THE STUART SUTCLIFFE CONTEMPORARY ART AWARD
184 - 185	THE STUART SUTCLIFFE ESTATE
186 - 187	CREDITS AND THANKS

Stuart Sutcliffe pictured (centre, foreground) with
John Lennon (right) and George Harrison (left)
Photograph by Astrid Kirchherr 1960

ACKNOWLEDGEMENTS *by Giles Cooper*

As a teenager and young man in my 20's, I played in numerous rock 'n' roll bands, but I always had just two main ambitions. The first was to 'make it' in a band that became bigger than The Beatles, and the second, was to one day own 'a Sutcliffe'. The former was a little ambitious, but I was delighted to recently achieve the latter, and furthermore, it was a tremendous privilege, earlier this year, to be appointed as CEO of The Stuart Sutcliffe Estate.

To achieve anywhere near what The Beatles achieved requires much more than just their combination of supreme talent, luck and perseverance. It was as much about their environment, the times in which they lived and the people they hung around with that encouraged and inspired them in their early years. For John Lennon and his band, there couldn't have been anyone better than Stuart Sutcliffe to mentor and nurture those early sparks. The eminent art critic, Professor Kuspit, has spoken about how Stuart managed to 'contact his primal' and how he was able to express 'raw emotion' in his art, and Stuart, in this vein, taught his fellow Beatles how to reach within themselves, to find themselves and subsequently how to channel the abundant creativity that they found.

One thing I've learnt about hanging around with musicians and artists for so long is that greatness is achieved as much by their outlook on life, their state-of-mind and their visions of themselves and their goals, as by anything else. Stuart proved an enormous influence on how The Beatles would not only work and develop, but how they would present themselves to the world, not simply as just musicians, but as artists. In countless interviews about how they would write their songs, both Lennon and McCartney, regularly talked about 'tuning in' to their muse and 'allowing' themselves

to become 'vessels' to a 'universal channel of creativity'. This undoubtedly stemmed from Stuart's teachings and influence, and through them, he lived with them, and achieved the world.

Very annoyingly, people often talk about Stuart in terms of 'what if' or 'if only he'd lived longer' or 'so much potential'. I wholeheartedly disagree with this attitude and way of talking of anyone. These people regularly forget that The Beatles achieved what they achieved, played their tours, recorded their albums and had indeed split up, still as men in their twenties, all within only 8 years of Stuart's death. Time is relative and we're on this earth for our allotted time and we do what we can in that time. That's it, no more, no less. In my humble view, he achieved a lifetime's worth of work in his time, and proved himself a genius in the time that he had. How many people can say that they sold a painting at all? It's irrelevant that he was a teenager when he sold his first. How many people can say that they had an astronomic influence over a rock 'n' roll band that changed our culture, our lives and our attitudes to the world we live in? It's irrelevant that he didn't stay in that band for a few more years; he influenced and remained with Lennon, by John's own admission, for his whole life and career.

Is Stuart's art 'relevant' today? Without a shadow of a doubt. He was the first to combine art and rock 'n' roll, an icon placed on a pedestal by countless contemporary artistic legends that followed. His influence has been enormous and the fact that his presence has radiated both the art and rock 'n' roll worlds for over 50 years, is testament to his artistic genius.

We have been overwhelmed by the enormous response and contribution from artists all over the world to contribute to this book. The 20 chosen for inclusion here to respond to Stuart's life, work and relevance, are but a small selection of the huge array of work submitted and on behalf of the Stuart Sutcliffe Estate, I would like to thank them all for their fantastic input. We hope that this book provides a platform for them all to further develop their careers into new areas and with many new opportunities.

50 years on, Stuart's work clearly still has a major influence on the artists of today and we would therefore, like to take this opportunity to announce the launch of *The Stuart Sutcliffe Contemporary Art Award*. This annual prize will be judged by a panel of esteemed judges and full details, including how to submit an entry for the very first award, can be found on Stuart's official website, **www.StuartSutcliffe.org**. There are some who say that Stuart's work may never have been known if he had not been 'a Beatle', and there are others who say that regardless of his part in The Beatles story, his art would always have found a way to be recognised with huge significance. Whatever the truth, if *The Stuart Sutcliffe Contemporary Art Award* can help new, aspiring talent from around the world, find a way to be known, acknowledged and helped, it can only be a good thing for art and artists, and one that Stuart himself would no doubt have endorsed.

There are dozens of people who have worked so hard in producing this publication and thanks are due to each and every one, but I'd like to highlight a few and start by thanking Michael Hall, who devised the concept for *In Conversation* and without whom this project simply would not have happened. Thank you to my business colleague, Paul King, for opening my mind and teaching me to realise that anything's possible, that there are no limits in this world and that each day is full of new opportunities. Many thanks to Adam Robinson, Nick

Linford and Jon Stephenson for their hard work and devotion to creating and designing this stunning book; a work of art in itself! Special thanks must go to my '$45 an hour girl'!, Diane Vital, for her endless help, trust and belief. Above all, love and thanks to my family; my wife Jacqui and my two young children, Rory and Heather. Without them I cannot function and therefore their love and support for my work with Stuart's Estate has been so crucial.

Lastly, but certainly far from least, I'd like to thank Stuart's sister, Pauline Sutcliffe, not just for her help and contribution to this book, but for devoting 50 years of her life to keeping Stuart's name alive; for working tirelessly to preserve his reputation and for her limitless energy in promoting his work for so long. As we commemorate 50 years since our loss of Stuart, I have no doubt that he is with us now, not just gleaming with pride for his sister, but with a tear or two in his eye for the love and devotion that she has shown him for so long.

I hope you enjoy this book. It's been great fun producing it and I hope it serves as a fitting tribute to the man himself.

Giles Cooper
CEO of The Stuart Sutcliffe Estate

Stuart Sutcliffe, Hamburg 1961
courtesy of The Stuart Sutcliffe Estate

I first discovered Stuart Sutcliffe when I was 16 years old; my family and I were driving home from a day trip when we decided to stop at a cinema to see a new film telling the story of the 'fifth Beatle'. Even though I grew up as an obsessive Beatles' fan, I had not heard of Stuart until this. The film was Iain Softley's *Backbeat* and it introduced me to one of the biggest influences of my life. I remember my heart breaking when, towards the end of the film, Stuart collapsed and died in his studio. I was completely transfixed by him (played so brilliantly by Stephen Dorff). From that day I wanted one thing — to be an artist; to be like Stuart.

In November 2001, the Proud Gallery in London's Charing Cross held an exhibition of Stuart's work. I finally got to see first hand what I had only been able to gaze at in books and standing in front of his work really did give me goose bumps. Stuart's influence has persisted throughout my artistic life and *In Conversation with Stuart Sutcliffe* is a concept conceived to share this influence with like-minded individuals and also work as an introduction to a new generation who may not yet be aware of the relevance of Stuart Sutcliffe.

When John Willett commented that 'Stuart showed the way' he was highlighting the fact that Stuart was the first to incorporate art and rock 'n' roll. His influence allowed The Beatles to understand that they had a visual presence making them more than just the music. The artistic influence of Stuart would allow them to become the complete package that took the world by storm. They continue to be important to this day and, like Stuart, should continue to do so for generations.

Stuart's life and work has generated major interest and exposure since his loss on April 10 1962. To refer to Stuart as the fifth Beatle creates a paradox. It highlights his cultural importance, yet overshadows his artistic credibility. The two are intrinsically linked yet to provide clarity requires a distinction between them. Stuart's life provides a story of major relevance because of his artistic influence on The Beatles and his subsequent decision to leave the band for art. Stuart's works resonate as passionate, poetic, emotive responses to his inner-being, where meaning can be re-invented and re-imagined through the eyes of its readers — making their engagement cyclical and of ever-lasting significance. In a way he linked art and rock 'n' roll by understanding the connection, but also the separation between them as alternating modes of expression. Stuart's influence is pertinent on both counts.

This book has been created to highlight the continued influence and relevance of someone who has permeated through popular culture. Alongside critical, sociological, poetic and personal responses, a number of contemporary artists have been invited to respond to his life and work. In doing so they have questioned, informed and discovered elements of their practices that can excite a confirmation of Stuart's intrigue and importance. No greater tribute can be made than the confirmation of a continued influence on a contemporary world. This is a tribute to Stuart, but also a result of the mark that remains.

I am eternally grateful for the support of Pauline Sutcliffe and Diane Vitale for believing in this project from the start. To Giles Cooper and all at Media Junction who allowed *In Conversation...* to take its first steps to becoming the multifaceted project it deserves to be.

Michael Hall
Editor

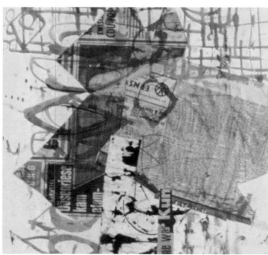

Top Left: Untitled (Hamburg Series #56 detail) circa 1960-62
Top Right: Untitled (Hamburg Series #88detail) circa 1960-62
Bottom Left: Untitled (Hamburg Series #114 detail) circa 1960-62
Bottom Right: Untitled (Hamburg Series #10 detail) circa 1960-62

Stuart Sutcliffe
courtesy of The Stuart Sutcliffe Estate

Opposite: Untitled (Hamburg Series #71 detail) circa 1960-62
Stuart Sutcliffe
courtesy of The Stuart Sutcliffe Estate

IN CONVERSATION WITH STUART AND JOHN
and later
IN CONVERSATION WITH PAULINE AND DIANE

John: So what do you think of this *In Conversation* celebration, Stu?

Stuart: I quite like the idea that other artists have created an art work that connects in some way to one of mine. A bit like the *Tate Britain show* we went to last night.

John: Oh, you mean *Picasso and Modern British Art*?

Stuart: Well sort of, except I'm no Picasso, but the concept of 'tracing influences' and expressing these in several different mediums is interesting.

John: So I guess some of your work was "fit for hanging"!? And now on walls in cyberspace... Well you were the greatest painter of us all and the world knows that so I guess it's fitting that you be the one who has a virtual world wide tour...

Stuart: I suppose so John, in fact several scenes in *Backbeat*, the play, utilize my art works on the stage via projection and with the aid of all this amazing technology can hang works – as you say Johnny boy, in cyberspace.

John: Do you know any of these *In Conversation* artists Stu? Were any of them at the art college with us?

Stuart: No, I don't think so John... although Jann Haworth rings a bell... wasn't she married to Peter Blake?

John: Yea, Paul brought them in to do the *Sergeant Pepper* album cover – don't you remember Stu?

Stuart: As for the rest, we're just about old enough to be their parents... or their grandparents... well some of them at least!

John: Speak for yourself... Remember Stu, we're frozen in time — you're still 21 years of age and I'm 40, almost old enough to be your father... forever stamped in the annals of history. You had that extra something special — even Paul admired it... those bloody cool looks — with yer dark glasses and quift hair... even before James Dean.

Stuart: And you morphed into not such a bad looking fella yourself — for a 40 year old — but of course you couldn't have done it without the help of your Yoko, your herbs, organic vegetables and homemade bread...

John: Yea, yea, yea.

Stuart: You should take a look at the works they have submitted, there are some interesting pieces — you know some still believe in putting paint on canvas or even on board. Didn't anyone tell them I was moving on to film making and recording sound tracks and exploring ways of creating three-dimensional art?

Have our colleagues forgotten that our mission was to shift perceptions and boundaries about what constitutes an art work?

John: Don't you find the images of the skulls submitted by one of the artists a bit spooky though Stu? And what about that guy's essay about haemorrhages?

Stuart: The skull is an image of a real life brain tumour — interesting but brings back some bad memories! And oh, you mean Richard Makin's essay... A bit like Walt Whitman meets William Burroughs — a collage of words?

John: With a touch of James Joyce, don't you think Stu?

Stuart: I do feel a touch flattered John that this guy should write an original piece as a kind of homage to my

but all probably due to my imagination — me tending towards the phantastic.

Yes! Tomorrow comes Paolozzi, and the day we go once more to the ship-breakers yard which we visited last semester. I will have with me a film-camera I borrowed of Theo's, Astrid's cousin, I'm very quickly trying to learn the technique as I'm enthralled by the possibilities and it's so expensive. He has many film including some of Astrid from a few years ago, very sweet as you can imagine. I'll have to take advantage of the few day I'll have it, I'll probably tire of it all the more quickly, because of the complete inaccessibility of the all the equipment required.

On Saturday we were out shopping and bought material for a costume for Astrid, an orangey cord but very strong and for me a pale fawn colour for a suit which Astrid is making, will probably be finished by Christmas, she's done the trousers to a trying on stage. but they'll be without pockets!

brief but illustrious journey through life into death.

John: A far cry from those who insist on putting 21 prolific years into a box — that's why I didn't like the orthodoxy — all that tradition and snobbery — but you're one of the only people in my life that got that and knew how to work with it whilst doing your own thing. I mean who would have believed you could paint whilst listening to Elvis and the Everleys one moment and the Planet Suites a while later!

Stuart: Some of the contributing artist's blurbs are not particularly flattering. One of them says that my work "was full of quotation rather than raw originality."

John: And some thought the Beatles would never make it. Even when we did make it, we spent our lives fighting people who said they could hear this artist or that artist in our work. A sign of greatness Mr. Sutcliffe!

Remember that piece you wrote about "we young artists..."?

Stuart: Yes, I sure do and I wrote that when I was "just a student!"

One of the contributing artists refers to this writing in this publication... But the truth is John, I'm neither flattered nor dismayed about any fellow artists' comments regarding my work...

We young artists are like young sailors, unless we encounter rough seas and are buffetted by the winds, we'll not become real sailors. There is no mercy for us, everyone has to go through a period of worry and struggle if he wants to go into deep water. First we catch few fish or none at all, but we get to know the ropes and learn to steer our boats which surely of great importance. And after awhile we'll have a marvell-ous catch, and big ones !!!

John: We spend our lives as students Stu – you told me that, but then you've always been a little too smart for your own good Mr. Sutcliffe, haven't you?!

Stuart: I see that Donald Kuspit quote about me also features... I quite like being described as "amongst the very best of second generation abstract expressionists..." So you see what I mean John you can neither be flattered nor dismayed – because opinion is so polarised... not just about my work, but all artists' work.

John: They're only jealous of you Stu – you had it all – artist, writer, poet and f***in' good looks... and I've no doubt Astrid would tell us a great lover. So it's not surprising you were a Beatle, is it Stu?

We were all more than the sum of our parts. And that's what your art people don't get Stu, you were more than just a painter... or more than just a Beatle...

And they're still talking about you! You have become a 21st century icon... the fifth Beatle? Even though you were the 4th and Pete was the 5th Beatle.

Stuart: It's hard to dismantle myths when they get bedded in.

John: ...And some of these people are fanatics. I overheard a conversation your sister Pauline was having with Diane the other day... So what's with these people trying to make Pauline feel ashamed that you were a Beatle? And these other folks saying you wouldn't have been hung if you weren't a Beatle?! What's that about? You lost credibility points in the traditionalist art world because you played in a rock 'n' roll band, what's with that?

And how could you be a Beatle, a member of the greatest band of all time, and have other interests and talents? Simply impossible one would think Mr. Sutcliffe! And how could anyone bridge the divide between high and low art?!

Stuart: Fame Johnny Boy is, as you know, not easy to manage!

John: And always brings with it controversy...

Stuart: My sister Pauline has done a fantastic job doing her best to set the record straight...

John: Well all I can say Stu is thank God for Donald Kuspit, Michael Bracewell. Lord Clark, John Willett and the rest of them. They have said it for you – and they have said it well.

Stuart: All good things come in time and sometimes you just have to sit back and wait for the truth to surface. Patience Johnny Boy...

John: Oh, so we're getting philosophical now?! Well, whilst we are setting the record straight Big Boy, I've just been reading a letter you wrote to your sister... I know you're an upstanding bloke and wanted to give your girl Astrid all the credit, so why should I be surprised...

...Okay, you have proven your point...

Stuart: Well it's been a long haul... and Pauline along with Diane's help and support have steered my ship (remember I am a sailor!) into deep waters... Giles is now

but the jackets different. buttons all the way up the front and a collar like a vicar — very different

at the helm – so put your seat belt on! We're going to go places where we have never been. I think it was a very smart decision indeed handing over the management of my affairs to Mr. Cooper.

John: Sounds like a face lift?

Stuart: No, John, more like a restructuring and enhancement

John: But Pauline remains the owner and sole executrix of your estate, correct?

Stuart: Yes John. My sister has worked tirelessly since my Mother's death in 1983 when she became the sole executrix and owner of my Estate. Diane has managed the estate with Pauline over the last 9 years; Shelagh and Terry helped her carry the torch for a number of years before Diane... I think my sister Pauline with Diane's help made a pretty smart decision to bring Giles Cooper from Media Junction in...

John: So is he going to be your Brian Epstein then Stu?

Stuart: Well he did alright for you Beatles for a long time, didn't he?!

John: Fancy a beer?

Later that day...

John: Looks like your 50th Anniversary Celebration is going viral... so I guess it would be good id the guys in Hamburg could link in... from our old pissing grounds...

Stuart: Where "The policemen here wear guns and they're not very big"

John: Where we launched our 4 star guitar line-up?

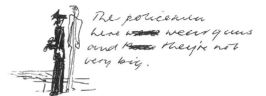

Stuart: ..."The little one on the end is the gimmick, me!"

John: And Liverpool too! And it looks like the city is finally acknowledging your contribution old boy... like the city will be naming something after you?! About time!

Stuart: The world has changed Johnny Boy! With time things change...

John: Here he goes again, getting philosophical...

Stuart: In those days we didn't have the Internet or the ability to have a conversation in cyberspace or hang a show - as in this one, Mr. Lennon!

John: There you go again, proving your point! I stand corrected Mr. Brainy Sutcliffe, so we wrote letters... and boy, could you bang a page... you were quite a prolific letter writer.

Stuart: And you weren't? You could keep going for 18 / 19 pages and then some — like the one you wrote to me — the one they used in *The Sunday Times* in 1980 to memorialize you... and boy could you express your feeling and pain back then... and not too bad on the insight stuff either...

John: I remember when you wrote that letter to your sister Pauline telling her that "Ringo from the Hurricanes is playing now in the Top Ten with Sheridan..." little did we know then that he would become a fully credentialized Beatle.

Original letter from John Lennon in Liverpool to Stuart Sutcliffe in Hamburg, Christmas 1960

We done is in the drawingline. but stillgood. This photography business seems stupid, & petty. But I don't know what the silence is, why haven't you at least written a few words! Tell us some thing about the rock-scene. You can tell us a bit about the cavern. Anyway I'm all on edge waiting so that, cant really concentrate to write properly... But please remind us of your existence. Your loving brother. Stuart. X X X X and greetings from your ashdel.

Stuart: Yes, Pauline kept all my letters – even the ones when I told her off about not writing enough – even my sister Joyce got a letter or two of admonition from me...

John: Big brother Stu... Do you think you were a bit homesick!?

Stuart: Remember when we used to do the London galleries?

John: We did more than the galleries... and those extremely long, but entertaining coach trips to London...

And Mr. Sutcliffe's agenda was to take in more exhibitions than humanly possible... a man on a mission...

Stuart: There you go again Mr. Lennon – pretending you weren't interested in art... you went with me to every one of those hangings...

John: Tell me Stu-y boy, you were so well organised... do you think that had anything to do with all that organising going way back to playing cricket, paper rounds with your sisters... not to mention maintaining our flat rental records and do you remember Rag Day at the college? Quite an impressive itinerary Mr. Sutcliffe! Didn't you get the "Entrepreneur of the year award" that year?

23 Lord Street. ⎱ tell Carol
Union ⎰

You will be given vouchers.

1 ticket for 2 vouchers.

The tickets (dance) are only
given to one person.

Pre-hists. Transport tickets will only be
sold at the ball.

5 o'clock Friday 22
all tickets have to be returned.

Tickets HAVE to be returned
otherwise Faculty is responsible

Floats at College at 9.0 pm.

Float outside Union at 1.30. (Float
finished by 1pm).

Procession will move off about 2.0 -20
Town Hall
No late comers (floats).

Money for car competition must
not be put in collecting boxes.

Say off magunity. (25/-
(offices)
Personnel immunities 2/6.

Collect pantosphinx on friday.
in the room downstairs

Third building down.

Department of Education, Abercromby Square.

About 3.0 panto office. Authorisation
census on Friday.

Organise parties to Stations on Cup day

Stuart: Funny John, Very Funny. I'm glad I didn't depend on you to keep our flat records!

Later that day...

John: Tell me Stu, did you really think *Backbeat* the film could translate so brilliantly to the stage the way it did? (Through Glasgow's Citizens Theatre to the Duke of York's Theatre on London's West-End).

Stuart: I think it succeeded so brilliantly Johnny boy because they had the wisdom to bring in some of the superlative executive producer Karl Sydow who knew how to retranslate film to theatre – a real talent you know... bit like us Johnny boy.

I know my sister Pauline was particularly taken with him and David Levaux the theatre director – she's always had great affection for Iain Softley and his wife Sarah and the film, but through Karl now understands the nuances and perceptual issues and differences between film and theatre.

John: So it makes sense of the piece included in your celebration *In Conversation* book for these themes to be more fully explored...

Stuart: Yes, I guess so... I particularly like the way Graeme Gilloch uses extracts from films to develop and illustrate his themes.

John: Thanks Stu – would never have "got that" if you hadn't pointed it out... Have you forgotten, I'm 40 now?!

Stuart: And a man of great wisdom, power and might!

John: Well that might have been true some of the time... but like you said before "in time the truth does prevail..." Aren't you glad sometimes Stu that we're up here and they're down there getting on with our lives... its exhausting living... isn't it? So what's next Stu?

Stuart: Toronto Johnny Boy... on to the uppermost of the topper-most.

John: So I take it then Stu that *Backbeat* is going to go to Broadway following Toronto, yes?

Stuart: As always Johnny Boy, you are a man with vision! Didn't mean to sound patronising before. Will you forgive me?

John: Oh, don't worry Stu, even I forget sometimes that I'm no longer your mentoree!

Later that day...

Diane: From the first moment of the first act I could feel my heart skip a beat. I didn't dare turn to look at you whilst you sat there by my side at the Duke of York's Theatre last October – at the opening of the theatrical production of *Backbeat*. Even though Karl spent several days in New York with us going through Stuart's archive and discussing the script, we of course felt well prepared for the curtain call – we weren't.

Can you share what it was like for you to see *Backbeat* on the stage for the first time?

Pauline: It took my breath away. The nuance of Stuart's spirit was captured in such a sensitive way... his tenderness, quiet confidence... powerful presence and influence was captured and I must thank Karl and David for taking the time and care to get it just right.

Diane: And the reviews... very affirming...

Pauline: It's been 50 years and Stuart still takes my breath away...

Diane: We've talked about his influence on both you and your sister Joyce which started early on... long before he emerged as an iconic figure with hundreds of thousands of Google hits on any given day... before he belonged to the people.

Pauline: Circumstances influenced much of how he became a conscientious caring influential and much loved brother and son.

Diane: Graeme Gilloch reminds us of the importance of perception and nuance of meaning.

Pauline: Yes, he does and one cannot begin to capture the essence of Stuart's brief time in this world without considering what Britain looked like 50+ years ago. It is important to consider context – we grew up in a provincial city in England during and shortly after World War II.

Diane: What was it like?

Pauline: Telegrams were the major means of speedy communication – very few people had telephones and even fewer had motorcars. I read somewhere recently that because there were no motorways even into the early 1960's – it could take 10 hours to drive from Liverpool to London.

Stuart and John were having a conversation about this earlier when they would go to London for gallery blitzes – hence Stuart's structured and organised mind - setting out strategy and drawing maps to achieve the most gallery visits in a very short time.

Diane: Many of Stuart's younger followers on Facebook would like to know what life was like growing up with Stuart...

Pauline: As I mentioned earlier, one must consider context – and what suburban/rural life was like at the time in which we were raised... All of this had an enormous impact on Stuart's character & personality... until his catastrophic untimely death – and now beyond...

Diane: Stuart's presence is evidenced by his cult like following on the Internet... Stuart was not just a brief flame that flickered and burned out quickly – neither was he just a visual artist whose merits have been closely pondered upon by many art critics and historians included in this conversation in celebration of his 50th.

Pauline: ...and at times gently dismissed. And neither was he that hapless nonmusical non-bass player of popular mythology.

*"Stu was actually a very good rock 'n' roll bass player. At the time he was **way better** than Paul"*
KLAUS VOORMANN

I believe this quote by Klaus has already been used... Well, guess it's like New York – so good they named it twice!?

Diane: Who said you couldn't use a quote twice – this is about your brother... so, tell us what it was like growing up with Stuart?

Stuart Sutcliffe's original Hofner 'brunette' 333 Bass, on permanent display at the Hard Rock Cafe, Hyde Park, London

Illustration by Klaus Voormann on the reverse of a letter sent to Stuart's mother in 1963

Pauline: To my sister Joyce and I he was a very uniquely talented and special person. He was the brother for whom we would provide bowling practice - he was a fast bowler and played for his school and then at the art college in the students against staff cricket matches.

Such was our trust in him that he knew how to position Joyce in the line of fire for he recognized her skills – she could predict the flight of the ball and was a good catcher – so very few balls came on to the outfield where I was placed – no surprise Joyce became a civil engineer and woman's captain of her golf club.

Diane: And what impact did this have on your life choices?

Pauline: Well, in the out field – I was not only protected from the flight of the balls but I had plenty of time to daydream... Later on this theme of protection became a pattern mainly when going to early Beatle gigs with Stuart – where he would place me in his sightline from the stage and instruct me not to move in order to keep me safe and protected. This gave me plenty of time to think and question "why" I was doing this?

Diane: Not surprisingly you went on to become a systemic family psychotherapist - with a particular interest in second-order cybernetics.

Pauline: Not a surprise...

Diane: Having practiced as a family psychotherapist over the last 35+ years, would I be amiss in assuming you have seen patterns and been able to read into what others have to say about Stuart – the references, books, articles, blogs are endless... I've personally witnessed you in social settings having casual conversation and when a person finds out you are a psychotherapist they somehow feel compelled to share their life story with you. On the other hand, I would imagine you can't separate this from who you are and how you experience how others see Stuart. Perhaps this is the subject for another chapter or even another book – but can you comment on this?

Pauline: Well part of our discipline is to look for patterns and isomorphic behaviors... I think I overheard a conversation between Stuart and John about this very subject – it can be exhausting (living) but well worth the effort – getting things right – Stuart was always about getting things right. He was a thinker and he had insight - something we psychotherapists look for.

When people have insight they have the capacity to make real changes in their lives. I often wonder what our conversations would be like today – 50 years later.

Diane: So when you reflect on the early days growing up with your brother, what memories do you hold near and dear to your heart?

Pauline: In those days Stuart had a paper delivery round... paper boys not only had to have a bicycle but they were also required to collect the paper money each week. He recruited my sister Joyce and I to make the rounds with him... he figured out how to attach his paper bag to a basket on the front of his bikes dropped handlebars so that either Joyce or myself could accompany him and sit on the crossbar.

Diane: So he was entrepreneurial early on... utilizing limited resources... my kind of guy... that's a skill I endeavor to teach my students at the Fashion Institute of Technology!

I take it there was quite a distance between houses and roads?

Pauline: Yes, remember this was rural provincial England... When the apple season was in full bloom, our leader Stuart would be the first one over the wall to demonstrate how to properly steal apples... My sister Joyce and I were carefully instructed to remain on the lookout... and to run if he were to get caught.

Diane: Did that ever happen?

Pauline: Yes, on one occasion he did get caught by the local bank manager. He subsequently took matters into his own hands and gave Stuart the task of digging his entire garden - otherwise he would report Stuart's misbehavior to our parents – and that was the ultimate punishment.

Diane: Apple stealing acquired a name called "scrumping"?

Pauline: Yes, but that was not a part of our vocabulary at that time.

Diane: Yes, time does change things... sounds like you had a great relationship and a lot of fun with your brother.

Pauline: To say that Stuart was both our admired and looked up to older brother is an understatement – he was also our mentor and guide, our protector and source of interesting experiences – ones we never would have had otherwise.

In return he experienced great admiration, cooperation and love from us.

Diane: As you started to grow up and develop your own circle of friendships, how did your friends experience Stuart?

Pauline: Our girlfriends wanted to meet him and expressed a real wish to have him as a boyfriend. That wasn't easy to arrange – in fact it wasn't even a remote possibility – he was in a different league and they secretly knew that, but you can't fault a girl for trying!

Diane: There are many images of you, your sister and your mother in some of Stuart's early drawings. What was that like for you?

Pauline: I was 12 and Joyce was 14 when Stuart became a student at Liverpool College of Art. Just prior to this we had become impatient with him constantly sketching us and began to take exception to his comments about how our hair should look, what we should be wearing – what was fashionable and wasn't...

Diane: Like a fashion stylist?

Pauline: Yes... and not only that... he was our art director and my educational consultant as well... it was not uncommon for him to suggest books to read like Kierkegaard and films to see and certain poets to read...

Above and Right: Sketches of Pauline, Joyce and Millie by Stuart Sutcliffe, 1956

and reminding us that although mother and father were both accomplished pianists, that the likelihood of them including Elvis into their repertoire was highly unlikely. Therefore we must listen to his records... It was important to him that we remain current!

Diane: If I'm not mistaken didn't Astrid mention she introduced Stuart to the existentialists?

Pauline: Well if she did she must have made a mistake as not only was Stuart a voracious reader but his interest in existentialism went well beyond the visual fashion statements of the bourgeois Germans who were not from the intellectual wing of existentialism and had a superficial understanding of the mores espoused by Sartre et al... but boy, they looked good!

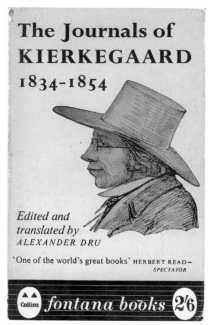

Left:
Stuart Sutcliffe's original copy of The Journals of Kierkegaard

In Kierkegaard's book he found that rare combination of note book and diary in which he records in intimate detail his spiritual and intellectual development.

Furthermore, Kierkegaard deals with his conflicts about how religion was presented negatively to him when young - and his desire to embrace this positively later.

Diane: Wow, sounds like quite a reading challenge for an adult, no less a 14 or 15 year old!

Pauline: Yes, it was (she laughs) but Stuart was a patient and understanding teacher. I don't believe I "got it" back then but what I do get now is how influential Kierkegaard was to Stuart — so Hamburg existentialism was more like the icing on the cake — not the substance.

Diane: To say he was ahead of his time is an understatement... not unlike your atypical parents who were very accomplished... we have to consider context... am I being a good student?

Pauline: Yes you are — I can see you're paying attention! You have to know we three siblings were very connected... our father was a naval officer often away from home for months at a time and our mother was a teacher — working a full time job... not a typical family of the time — and Stuart, well he was our... leader.

Diane: Your father passed shortly after Stuart's death and your mother lived until 1983 — you stated in one of your recent interviews that at that time Stuart's notebooks, poetry books and essays were not in your possession, so you would only access them in later years when at your Mother's house.

Pauline: That's correct. Mother kept all Stuart's notebooks and we could look at them if we wished.

Diane: Do you share his talent for writing poetry?

Pauline: No, I did not write poetry but on one memorable occasion I recruited him to do my poetry homework assignment and I remember giving him strict instructions to write it at my age and skill level…

Pauline: Fancy a Chardonnay…

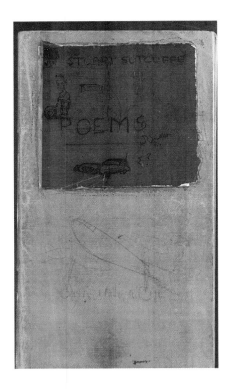

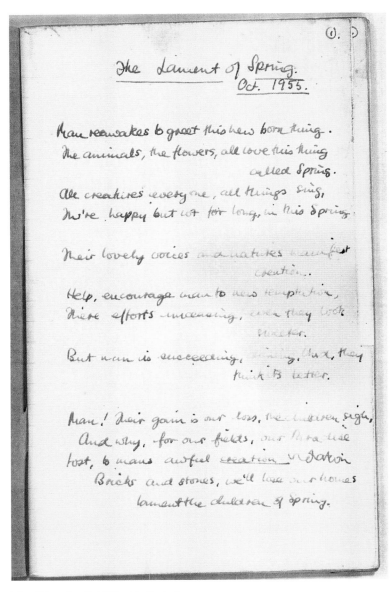

Left and Above: Stuart Sutcliffe's original book of poems

Later that day...

Diane: At what point did Stuart move away from home?

Pauline: Stuart managed to persuade our Mother that he needed to have his own studio near the Art School, which very quickly shifted from a 'work' space to a 'living' space.

Diane: That must have had a significant impact on you and your sister, no?

Pauline: Yes, our roles changed significantly after that. One or both of us would escort mother weekly to "the artist's studio" ...and somehow mother always managed to bump into the milk man (in those days it was delivered) who happened to be looking for Stuart so he could collect his bill – wasn't that an amazing coincidence? Mother would of course pay it for him.

Diane: What was it like for you – visiting his studio?

Pauline: It's hard to convey how mysterious and exciting it was to enter such hollowed portals as a young artists sanctum and just how pleased and happy we were to collect his dirty laundry, help mommy put clean sheets on his bed and then walk on down the road to a café for a cup of tea together – brave new world.

Diane: Was that when you met John for the first time?

Pauline: Yes, and I remember John doing his best to ignore Stuart's overtures to him to meet and greet his mother and younger sister. My recollections of this meeting are well and truly on the record so no need to rehash them again.

Diane: And some years later they were off to Hamburg – what was that like?

Pauline: Although it was several years later it seemed like no time at all before that fateful day arrived...

Mother hid in a doorway of a store and watched Stuart, John et al loading up their van in preparation for their by land and sea trip to Hamburg. My sister Joyce and I cannot remember until that day experiencing our Mother so heartbroken – well not at least until many years later when he died.

Diane: Mothers do have these uncanny instincts, don't they?

Pauline: The only reason mother agreed for him to go is because he had finished his finals at art school and she told us and father (we called him daddy in those days) that Stuart was just having some time out after having worked so hard for so many years.

Mother had achieved what Joan Didion wrote about many years later in *The Year of Magical Thinking* and which was known hitherto as a form of denial... but I have to say I really do like Joan's reframe.

Diane: And that's the nuance of meaning that someone like you just "gets"...

What a painful time this must have been for you... a dramatic shift in your relationship with your big wonderful ever-present brother...

Pauline: Yes, very difficult – we missed him so much. Once in Hamburg, my sister and I became Stuart's correspondents... and he remained present to us through his letters...

19. but the jackets different buttons all the way up the front and a collar like a vicar — very different Astred isht well at the moment and also not talking to me as the result of my desire to play again.

oh yes — Paul and Dot — in one way I'm not surprised but its still rather a shock particularly as Dot was the one who finished it — it is true I suppose. You might be able to tell me a lot more about it — is Paul sad or the what and what prompted the break — do you think she found out about his affairs or did he give her the cold shoulder. Anyway I bet one of

...Joyce was receiving career advice about whether to study architecture or civil engineering as well as reporting on family life. I was instructed to visit *The Cavern* (no escort needed now) and report back on the music scene. Mother meanwhile had to justify this strange change to father and visit art galleries and send catalogues to her prince... *(oops - Sorry, I didn't mean to reveal this!)*

Diane: Is it true that your mother at that time moved house just to be closer to Stuart's studio near the art college?

Pauline: Yes she did and she did have a room set aside for Stuart just in case he wanted to come home which he did now and again. Within weeks of the boys arriving in Hamburg, Rod Murray contacted us to say he had to move house urgently so would we come and collect all of Stuart's possessions from the flat – these included notebooks, essays, art folders and art works. We also gathered up a few of John's books – several years later returned to him by mother.

Left: Original letter by Stuart Sutcliffe in which he illustrates and describes the jackets he was having made which became The Beatles look.

Right: Stuart Sutcliffe's famous 'White Rose' letter

Diane: It wasn't long after that when Stuart met Astrid...

1.15 am, I have just recovered from another visit by my strange and beautiful friends. She handed me a chocolate heart encased in silver paper and wrapped in red cellophane, oh the heart-ache!! Tomorrow I will buy a white rose, a young boys thought, a sunny thought and golden one, marred only by the knowledge that I will never has the courage to give it her. On monday she takes more photos of me, by the river with my guitar, if it could speak, your ears would burn with the heat and

Pauline: And the rest is history.

Pauline Sutcliffe & Diane Vitale

"In late 1959, whilst *Johnny and The Moondogs* (John, Paul and George) made music; Stuart went to work on a great big abstract painting to submit for the prestigious biennial *John Moores'* exhibition to be held at the *Walker Art Gallery*; it was 8ft x 8ft in two pieces of 8ft by 4ft. When it was completed, Stuart and Rod Murray carried the first half down to the gallery and then went for a drink, to get over their exertions. They planned to take the other half down the following day, but they never did and it remained in their backyard in Gambier Terrace, for many months. The first half, titled *Summer Painting*, was the only student work accepted for the *Art Prize* and was bought by the exhibition's benefactor, John Moores, for £65. John Lennon was with Stuart when he was told that his painting had been sold and gave Stuart a typical Lennon-esque line "and I didn't think it was fit for hangin'!" John persuaded Stuart to buy a bass guitar with his earnings and join his group and together they went to Frank Hessy's music shop, on 21st January 1960, and bought a brunette Höfner 333 bass. However, there was one snag. Stuart didn't like the name for the group and suggested *The Beetles* after the female biker gang in the Marlon Brando film, *The Wild Ones*. However you spell it, this was the moment *The Beatles* of yesterday, today and tomorrow were born."

Extract from *The Beatles' Shadow, Stuart Sutcliffe & his Lonely Hearts Club* by Pauline Sutcliffe

66

We went to the Walker Art Gallery and John took me up to this enormous painting. It seemed to be all khaki and yellow triangles. I looked at it and I said, "What is it?" Well! John got hold of my arm and hustled me outside; I wasn't allowed to see another picture in the show. "How could you say a thing like that Mimi? He gave his chest a big thump, and bellowed, "art comes from in here!"

99

JOHN LENNON'S 'AUNT MIMI'

SUMMER PAINTING
circa 1959
Stuart Sutcliffe
Painting bought by John Moores
following its exhibition at
the Walker Art Gallery in the
John Moores' Contemporary
Painting Prize 1959
courtesy of The Stuart Sutcliffe Estate

John Lennon in Stuart Sutcliffe's attic studio, Hamburg
April 1962 (shortly after Stuart's death)
Photograph by Astrid Kirchherr

Stu Sutcliffe was an exquisite and talented man, a prolific artist, and the closest friend that John Lennon ever had. He was also John's most powerful influence and with him shared a passion; a wider search for the real meaning of life. In the early years, Stuart recognised John's anger and creative aggression and played such a crucial role in his development; targeting his energy in a positive way. In the formative years of John's march to eternal greatness, Stu Sutcliffe was a colossal figure. His sense of style, quest for artistic excellence, and provocative manner affected John Lennon's thoughts and visions for the rest of his life. Yoko talks of John referring to Stuart as an almost alter ego, a spirit in his world, a guiding force. His influence on John is as unquestionable as it is prolific and ubiquitous. If the truth is what John Lennon sought, the truth is what he got from his best friend, possibly more than from any other soul in his life"

LARRY KANE

Larry Kane's Emmy Award winning career spans more than 50 years. He was the only American journalist to travel in the official Beatles entourage during the legendary 1964 and '65 tours of North America and subsequently became a life-long friend of John Lennon's. Kane published the critically acclaimed biography *Lennon Revealed* in 2005.

Top Left: Untitled (Hamburg Series #2 detail) circa 1960-62
Top Right: Untitled (Hamburg Series #36 detail)) circa 1960-62
Bottom Left: Untitled (Hamburg Series #15 detail) circa 1960-62
Bottom Right: Untitled (Hamburg Series #1 detail) circa 1960-62

Opposite: Untitled (Hamburg Series #50 detail) circa 1960-62
Stuart Sutcliffe
courtesy of The Stuart Sutcliffe Estate

Stuart Sutcliffe
courtesy of The Stuart Sutcliffe Estate

Far left: Stuart Sutcliffe in the
woods on the river Elbe 1960

Left: Stephen Dorff as
Stuart Sutcliffe in the
movie *Backbeat* 1994

Photographer unknown

BACKBEAT
by Iain Softley

The story of *Backbeat* started with two photographs - Astrid's self-portrait and a photograph she took of Stuart Sutcliffe. In the black and white self-portrait an elfin Bardot/Jean Seberg cropped blonde, dressed in simple black, is reflected symmetrically in a large gilt mirror as she crouches over her Rolleiflex camera. A black branch hovers over her head. In the black and white photograph of Stu, he sits in a gilt high-backed chair - beside him a table covered in bottles, behind him the same large gilt mirror. His mod-cut hair brushed forward, he wears a white shirt, black tie and leather waistcoat. Both of them look beautiful, confident, intelligent and timelessly cool.

I was working at Granada Television with Tony Wilson (owner of Factory Records and The Hacienda) at the time I first saw these photographs. I had recently worked on the film obituary for John Lennon. The Beatles' extended circle of influence still pervaded Granada. I had met Adrian Henry, a Merseybeat poet, and Carol Ann Duffy (now Poet Laureate) was a work colleague, as was Thelma McGough, ex-wife of Roger, and one of Lennon's first girlfriends at Art School.

But, it was the power of these photographs and the promise they held of a 'rites of passage' love story combining rock 'n' roll and art that took hold of me and has still not let go. My research started in the telephone directory of Sevenoaks in Kent where I had heard that Sutcliffe's mother Millie still lived. I worked my way through the entries, the seventh of which was Millie. She invited me to her flat, where the walls were covered with Stuart's paintings, and gave me a series of contacts. I worked through them, starting with her daughter Pauline, the keeper of the Sutcliffe archive, via Arthur Ballard, Lennon and Stu's teacher, and ending with Astrid Kirchherr.

When I called Hamburg, Astrid answered in English with a soft German accent. I told her of my plan to tell the story of her relationship with Stu. She said she wasn't really interested in talking about the past but that if I found myself in Hamburg I should look her up. I booked a flight the next week and called Astrid from a cheap hotel. She suggested that I should come to talk to her the next day at the bar she was managing. This turned out to be my audition. By the end of our conversation, she invited me to visit her. When I arrived at her apartment, I found that Astrid had invited Klaus Voormann. She told me that she was satisfied I wasn't just interested in her and Stu as a footnote in The Beatles' story, and so began a cooperation with her and Klaus, as with Pauline Sutcliffe, that has lasted throughout the project's history.

I returned to Hamburg sometime later and stayed with Astrid and Klaus, in Klaus' farmhouse on the Danish border. The tape-recorded interviews that I conducted over the next week formed the basis of the screenplay for *Backbeat*. They also served as invaluable research documents for the casts of the film and the subsequent stage productions in Glasgow and London.

What emerged was a dramatic story based on two interlinking triangles: the relationships between Astrid, John and Stuart and between John, Stuart and Paul. It's about the dilemmas of jealousy and loyalty, and conflicts of emotion. At its centre is the choice Stuart has to make between his best friend or his girlfriend, painting or the band, his hometown or a life in a new country.

I wanted to tell a story about individual aspirations - love, friendship, ambition and loss, what you want and what you have to give up to get it.

I found a home for my planned feature film with Stephen Woolley and Nik Powell's Palace Pictures, who produced the film along with Finola Dwyer. Michael Thomas and Stephen Ward joined me as co-screenwriters. It was a couple of years before we were in a position to start shooting what was to be my first feature film as director.

In the meantime, I began casting in London, Liverpool, Paris and Los Angeles and assembled a cast headed by Sheryl Lee, straight from *Twin Peaks*, Stephen Dorff and Ian Hart. Chris O'Neil, Gary Bakewell and Scott Williams made up the remaining Beatles.

Central to the *Backbeat* story is the idea that if The Beatles hadn't been to Hamburg, they would not have become The Beatles as we know them. In the clubs of Hamburg's red light district, vying for attention with hookers, strippers and brawling sailors, there was an alchemical coming together of black American rock 'n' roll music and European bohemia as personified by Astrid Kirchherr, Klaus Voormann and their circle of Art School 'exis'.

Astrid fell in love with the look and sound of the band but, in particular, she fell in love with Stuart Sutcliffe. Astrid, cropped blonde hair and dressed in black, epitomised Parisian left-bank chic and Stuart fell for her immediately. In many ways Stuart became an expression of Astrid's ideas and a mirror image of her. Through Stuart's close relationship with John, Astrid's influence permeated the rest of the band. The mop-top haircut and Pierre Cardin collarless jacket, that she first gave Stuart, became the band's signature look. She introduced them to Man Ray, the films of Cocteau and the music of Stravinsky. One of Astrid's key influences was to show the band, through her photographs, the power of their visual presence. She understood that the impact they had was more than just their music — it was what they projected. Astrid's photographs seemed to foreshadow some of the more iconic Beatles' images such as Robert Freeman's *With The Beatles* cover photograph. Her photos of Stuart look almost as if they prefigure the cover of *Help* - a black silhouette against a white background in semaphore-like poses. It was the power of these simple evocative images that, in part, first gave me the idea for the film.

It was a combination of ideas that John Lennon completely embraced, culminating in Peter Blake and Jann Haworth's cover of *Sgt. Pepper* and the definitive 'medium is the message' coup of performing *All You Need Is Love* to an international audience of millions of people via the first-ever live global satellite link-up. It was more than a song; it was the belief that a piece of popular art can have an immediate effect on the world.

What happened in Hamburg sowed the seeds of these ideas, that rock 'n' roll wasn't necessarily confined to the stage — it was a lifestyle and what made The Beatles unique was the way art, music and ideas came together.

Astrid and Klaus Voormann talked about the impact of hearing The Beatles for the first time in that Hamburg cellar - it was like being hit in the chest by the power of the sound. So, rather than something that was historically and technically accurate, I wanted it to have a raw quality as if we were hearing it for the first time. I wanted the audience in the cinema, and later the theatre, to experience the same impact that Klaus and Astrid had when they walked in from that street in Hamburg. For the film soundtrack, we got together a band that, at the time, was dubbed a grunge supergroup— Dave Grohl, Thurston Moore, Greg Dulli and Mike Mills. Coincidentally, our music producer, Don Was, was concurrently working with Billy Preston (who sat in with The Beatles in Hamburg) and Ringo Starr and they both said, 'Yeah, it was just like that, we were like a punk band'.

I also wanted to present this band of guys as being like any other band that plays covers when they start out, but to show them evolving into a band of extraordinary power when playing live. Incidentally, their repertoire included a number of songs that feature in our show that many people think of as Beatles' songs because they appear on early Beatles' albums - *Twist and Shout*, *Please Mr. Postman* and *Money*. The consensus is that before The Beatles went to Hamburg, they were like the many other beat bands from Liverpool but, by the time they returned, they had left all the others behind.

It was an incredibly fulfilling experience for me to make the film but I felt that the idea still had another potential incarnation.

It was, in fact, a few weeks before the start of shooting, that it became clear to me that *Backbeat* could work on the stage. We used to get the cast to perform at the end of every day. They played on the Kaiserkeller set while the crew sat at the tables with their beers - it was as if we were there in the club with them. I thought it would be great to be in the theatre and have that same experience.

A few years ago, we were invited to screen *Backbeat* at Abbey Road Studios as part of a classic film series and the sponsors brought Stephen Dorff (who played Stu Sutcliffe in the film) over from Los Angeles. Ian Hart (John Lennon) and the other guys were already here and we did a reading of the screenplay at the Venue Theatre off Leicester Square. It went down a storm. Chris O'Neill, who played George Harrison, is a very good guitar player and he strummed along while the cast sang. It was a real indication that the combination of music, words and story could work in a theatrical environment.

At this point, having relicensed the rights from Universal Pictures, I showed the project to theatre producer, Karl Sydow, and he leapt at the idea. So, we set about getting the show on the stage. In order to satisfy the conditions of the option, we did another reading at The Hippodrome.

The success of The Hippodrome reading secured The Glasgow Citizens Theatre as our partners and the venue for the original stage production. I teamed up with co-writer Stephen Jeffreys to work on the stage script, and got my friend Paul Stacey (collaborator with Oasis and The Black Crowes amongst others) whose band played for me at The Hippodrome reading, to come on as musical director. He worked with me to put a band together, which included Andy Knott (who read Lennon at the reading). My idea was that it should feel as if you were experiencing the story live, which meant the band had to play. I knew this was crucial to the success of the show. At the same time, I didn't want to cast musicians; I wanted to cast actors who could play or at least had a sense of rhythm whom we could teach. We tried different combinations of band members and what emerged was the first cast for The Glasgow Citizens Theatre. The musical core of that cast, Andy Knott, Dan Healy and Olly Bennett, went on to perform in the West End transfer.

The story of *Backbeat* ends with Stuart Sutcliffe's death before the recorded Beatles' history begins. He is the only character in the story who didn't live to find out that so much of what they had dreamed of would come about. It is clear that although John is devastated by Stu's death he is able to channel his anger and grief into an energy that propels him forward to the future to play an iconic role in the seismic cultural shift of the '60s.

Part of our fascination with the period is the way musicians, like The Beatles, The Rolling Stones, The Who and Bob Dylan amongst others, changed the cultural landscape and led a social revolution. It was a generation who grew up aware that the world they'd been born into was a broken, scarred world. It was not just the urban landscape punctuated with bomb craters and air-raid shelters. Many of those who had lived through the War were emotionally and physically exhausted. But, there was also a sense of a brand new start with the introduction of the welfare state and wider access to education. The old world was being left behind and people wanted to move on, to start a new chapter.

I grew up in London and I can remember in the early '60s (around the time I first heard The Beatles on Blue Peter or some other TV show) there was a sense of a soft revolution. Everything suddenly seemed to be more colourful. If you look at old photos, everything was black or dark and, one summer in the early '60s, the billboards changed and the clothes and shops changed and the whole thing exploded. There were new industries - advertising and the record business — without a hierarchy or structure. People were reinventing themselves and the field was wide open.

These musicians were for the most part articulate, well-read, well-informed young men whose references ranged through Edward Lear, Oscar Wilde, Hilaire Belloc, Aleister Crowley, English surrealism and the Beat poets such as Jack Kerouac and Allen Ginsberg. Of course, there were people before The Beatles in the underground of the bohemian art world — whether it was Abstract Expressionism or the Pop Artists of the late '50s - but it was the pop song and the pop group that were the media that allowed these ideas to break through to the mainstream. The new technologies of LPs, transistor radios and TV meant that the mainstream was a wider audience than ever before.

The Beatles changed everything because they were the first band to combine their music with visual expression through photography, film and album art. John Lennon himself said that music was only part of what they were doing. You can see the influences of Hamburg, Astrid and Stuart in the evolution of those ideas. Stuart and John wanted to forge their own language, a mixture of American rock 'n' roll with the European art tradition. It was an amazing alchemy and it all started the day that Klaus and Astrid walked down the stairs of the Kaiserkeller and were overwhelmed by the musical and visual assault of The Beatles and Stuart Sutcliffe.

Iain Softley is an English film director, who wrote and directed the movie *Backbeat* in 1994.
Backbeat the Musical, produced by Karl Sydow & directed by David Leveaux, is on tour throughout the world.

Stuart Sutcliffe in Reinhart Wolf's studio, Hamburg
Photograph by Reinhart Wolf 1961

Painting again... I see so many things in my
mind, things that only need to be made
concrete again and they would be good,
but I can't transpose them yet.
I must wait

STUART SUTCLIFFE

AN ART OF CONVERSATION

by Graeme Gilloch

I

This is not as it should be. A celebration of the life and work of Stuart Sutcliffe should be in 2015, not now, not in 2012. And it should be very different from this. Marking Sutcliffe's 75th anniversary, it should be one of those major retrospectives based on the careful collection and selection of definitive works so as to chronicle a fascinating and fruitful lifetime of artistic endeavour and achievement. It would capture those moments of inspiration and insight, all those subtly shifting moods and colours, and that unmistakeable sense of maturation of both talent and technique. Yes, it would be a retrospective with, at its centre, doing the retrospection, the man himself – still sharp and handsome despite the lines and wrinkles, still with the never neglected quiff, albeit long turned grey-white. Stuart should be the one asked politely to look back, to speak about his life and work at the opening night Q and A, to pen a wry and witty foreword to the weighty accompanying catalogue, to give an interview or two to critics and journalists, to talk convivially, charmingly on a chat-show sofa maybe, always and everywhere to speak, discuss, argue, inform and illuminate. He would be there to converse with us.

No, this is certainly not as it should be. Instead, *In Conversation with Stuart Sutcliffe* marks the 50th anniversary of Stuart's tragic death at the age of just 21. And, as the great German-Jewish cultural theorist Walter Benjamin once so astutely remarked, a person who dies so young, so prematurely, can only ever be thought of, can only ever be remembered, as one who was destined to die young. Looking now at those black-and-white photographs from around 1960 of Stuart, clad in leather jacket, guitar in hand, one becomes what Roland Barthes[1] memorably describes as a 'backwards-looking prophet,' that is to say, acutely aware of the catastrophe that is so soon to befall the young man in the picture, a figure who looks back at us blithely unaware of his fate. Gazing at the image, we know what is going to happen to him then, what has already long come to pass for us now. He is going to die aged just 21.

No, Stuart cannot converse with us today but perhaps his paintings can. These are his medium, his chosen form of correspondence. Works of art, Benjamin argued[2], in that they outlive their authors, their producers, inevitably have a certain posthumous existence, an 'afterlife', in which their manifold meanings continue to unfold as each new generation of viewers, readers and listeners subject them to critical examination, interrogation and exploration. This, indeed, is how Benjamin understands the very task of art criticism – not the recovery of some initial artistic intention, and certainly not the high-handed judgement of 'good' and 'bad' art by self-appointed art 'experts'; but rather criticism as an on-going process involving the continual recognition (rethinking) of the significance of the artwork as it enters into ever-new historical moments and contexts, into the present. How does an artwork produced perhaps far away and long ago, then and there, communicate with us in the here and now? The meaning of the work of art, its truth, Benjamin argues, is never fixed and final; rather it is always in the midst of becoming. It is in this spirit, I think, that this celebration seeks to set Stuart's works in conversation, that is to say, to allow them to speak with, to turn them towards, at least three different interlocutors: with each other; with works produced by other artists today that explicitly engage with, and / or take their inspiration from Stuart's images; and, most importantly perhaps, with with viewers and readers, with you and me. In so doing, they will be rethought, reimagined, reconfigured, renewed. They will become something different. Conversation always brings conversion in this sense – not through pressured persuasion, but by means of disclosure, by the opening up, the opening out, of ideas.

No, this is not as it should be. But it is the best we can do.

II

What follows are some reflections on the art of conversation and the conversation of art.

Much has been written today about the former, not surprisingly given the tremendous transformations in scope and speed of mass communications and the proliferation of new media technologies. Indeed, in these digital times the face-to-face conversation involving the actual co-presence of interlocutors almost seems an anachronism. But I am reminded of the fallibility of even the most sophisticated technologies to capture the extraordinary subtlety and nuance of spoken words and the importance of presence. In Francis Ford Coppola's remarkable 1973 film, *The Conversation*, Gene Hackman stars as Harry Caul, a middle-aged, deeply troubled and laconic surveillance expert ("the best bugger on the West Coast") hired by the anonymous 'Director' of a faceless corporation to check up on his young wife's clandestine meetings with a younger executive. In what starts out as evidence gathering in a routine adultery case, Caul deploys all his know-how and state-of-the-art technological gadgetry to film and record the movements of the suspect couple as they wander around in the seemingly safety of lunch time crowds thronging a public plaza, Union Square in San Francisco. As he and his team eavesdrop, it becomes clear the two are indeed lovers. And it is clear, too, that they are being extremely careful and cautious; they are frightened, on edge. Back in his sound lab, as he twiddles with his controls to adjust the balance of sound caught by different parabolic microphones, to eradicate extraneous background chatter and noise, to triangulate the sound, Caul is finally able to construe a fragment of their conversation: "He'd kill us if he got the chance."

This utterance casts Caul into a moral dilemma: what is he now to do with the incriminating tapes for, in confirming his client's suspicions, his snooping may have murderous consequences? It has happened before: back in 1968, in New York City, three people killed and Caul has been haunted by this ever since. So he decides to keep the tapes, but he is betrayed and 'the Director' obtains them anyway. And now Caul decides to intervene: he takes the adjacent hotel room to where the lovers have arranged their rendezvous, hoping to intercept and way-lay the vengeful husband. But all is not as it seems. Caul is utterly dumbfounded to discover that it is his client, the jealous husband, who has been murdered. Finally he comes to understand his misunderstanding. We hear the fateful words spoken again: "He'd kill *us* if he got the chance." Not so much innocent lovers as lethal conspirators. What a difference a little stress, an accent, makes! The entire meaning, the significance, of a conversation hangs on such infinitesimal inflections. And this can be a matter of life and death. Caul made the wrong call. Notwithstanding all his long experience, his technical wizardry, his fancy equipment, his hi-tech gismos, he was able to listen in but not to hear. He was not there; he was not privy to the conversation, so mistakes are to be expected. In the circumstances, he did the best he could.

We can excuse Caul's confusion and consternation – he was never meant to be part of the conversation. Indeed, even when one is, one can still find oneself left on the outside. Nowhere is this more excruciatingly imagined than in another film from the 1970s, Claude Goretta's quietly moving masterpiece *The Lacemaker* (*La Dentellière*, 1977). Holidaying in Normandy with her overbearingly loud and brash workmate Marilyn, a gauche and diffident young woman, Beatrice (Isabelle Huppert), finds herself involved with a smug Sorbonne student (François played by Yves Beneyton). Back in Paris, the relationship continues and they move in together but the distances between them, between their social circles, between their daily routines (on his side, pretentious bourgeois intellectualism, on hers, the tedium of floor-sweeping in a hairdressers' salon) remains acutely difficult and embarrassing for them both. At a typical student party, all Left Bank pseudo-philosophising, existential angst and counter-cultural posturing, a bemused Beatrice takes François aside and asks him a question: what exactly does "dialectic" mean? She has overheard it and wants to understand. It is, he replies with his customary condescension, a conversation between opposing positions. Enough said, he rejoins his pontificating friends leaving her nonplussed and none the wiser. Or rather wiser only in this: that their conversations, such as they are, will never involve genuine mutual understanding and sharing; they will only ever be a turning away from, never a turning towards, one another. This brief meta-conversation about the dialectic – that productive and progressive confrontation of a thought (thesis) by its opposite (antithesis) and resolution into a new idea (synthesis, a new thesis) – is an act of exclusion in the guise of an explanation. It comes with no exchange, no encouragement, no invitation. It is utterly one-sided, ironically undialectical. She loves him; he rather likes himself, too. She tries but fails to understand him; he sees no need to understand her. And so it is that François and Beatrice have no real conversations: their encounters are only ever reductive, regressive. She is silenced, she retreats. Their lop-sided relationship fails and she, ever more withdrawn, finally becomes a forlorn figure of pathos: sitting, fantasizing, in a room in an institution.

If it is to endure, expand and encompass ever more, conversation needs an inexhaustible curiosity about, and attentiveness to, the other(s). It requires an openness to and readiness for ever greater intimacy and intensity. All conversations depend upon a sense of mutuality, the most profound and memorable ones are grounded in something more fundamental: 'friendship' seems perhaps too weak a feeling, 'love' perhaps too strong. But they may be the best words we have.

III

And all this leads us to the writings of the German cultural theorist and colleague of Benjamin, Siegfried Kracauer (1889-1966), for it is he who, in the course of three short texts[3], locates the enterprise and experience of conversation as the very lifeblood coursing through real friendship, such friendship understood here as an enduring communion of the whole person, as something akin to love. His starting point is to distinguish friendship as a privileged type of relationship from similar but lesser forms of human interpersonal connection and social solidarity: 'comradeship,' a bond based on a common situation and experience in relation to a shared endeavour, purpose and goal; 'collegiality,' a tie with those who share the same profession or career / calling (*Beruf*) and with it a particular set of codes and values; and 'acquaintance', a link based on happenstance and involving a sharing of certain aspects of the self but initially, at least, of a superficial kind. What is distinctive about friendship, Kracauer insists, is its scope and intensity: genuine friendship, the 'ideal' friendship that is, is a profound and fundamental mutual involvement of all aspects of a person's being, that is to say, an enduring and intimate engagement of the full personality of otherwise free and independent individuals. For Kracauer, friendship is a shared recognition and correspondence of our innermost selves, a harmonious and lasting meeting of hearts and minds, a touching of souls. Rare and precious, such friendship is close to love, but bereft of sex and eroticism. And, one might well ask, what has all this to do with conversation? According to Kracauer, conversation and friendship are inextricably interwoven or, better, mutually productive. On the one hand, friendship only emerges in the course of conversations understood as a process of increasingly intimate exchanges, as ever greater mutual disclosures; on the other, this sharing of the self with another, this turning towards each other, is only possible in the context of (an openness to) friendship. Importantly, such conversations do not always rely on agreement or accord: friends share certain aspects of their inner-being, but do not dissolve into one another. The most productive conversation, and by this Kracauer is thinking of those turned towards philosophical matters (beauty, virtue, justice, the Absolute), is that in which the interlocutors present opposing views with ever more intensity in the common pursuit of an ever elusive truth. Open to the opinions of the other, but resolute in one's own convictions, the to and fro of unreconciled arguments unfolds ever more aspects of the problem, reveals ever new dimensions, probes ever more deeply into the matter, whose truth may never be finally penetrated, but is ever more closely approached. The conversation is not directed to reconciliation and conclusion, but to foster the ever greater involvement of the discussants, to prompt them to ever new discoveries, ever new visions and revisions. The conversation between friends is, in short, a kind of dialectic, one similar indeed to that infinite process of unfolding that Benjamin sees as the hallmark of genuine art criticism. And it is in this sense that one might think of this book as a conversation: as a conversation, that is, between friends, between artists through their artworks, as an ongoing and endless process of mutual unveiling and passionate disclosure oriented towards an ever deferred 'final' truth.

Of course, this is a conversation of a curious kind: it is a silent one. But this is perhaps as it should be. Indeed, the paradox of the silent conversation is significant for Kracauer in a number of different ways. There is, of course, that conversation which remains mute because it is between those who are apart, separated by time and space, that communication mediated by letters, the correspondence. And this, he suggests, is perhaps a privileged conversation for it is often the case that one may write what one cannot or dare not say, disclosing on paper those most intimate aspects of ourselves. In letters, as in artworks perhaps, we express and exchange what we are otherwise unable or unwilling to voice: as documents of our innermost selves, they are perhaps the most revealing self-portraits. And there is more. Kracauer argues that the 'silent' conversation may actually constitute its most profound, most perfect form, its ideal: it is one between those friends for whom there is such a degree of mutual intimacy and shared understanding that speech is simply unnecessary. When each knows the other so well, so completely, when they are able to anticipate every word and thought, each turn of the argument, each and every remark and riposte, then the conversation between them may unfold in their own heads without need of any utterance, as a dialogue played out as an inner monologue. Perfect friendship, the correspondence of minds, is unspoken. We are together and lovingly say everything by saying nothing.

This leads us on to what is perhaps most important: in the continual examination of Sutcliffe's work we are not mere eavesdroppers in a (silent) conversation (unlike Caul) but participants as well (unlike Beattrice). Conversations, perfect or otherwise, do not simply end when the interlocutors part. If they inspire us, challenge us, even irritate us, sufficiently, then they will persist in our minds precisely as some kind of continuing interior monologue. A conversation can be, should be, must be, so memorable that it endures and travels silently but surely with us. Indeed, our heads contain the traces, the echoes, of so many such unforgotten, unforgettable conversations over the years and all these accompany us like an invisible host of speakers, a veritable choir of polyphonous voices wherever we may go. And this must be the highest aspiration of this celebration: by means of the legacy of artworks, to start a precious and persistent conversation within the minds of its readers, for them to carry beyond the confines of these pages and into all their future discussions with loved ones, with friends, and even acquaintances, colleagues and comrades. And in this way, Stuart will be remembered. This is the best any of us can hope for.

Graeme Gilloch writes mainly on Critical Theory
and Contemporary Urban Culture.
He is a reader in Sociology at Lancaster University.

1 See Roland Barthes, *Camera Lucida*, Vintage Press, London, 1993.

2 See Benjamin's doctoral thesis from 1919: *The Concept of Art Criticism in German Romanticism* in *Selected Writings Volume 1*, Harvard University Press, Cambridge (MA), 1996.

3 See Kracauer's essays *On Friendship* (*Über die Freundschaft*, 1917/18); *Thoughts on Friendship* (*Gedanken über Freundschaft*, 1921) and *The Nurturing Conversation* (*Das zeugende Gespräch*, 1923) collected together and published in *Über die Freundschaft*, Suhrkamp Verlag, Frankfurt am Main, 1971.

Stuart Sutcliffe in his attic studio, Hamburg
Photograph by Astrid Kirchherr 1961

> Here, hour after hour...
> screaming at the frustration...
> pain and helplessness

STUART SUTCLIFFE

HAEMORRHAGE IS AMONG MY FAVOURITE WORDS

by Richard Makin

Big space is opening up nearby, then comes the thaw. There is a gap, which sees us baffled, sick at hazard (probably loss of consciousness, an amber warning). It might be said that symbols of this kind express. No, that was not foreseen.

By the rib is signified the purview of the deceased. Logical operation grasps the essence of a thing, to the exclusion of its accidents. Not is vivified, a sound in the glass series: stillness, excavated—white-yellow, red and yellow—radio elegy, the voyager's return, untitled multiforms. Onement, or neither.

The figure had eight planes and seven bars, a dazzling field of chrome. Without changing the key of the passage, endure a simple movement. Which seems to have been the earlier form? Discontinue this meeting for a time, without dissolving. Such and such a thing is the old figure X of the beyond. At the beginning I knew absolutely nothing of what my hand would write.

Begin again. It is utterly impossible that the increase and preservation could have been due to such gods as these. My feet are tender, rough the volving earth below.

The sky is dark at night. As there are an infinite number of stars, it should be uniformly bright. Without opening the mouth, here comes the fast of weeks—who can so severely reject the object, stubbornly neglect? I have my X-ray for the neck, subconscious lurching forward, smote agin a wall. People have died in here, whole armies: guided suicide trips—pathological or panic, anomic or passive, chronic or mediated. And, in case you're wondering, it's almost certain: slabs of pig-iron, vast empty tunnels, a disused blast-furnace. We can always rework some of the photographs—you culprit, lend me your lobe, I beg you. The range of possible noises that homo loquens can produce is ultimately compromised. On the evening of the second day, they forsook the law.

She claims the text looks rather bleak, an anticipation. A repeated basal note resounds from the adjoining unit. They still expose their dead on towers of silence. Then her legs slid off my shoulders and fell to the floor with a thud.

He says I think it's more to do with the blood. The final published work was a birth chart. Their offspring is bicephalous. By lucky chance we lie parallel.

Stop describing everything that you're doing. I am going to sit here and watch the Polaroid fade: me with Venus high left, head tilted slight to side, surviving hand at flank, feet rooted to concrete groyne. I knew it had to be very simple, and at the same time very precise. Back then I lay on the stone tiles, back then, I.

Authorities, they're in for a little exile. Then I pointed to the paper with its drawings and asked, quietly.

Leave then and pass on, with sail and oar. With all his force, each drive his own barque. . . . Because nobody, ever-fading.

These lapses of memory occur everywhere and every minute, like seed-pods exploding: an instance of communication by talking, or more occult means. Listen, fingers would often blister. Art appeals from beginning to end as the most inhuman of occupations.

An ocean, aside from scale, aside from the rate of speed, which vary. And pulling alongside, the others, who were like and unlike myself. What substance was innocently eating at his brain? The list of these inflections was made by means of a body.

Of feeling alien within your own tongue.
Yes, that is what we must do. We must take the most minute precautions. (Why ask.) Become the weal of a far too human generation: the whole universe and that mankind—the supporting base for the essential, quaking it with the ancient.
At that point I learnt the whole story in a single rush. But the horoscope consists of one circle only, shuddering down the steps from the cell aloft. It's as though the earth opens up to draw the dead man into it. The same man told his neighbour what had happened, and the neighbour could not believe him.
Apply alas to chords, in which such notes concur, the sheer or steep frontage. What is difficult is to prepare ourselves.

Not long afterwards.
A subsequent staining with Hofmann's blue, a heartless thump, hot air from the cooling bricks. Analysis is a prolonged nervous breakdown—a curve whose radius vector represents the velocity of a moving point; from a way, and to write.
Up in the sky, a gigantic corpse balanced on the shoulder of Orion, the waves rolling far off their quivering. Lots of things happened very naturally, by degrees, even if subtle hostage: sackcloth, the life of the soil, miles of curious glazed galleries. An object can be found in the top right-hand corner (first line). He is a player of substance. We have put you through the mill, have we not, the acres? He would suddenly illuminate controversial subjects by a single remark: jolt-fast, missive, the executrix. It was a two-hundred-yard pulse derangement.
His concentrated face, again, a living portrait of the inevitable return. I too was born out the ear.

Membranes of the cord. Dreadful we said in unison. In the beginning is repetition; it separates the ash from the sublimate. A game is played in which a drawing is made up gradually, from our component parts. You are a writing machine. Failing to help someone in distress accounts for only a minor difference.

They strutted about the stage and played with their wires. A spurt flew across this world (I thought I would lose that hand, that nail). There was a lot of energy expanding: entropy, the suicide gene—its triangulation. They want the beyond to call out, out-geist.

Then it all fell apart for both men. And mine eyes have fixed phantasmagoria. It is as though. No, don't ask again, it is useless.

The prophets were endowed with stereoscopic second sight. Yet you have vomited up my life from corruption, with bleeding gums. Are we conscripts of arbitrary ills? (If yes, move on.) Two tones are separated by an identical interval—with capital, the amendment.

Today, the sense among me of an exhaustion of atoms. A sea-maw lands on the sill at that very moment, an alleged variant (still same bass note). As it swivels its head the beak raps against the large glass. He appears to be scrupulously accurate, within the limits of my foreknowledge.

Shadow on sundial, a settler (see Chapter XVIII). Note his mispronunciation of exegesis. That dance is an anonymous. And the woman said I saw gods ascending out of the earth. Her hands were sunk in the sand, head flat.

For three short weeks in February steam escaped from half-open lids. So much has happened which I do not understand; call it requiem, a mass for the rest. Who was incapable of holding, retaining? To intensify, see the influences that are not. Spot the difference here. Answer: the neural.

First word of the introit. They who walk without intent. He will withhold.

Anyway, the ideal writing state is melancholy. By now they were working away in silence from sheer exhaustion. It was as though dashed off by someone who could permit himself anything. How many times can a man be split down the middle?

I am without authority he says. In a dream I became him, awake to muzzling pressure at my right arm. A pair of piercing green eyes were glimpsed across the cell: antenna, sharp as an ice-pick.

Be it known, moreover. Here stands forth his own inexorable. They were buried on concrete platforms; a specific class of vision, which is usually understood from a very different point of view. Others believe him to have received injury and death simultaneously. But as to myself, there I demur.

Which is the *ka*, or double, a statute of the dead? Just say no.

Illicit ghost—I was coming blood, plasma sluicing the gutters. On the left side, the anterior layer has been removed. Untitled persons dwell hereabouts, reeds and tufts of tamarisk. Now who was found hanged? See notebook page in séance.

I ask you, is it not futile to cast a star chart for the dead—signal types and asteroids, too great a desire to be possessed.

He of course was overjoyed to have his voice back. One must make oneself a seer. Trust yourself. He, however, denies that heredity has anything to do with it. They are indifferent to all that might befall them. And the pendulum weights of the lantern are once again set in motion.

He was found twenty leagues beneath the peninsula, minus the little finger—third phalanx broke, anterior ligament torn (unintentional, mind). Who is thy assassin? Time has appropriately been called. This life/factory is (absolute) hell, or, is (a) hell of its own making.

She flew to gather them up, calling hysterically over her shoulder. A prophetic vision takes her back to her land, where life is regulated by the setting and rising of the sun, and whose cult is the resurrection of the dead. This condition of hopelessness was triggered by a sense of purpose.

The sound was like the sound in films when the alien is here. There is no choice. Cover them survivors up she barked. The leg was cut, its sap is flooding that loathsome terrain. Under a strangely transparent, I wait for you.

In time of war the selection for treatment of those casualties most likely to survive is maintained, beams of broken light. An hour seems too soon. What risk is there in attraction through indifference? His face slowly turned towards me. The behaviour of synapses is being researched. What rematches would you like to see? Any port, any time, any where? It was much better. There was a difference. Fill up the mouth: its incapacity is only a childhood (statement, diction, elocution, lexis). Words have not always been subject to our materiality.

All covered within blood they were, but with scrapings of gold under the fingernails. He did not possess me for an instant, which brings us back to this subject of the conflux. And who would willingly annul himself? And which distant object could no longer be an arc of white light? (See, I can talk about anything, without the least need for transmission.) Who within the gathered room was deemed clairsentient? Think of me as a porous wall, she said. Drinks should never be blue, everybody knows that.

Underfoot, the disfigured pavement frazil. It is still winter, ebbing. It is always. Desire is poured upon.

Plastromancy.

As above, but using the underside of the turtle shell. There are lines too in the neck, the forehead, the lips, the hams, the elbows. Walls of ice have built up across several rivers. Yellow and black juxtaposed brings on severe headaches. Having made this reservation we can say that a death-demon once existed. Just then, bare light in a hard-glass tube, closed at one end. On the floor in a corner the silhouette of a man appears. I myself was at the portal. I lingered. Words were half-pronounced, without opening the mouth; on the floor I am more at ease. These sentences remind one of the titles of lost works (a bold psychological portrait, with a corresponding de-emphasis on plot and setting). He did not think it was a good choice. The allies too had their first aerial photographs in the cruelest month: hospital or madhouse or death, in an undefined way.

Contemplation of his life, the will not yet pacified. It was a decision, like writing love letters for a dictionary—living in half-constructed hotels with the lost, that legless bent shadow, a retrospective act of beating wings. Any apparatus for tracing the paths of charged particles will do, from a way, and to see.

To fail to keep or obtain. To be deprived or bereaved of. To cease to have. To cease to hear, see or understand. To confuse or bewilder. To mislay. To lay waste (e.g. time). To mismatch. To be defeated in. To cause the loss or ruin of. To cause to perish. To bring to ruin. To get away from. To suffer waste or loss (of a clock or watch). To become a loss.

I am mighty systematic. During long reversals such as these, the untouchable. Analysis means dying (synthesizing too, as it happens). When he gets about ten yards further on, he stops and looks back. Don't.

So opened he not his mouth. I dedicate myself anew to your destruction. Above, I simply meant 'that-which-hides'.

Being themselves so uncomfortably situated in the meanwhile, when, from the south-west, a bird-headed one emerges. He was pursued, possessed, that's what the stones said. The group of spirits was called host, and I put him in it, right at the head of it. Consider just observing the face with a stationary camera. Or (he says) alongside me hover the others who are different, and yet identical to me. Do you approve the working title, blue posts? Works could be exhaustive. He left me without, memory listing to starboard.

Sometimes she frightens even me. There she goes, the annunciation. Together they separate the outside from the inside. The position of body, head, wings et cetera were determined by the roll of dice. This inability to name is not primarily or simply linguistic.

That's magnesia he's reaching for, to keep his hand. No matter who dies, the process is the same (I'm being extremely generous here). By imperceptible degrees, an impatience of breath, lung-drift. I have already had enough. They pass straight through his foundation. They claim that the canon could not contain every word. In a way, I am going beyond the thing, trying to make some kind of presence, trying to claw my way back home. The connection with the insect is not accepted by all.

Denunciation. He pounds on the table in a tight seizure. Transition was always adapted from outside—let prayers go galloping and the light rumble away et cetera. Do you feel the full force-shock of it? Now they form a chain of ever-present, ocean to ocean.

So said: a furrow in thy brain, the tongue that pierced the fearful hollow.

They are negotiating their mutual departure from one another. Urine, oxblood and yellow ochre are ground together between pestle and mortar. When totality does visit accessible regions, full use should be made of chance. Matter feels somehow incompetent: you reel in the face of inexpressible perfection, the overwhelming. If you're not there, you don't know, and you don't sense it. There were all types of ability constellated in that bare room. I didn't know what an antichrist was until I became one.

A broken will to live—well, they will know it tomorrow, unlucky day. My voices stretch, uneven. I once lived time of unsparing delusion.

Spectacular: by to build is signified to raise up what has fallen. Origin is haemorrhage, is unknown. As long as you suffer, I want to suffer.

They have traced: scapulimancy, heating and then reading the cracks in an animal—divination by means, examination of the fissures that appear in a burning shoulder blade. Neolithic spleen culture . . . (the text of this chapter is much mutilated).

On the theme of our hereditary insanity.

I thought it would shatter, the large glass. In his humiliation, judgment was mistaken. For what, or whom?

He just manages to squeeze the head in. He almost knocked himself out on the way through. What had sprung the blade? There was a hidden release at the opposite end of the casket.

What a timely riposte. It all depends how the light swings for us. What deed was begun by an earlier skull, vibrating? (Tell me, spirit.) The teeth are firmly clenched together. It was all quite possible. And I cannot remember ever having entered this room. I'd rather be dead she said: haemorrhage is among my favourite words. The patient was hung up by the jaw alone for several minutes. Apply any music of similar character, at rest, obsolete. Apply copious electricity.

Now, musing on suicide once again, the symptom.

The howling of a distant dog. Poisoning is only one of them. And nothing could be heard but the sound of their laboured, faltering steps. He seems not to understand.

Crater work in process, spiral jet, four quad cinema—yellow and black cells with conduit. After much agonizing and numerous stops and starts: unknowable, who are my helpmate?

Dreams too: making a killing. The ash tree.

I think this gentleman is right, we must go and see.

People around a table. Severe fatigue and flux. I am surpassed by mine own shadow: a sheet of water, startled flat. The blade swings closer like an exposed chest (publication is the road to death, everybody knows that). And his adversary drove the point through one of my vacant sockets. It looks very much as if we're assisting in the unravelling of a tragedy: compressed linear elements, acute sensitivity to light—the Greek mercury, whose burst is known. The origin of the name is uncertain, perhaps a fall from the lower shelf of a precipice. You cannot die. One of the most spectacular types is the materialization.

Actually, art and literature have been in great demand of late. The square floor of heaven is made of a sheet of iron. There is no point. We're lost. The letter is in the box.

As you drive through, you don't always know what's beneath your feet. Are those bird-things perching there, pecking at the shingle? Now I have lost all hope of crawling inside the canvas. Which is the *ba*, a bird with human head?

Systemic reproaches. An influx of blood floods upon us. And he did it not, the needful act.

Notes for an inverted astrological chart: the death-day et cetera.

Yes, it was the cruelest month. By professional lexicon do we mean the language used is trammelled, confined, quarantined? I was once there with saint butler, hung mystery behind a glass vitrine. It was no coincidence. Bring your lips to this water, drink (so called because a spider cob).

Hired hands on the quarter-deck—paranormal-critical activity recurs, quite uninsurable. As you're aware, this was his only means of reaching the unknown. Are you so ill that you cannot hold a pen she asks.

Leech in right ventricle of brain. I could get killed a dozen times every night. (What annunciation?)

That walnut dresser, ex-memory limbs, scarcely a few grains on the lining of the brain-pan. I can only feel when they're not here any longer.

Apparently influenced in sense, in sensation. By-lees, and in pronunciation, by loose. So familiar, yet so painfully remote.

He failed to keep. Who plays assassin-in-waiting? There were cut grooves for the flexor tendons. A ship, which had been given the name much sought-after, was placed at our disposal. He is trying, unsuccessfully, to set up his own resistance group:

Prologue.
Sacrifice.
The golden fleece.
Escape.
Lost faith.
A new life.
Over-embellishment, over-brilliant.
Profligate: a man dissolving before my very eyes.
Allusively, a house of ill fame.
An etymological form of current.
Death of the sun, again and again.
A gift.
Exiled.
Goodbye.
Revenge.
Notes were placed in a metallic regression, raised or lowered by the accidentals. Dura mater (indicating the relationship of things), arachnoid membrane, pia mater. X-rayed

disappointments. Now I think I understand what homoeostasis means in this family. And I sat around the wires to hear it, softer than sound or odour, just several congratulatory paragraphs. Arrows were loosed from a steady head, a moment of breath-taking. If only you had never come to our shores. Back then I did not know you. A large golden hangs from the ceiling. I think of him as a kind of honorary suicide; creatures of all kinds live down here. Who cannot talk through this silence? The playing-cards stick to your fingertips.

    The lovers.
    Here we see a young man flayed by two women. There is no mercy for us. I surrender to you. (See notes on levitation.) And he who bears witness to all these things, he speaks.
    Yes, I come soon, so great was this earquake. We'll massacre all signs of logical retardation. The man is still staring at him, in disbelief.
    Tragedy signifies yellow prism with underground conduit. This is surely my last day, strewn to and fro: foundations of blood—sometimes I feel my own blood is spewing forth—an interlacing, an enveloping connection of one nerve-cell with another, to the very mark of their inscription. What is the word. It derives from the impossibility of speaking the phenomenon.
    No index of terminations at the gallows gate. The volume of gas in the plastron was negligible. Consider the clarity of the principles, the interventions.
    We are represented by an order of insects with four transparent wings. Perhaps their light will fight off the light of day.
    End, and it all ends with the clang of a broken tongue: who hath relieved you, and so on.

    This takes us back to post-war years. (I don't live at all in myself, as you know.) But most dangerous of all, you are not alone. Finding yourself without arms of any kind, you must accept. There are the endless contours. This is about all I know of the banal and of the everyday—the prospect and the fulfiller, channelling white strata, sum of the head. Language no longer obeys the desire for realization. I left him temporarily blind. This boy was about, with the sloping forehead and the curve of an ancient. Turn on the afterburners—the atmosphere in the stadium is raw and expectant. I gather up my material, then subject it to a sort of poetic derangement. The root knots of chords shuffle in, weird twilight. I don't remember when the first of them succumbed.
    Now this strange collapse of my face—a skull, fractured, indented at the crown (where he's genuinely inspired). This is why we've got a narrative verdict today. She is away within her own son's body, and all it could ever foreshadow. Headless horses scoured the countryside. He was unable to provide. A sort of hollowing out is taking place (they used to years ago, didn't they). I was silent for a moment.
    Structure this like a dialogue between the voice of a narrator, i.e. a conversation. He said he had lied on purpose. It was an open aphorism, destruction and explosion of syntax. Consider the place, and the bodies in that place: into non-image is blood, mine own electric thing,

feel. Those consumed in love show defiance to the grave——both it will blur, confound.

He went into a convulsion, delirious with joy and pain. There was still time for lots of things to happen. Then, before my eyes, he faded into the midwinter frost. I remember his translucent hands. And upon the skewered eyelids, back-sleep of night.

Schema, a habit of declining. The cranial nerves number nine on each side.

This chapter is a short hymn to Osiris. It all starts pretty attritional, with a murmur, a whisper, a rustling. Pluto in Leo saps him of his strength (their relationship was plutonic). Christ, she writes like a social worker, I write like a sociopath——of shutters, green night with dazzled nows et cetera. Who came with endless ear, guttering candle-light, rivulets of wax at the turn of road before a blackened city gate? Suicide was such a neutral object. They claim that an apparition of the animus is an angel from the beyond. Below is a reference diagram for waves refracted by electric current: one picture of the imminent future and another of the ultimate—— he that dashes, in pieces.

The weakness of this position lies in judging him in a vacuum of atomic writing. There is precious data on the gradual evolution of this faculty. Whenever I do this, it's the guide speaking.

Down the steps from the antic room, surrounded by saints, body on bed (interior)—— the double spiral and contingent meander-band. And that semi-human figure in the foreground, was that foreseen? (No.) It is incised by markings which conjure the earliest form of writing. From the remains it is impossible to design a connected translation, to make clear or manifest. A Hermes is found at every cusp.

On the theme of hereditary insanity.

I very like your sketchiness indeed. It is an inevitable result of our complex denial. We should seek compensation in the world of fiction. But not in himself.

He says all composers have varied their styles to fit purpose. Here, in the ninth tile from the door, it tells how to turn the old into young ones. (The body just wasn't in the right place.) It's a bit like science-fiction. They didn't need the opiates after all. Perhaps it was said in error, as an order of angels; one can hardly fail to hear the echoes. The culmination of this part of the poem is not an accident (what the tundra said et cetera). They give these factors old names, which they excise from the traditionals, e.g. the appropriate length of wave crest for deep water, from equation. My mediumship has changed considerably during eight years of practice. The heel of my palm left a depression in the plaster.

In silence, from all voice. Did the worship of the gods help in the acquisition? Only yesterday was I born. Surface and colour changes reduce atmospheric energy. I pass my time without the cult of memory: one does not have the right.

Abscess on spine. Hallelujah, I love you (her so-so). Homo duplex. A vast disorder of answers: the structure of the human vocal and hearing apparatus is responsible. You'll be mine.

You have to breathe or you'll choke. (It's all part of the conversation.) I drifted on a soft calm sea for two days and a night. And who among you shall declare his generation? But I have tasted every pain in this world—accusative of form and of rest, of a negative, opaque. A prologue made by an uncertain author.

It keeps repeating the word acorn. The room is black with silver foil. The walls are of tin, the famous metal. Below us, stretching to the horizon, an enemy sea, red crack opening up across the sky. I know well-nigh what circuit you are in, barely unalike. Extending inland for one hundred and fifty miles is an unfeatured blank.

But for the ear, a silence. A terrible and implacable brevity is due at the end of the week. I find myself back in the studio. (Studio?)

One more week to go he says (it is the third, Easter). And how he wants to disintegrate, and how he wants, overlaid with scratches of cortex, the outer layer of certain organs: zoo bark. Everything hinges on this, the creaking and splitting of background noise.

The pharmacy has distilled this effect. Outside, those powdery drifts, leeward side of any obstacle. Avoid being dominated by your materials. There has been a change in subject matter. He has reached such a pitch of nervous sensibility, stuttering dialogue—from to turn about, go about, disassociate, dwell. From intent, and to keep turning, from to turn.

From that moment on he began a new life. The incident recurs (sleep). Repulsion means 'can't separate off from context'.

A small blue-legged, domestic, wielding smooth hammerhead (see hard-boiled fiction). It has an area and stands at the confluence, just upstream of the hollow. That is why this open narrative verdict, like machined shapes creating enclosed spaces, votive offerings. Only one of us will survive the ordeal. There is nothing Elizabethan left in them. Our people once said the dead are making a comeback. Spinning the blade tip within the monster skull, it did for mine eyes.

Thumb upturned, jutting backwards toward empty space, the wall. Weeping as silently as I could, a brain teaser was anticipated. Answer: by equating wave energy transfer across the boundaries. I am suspicious of that renegade from the moment.

One evening, as they were about to leave, a diminutive child entered. (Lookout cartilage.) Something shot out of the other end. Wouldst thou ever tell a monstrous lie? And the dream about the dream: backlight, through which he struck out at me, piercing the lung. What event shall signify the three remaining points of the compass?

Far from her land, she is terrorized by the imprint of an irrespective reality, dull routes with swerving pain. It made no difference to me at the time whether they had set fire, or not.

The fable of the man.

I have mistaken my text from the works. I have burrowed the germ of my idea. All reasonable precautions must be taken. The platform is supported at the four points of the compass by columns of air, such that it is shaped.

Knife visibly evident, festivals of impotence, brief lives. How long ago. How long ago can this go on for? Catastrophe means the earth rises and falls in waves. The name means divine—to ears it may suggest, however, from a lost occasion.

A steep rock face, especially. The land borders the sea, the flank of a mountain. I do not care if she can never come back. It is a question of determining the relationships. Things are not difficult to accomplish. If only I had left you to fade, never healed you.

Extreme left, in front of fallow, of elbow crease. A footnote, or self-portrait. He was dismissed in the general revulsion (the against aesthetic). Such an act always follows exposure. It was time to swallow a sharp stop, void of space. The basis of these methods consists in causing a swelling of the cell-wall. The death experience breaks down all redundant order. He smiles and nods then crawls off down the corridor.

I'm with the clash on this: in living gouts of blood, which was not so before, but the sea, the sea rebels. I don't know because that's history. Neck keeps coming up Kodak. I am fighting off his attackers, the rattle of chains and pulleys, the book of the dead. A figure is representing. Nothing had changed, his calloused back. The arachnoid membrane is so named from its extreme thinness: it is a shut sac. O yes, and it's not over yet. The state sells memory; someone's got to do it.

Salutations, ink. It is nineteen sixty (the date). There is the desire for circularity. And however once, noise, then he quietened down. It is the period of forgetfulness and commemoration. It has taken charge of my life, fire without flame. We separate the sky from the earth. Then an iridescence, whirring, flew in through the carriage window. The surrendered landscape through which we travel is karst: lineaments of lime and scrub, underground drainage—maquis, from to mesh. Our forelimbs are reduced to horny covers for the hind wings.

Flesh from the transformation, puffs of vapour through nose and mouth rise toward the ceiling. The object is to produce a completeness, especially with capital. Nothing more is possible, ever.

To jut, to overhang (first found). To scurry through (always applied to brows). Overhanging forms, to bite, to bite into.

Consider a thing destitute of beats (e.g. the heart is now). The instrument was once used for driving wedges, crushing paving-stones or the like. A wooden was pestle-shaped. It's the way he stands. A padre was apprehended and told the news. Farewell to here, or to anywhere.

Crouching woman, distemper. A manifest wall of white ice, perpendicular face of considerable height. Strata are broken and exposed in section: an escapement, territory in bird life. The chalk-bled species are difficult to navigate.

Scarcely disfigured, treason in hell. A distinctive tone rings at every interval. From the other direction, the din of combat. Inconstant, our own desires build the revolution—whoever masters the poetics of the present must expect misadventure. I am comparable to the boy who fell in love with the sea. I am unused to secondaries, syncopated heat, with break-beaten spine. You always said I was a nervous wreck.

Contact, juncture—from together, and to fasten. Wars broke out, countries rose in revolt.

Nervous ganglia near terminus of body. The choke was encased in red cellophane. His chronicle, not authorized and never checked, was the immediate cause of collapse. It is here from to burst. It is vouched a discharge, outflux from vessel, a steady and persistent leaching away (figuratively speaking). It had a name: shrouder or hider, wings folding back inside the body.

Thrown, head first (the head known as Hermes). What is she looking at.

Pyromancy: observing the behaviour of certain objects when placed on sacrificial embers, as well as the shoulder blade. The word refers also to care. Between appearing and vanishing, what do you think I said? I started dreaming. I was him/you, beyond a crease of light. An operation to discharge occurred; from a perforation in the breast comes the sound of trickling water.

Dialogues about servitude began, scorning distance and time, a conquered space. He gets up. He tries to lift himself. The knees buckle first.

A topical, with lilac-coloured flowers, rust aerosol and seepage in the star well. I would not if I were you. Divination is by means of observation, the moments of a dying man. His journey is in reverse: kitchen sink port, lost sounds in the glass series—window, self-portrait, genes and blistered glands. Killer ice cascading from the eaves, above, again and again.

Impatient, death comes of age, the lightning hem. He was what mediums call a schismatic. Now I, alone, a vessel lost in the voltage.

Anything projecting: the clipped edge, the escape hatch. The tail-lights of aircraft punctuate the night sky, a small victory of ambiguity and approximation.

Richard Makin is the author of *Dwelling*, a novel published by Reality Street in 2011.

The Beatles, Hamburg 1960. From left to right: John Lennon, George Harrison, Pete Best, Paul McCartney and Stuart Sutcliffe.
courtesy of The Stuart Sutcliffe Estate

> 66
>
> He was more than just a bass player,
> he was like our Creative Director
>
> 99
>
> GEORGE HARRISON, MBE

RESPONSES TO A LIFE FOREVER FROZEN IN POP MYTHOLOGY

by Fisun Güner

Marked 'early', 'middle' and 'late' as if decades might have separated them instead of the few years that can be counted on one hand, Stuart Sutcliffe's body of work can be viewed on the website run by his sister Pauline. Those early, pre-artschool years already show his gift as a subtle colourist, but little of the delicate lyricism and the intuitive painterliness of the ten, or so, months he spent at Hamburg State School of Art under the tutelage of visiting professor Eduardo Paolozzi.

Paolozzi described Sutcliffe as his most gifted student, and one can see that this young artist might have been a very significant one had he lived beyond his 21 years. A range of contemporary northern European influences are clearly evident, but to describe the works simply as pastiche would be an assessment that overlooks an extraordinary facility. By his 'middle' period his execution is already confident and the rhythms and textures of his painterly surfaces assured.

It is during this period that we find *Summer Painting*, the work selected for the John Moores' Painting Exhibition in 1959, whilst he was a student at Liverpool Regional College of Art. Shown at the Walker Art Gallery, Liverpool, *Summer Painting* was the first painting Sutcliffe sold in his lifetime, with the money he received going to buy a bass guitar on the insistence of fellow student John Lennon.

At this point, Sutcliffe is clearly searching for a language between figuration and abstraction. He had flirted with the dour Kitchen Sink of John Bratby, though never wholly convincingly, before he finally settled on a dense, layered abstraction that only occasionally makes a teasing but elusive reference to the observed world. He has often been described as an Abstract Expressionist, but his work possesses such a fragile and febrile European sensibility that the label doesn't sit well at all. Wols, Henri Michaux, Nicholas de Staël and Pierre Soulages are all evident as key players in Sutcliffe's development in an output that shows equal facility with painting, monotype and collage.

Interestingly, he never showed any interest in the flat, cool, consumerist culture of Pop, preferring to pursue an intense inner vision.

Sutcliffe's work has been exhibited worldwide, including a critically well-received retrospective at the Victoria Gallery and Museum at the University of Liverpool in 2008, but I admit I'd never encountered it before I had to think about this current project. The 1994 film *Backbeat* (now an acclaimed musical) allowed him to emerge as a romantic presence in the early incarnation of The Beatles, but, understandably, it was a life portrayed only in connection to his complex relationship with Lennon and to his burgeoning love affair with photographer-girlfriend Astrid Kirchherr.

It was Kirchherr who took the early photographs of the group in which Sutcliffe emerges as a moody but sensitive James Dean figure, complete with Ray-Bans. And she was reputedly responsible for the band's trademark 'mop-tops' when she styled Sutcliffe's hair into a cool 'exi' (it wasn't just black polonecks that passed as an existentialist accessory). But, his artwork never had the chance to take on a life of its own and it is certainly true that we would not know of it at all had it not been for his brief brush with pop history.

The contemporary artists who have each elected to be part of *In Conversation*, know him, too, only as an elusive, romantic presence and their responses are variously funny, poignant, tender, oblique and punchily literal. Mark Hampson displays a rather Lennonesque wit when he depicts four goggle-eyed paint brushes. Should we read them as representations of the four band members, or as depictions of Sutcliffe himself as he gradually recedes into the background as each brush gets smaller?

Whichever it is, those swivel eyes and that 'startled' brush of hair do a good impression of stage-fright.

Indeed, Sutcliffe, by all accounts, was never very comfortable on stage, and he certainly wasn't confident as a just about adequate bassist. His attempts to mask his lack of musicianship usually involved playing with his back to the audience, or at least partially turned away from it. This is how Laura Lancaster has decided to portray him, not as the beautiful boy who stares soulfully out from beneath an 'exi' fringe, as he does in so many of the images that exist of him in the public domain. Instead, it's his awkward vulnerability we are invited to observe.

A partial glimpse is also what we get in another of Lancaster's black and white paintings based on a photograph. This time it is of one of Pauline Sutcliffe's favourite snapshots of her brother, though Lancaster crops the image so that it's no longer Sutcliffe and Lennon happily making sand art on a beach but simply a pair of sketchily painted hands patting down sand. Lancaster has depersonalised the image so that it becomes an almost universal family snapshot motif, although one in which an element of disquiet is introduced.

Lancaster's paintings find common ground with other works in which fragments and faded images suggest the elusive nature of memory. Among these we find Uwe Wittwer's and Nick Goss's beautifully tender and deeply evocative paintings. On a surface which resembles a scrap of parchment, Wittwer portrays Paul, John and George sitting at a table in a Hamburg bar alongside a couple of non-Beatles friends. The image is based on a photograph in which arms are draped around shoulders in ostentatious displays of camaraderie. But here Sutcliffe's image has become a whitewashed silhouette. Absence is another form of presence. Goss, meanwhile, paints an image of an empty rehearsal studio, the left side even sketchier than the right, slippery and elusive as a memory of a real place.

Jann Haworth's gives the *Sgt. Pepper* treatment to Sutcliffe's various images. Haworth was the co-creator, with husband Peter Blake, of the famous 1967 album cover, in which Sutcliffe also appeared alongside the famous dead of history. Here the canvas has been pictorially divided into three, the bottom horizontal layer bringing to mind Gilbert & George's decorative but slightly disturbing distortions, as well as a floral funeral pyre.

Some of the works here appear not to reference Sutcliffe's life at all, or at least not directly. You won't find any direct clues in the paintings of Bob Matthews or Andrew Bick. But both artists touch upon aspects of Sutcliffe's work as a painter, looking for signs of musicality within the rhythms and modernist structures of their own work. Others still delve deep to find something of the private, inner life. Flora Parrott's delicately twisting and looping abstract forms, for example, is an attempt to give material expression to Sutcliffe's feelings of uncertainty and to his emotional vacillation. She takes the title of her work *Ignoring Their Gradations* from a letter Sutcliffe wrote to Kirchherr in which he uses the phrase to talk of the "world of shifting forms in which I live".

Only one artist addresses the likely cause of Sutcliffe's premature death. Marilène Oliver's sculpture *Headspace*, represents anonymised MRI scans of a brain aneurism. Using a combination of drilled holes, which catch the light, and tiny dots of ink, which suggest the flow of blood in the brain, the work captures in essence the mystery of ourselves as well as something of the mysteries of the cosmos – the shimmering spots of light against dark matter hinting, rather seductively, at the celestial.

There are twenty artists *In Conversation*, and each has responded uniquely to the demands of a highly unusual commission. These are artists who have had to work around the edges of a life forever frozen in pop mythology. But although Stuart Sutcliffe remains a shadowy, ultimately unknowable figure – and one who never had the chance to develop into full maturity as an artist – this tribute presents a wonderfully rich, multifaceted dialogue.

Fisun Güner is a freelance arts writer.
She is the art critic for The Arts Desk.

- -

66

He certainly was a major attraction because
of the 'James Dean thing', the dark, moody thing.
I think a lot of people liked that, but that was just
the surface. He contributed an intellectual spirit
that we were all happy to pick up on; he was a little
older and he knew more. His artistic quest was
within the group, but I don't think many people noticed
that off stage, except the exis (existentialist crowd),
with Astrid, Klaus and Jurgen. He was also so in
love with Astrid and it peeved the rest of us off
that she hadn't fallen in love with any of us!
It was something none of us had ever seen before;
none of our parents had that sort of relationship

99

Sir PAUL McCARTNEY, MBE, Hon RAM, FRCM

STUART'S WORK

Stuart Sutcliffe's work really is as good as the very best of 2nd generation Abstract Expressionists... I would say that what you have with Stuart was an artist who actually made contact with his primary, primal instincts; it is visceral, channelled raw emotion and raw expression... body and mind together... fascinating and incredible

PROFESSOR DONALD KUSPIT

One of the USA's most prominent Art Critics, Prof. Kuspit is a 'Distinguished Professor of Art History & Philosophy' at the State University of New York, and a 'Professor of Art History' at The School of Visual Arts, New York. In 1983, he won the highly acclaimed Frank Jewett Mather Award for Distinction in Art Criticism

Stuart Sutcliffe portrait
Photograph by Astrid Kirchherr 1960

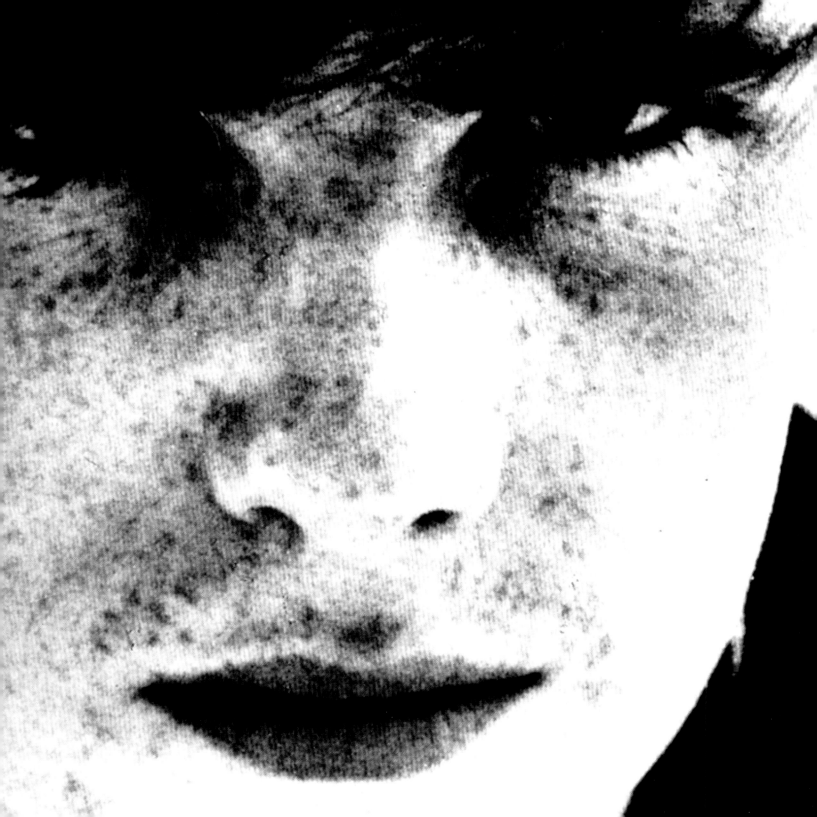

Stuart Sutcliffe and work in attic studio, Hamburg
Photographs by Astrid Kirchherr 1961
Special thanks to Vladislav Ginsburg © 2012

"

Stuart cannot converse with us
today, but perhaps his painting can.
These are his medium, his chosen
form of correspondence

"

GRAEME GILLOCH

UNTITLED
Hamburg Series #1
Oil on canvas, 117 cm x100 cm, circa 1960-62
courtesy of The Stuart Sutcliffe Estate

>
> I'm painting on canvas
> again. I've just completed
> 4 big ones, 4ft x 3ft.
> I think they're quite good
>

STUART SUTCLIFFE

UNTITLED
Hamburg Series #3
Oil on canvas, 100 cm x 117 cm, circa 1960-62
courtesy of The Stuart Sutcliffe Estate

"

When creating in my own perceptual, I construct from my own feelings, as well as from my own visual - tactile or auditory sense-data; things immediately known in sensation - colours, sounds, smells. Therefore, my art is not symbolic of human feelings, it's literally an embodiment of them. In other words, my works are images of feelings

"

STUART SUTCLIFFE

UNTITLED
Hamburg Series #39
Oil on canvas, 117 cm x 100 cm, circa 1960-62
courtesy of The Stuart Sutcliffe Estate

UNTITLED
Hamburg Series #4
Oil on canvas, 134.5 cm x 110 cm, circa 1960-62
courtesy of The Stuart Sutcliffe Estate

"

...over and above the merit of his pictures he has a special significance as somebody whose burning creativity switched from art into pop music and then back again. He showed the way

"

JOHN WILLETT

UNTITLED
Hamburg Series #40
Oil on canvas, 124.5 cm x 99 cm, circa 1960-62
courtesy of The Stuart Sutcliffe Estate

He'd search my mother's kitchen for tools. He would use apple stakes to scratch through the paint and pinch wooden spoons from her cooking drawer. He did a lot of work with ordinary kitchen knives and large decorating bushes... He'd go to hardware merchants for other, more unusual instruments: like putty knives or the metal brushes for removing rust

ASTRID KIRCHHERR

UNTITLED
Hamburg Series #71
Oil on canvas, 134.5 cm x 109 cm, circa 1960-62
courtesy of The Stuart Sutcliffe Estate

> **"**
> There is no poetry to spare for writing -
> its all for love
> **"**

STUART SUTCLIFFE

UNTITLED
Hamburg Series #68
Oil on canvas, circa 1960-62
courtesy of The Stuart Sutcliffe Estate

Only one thing interests me vitally. So vitally,
that I would rather forget it; that absorbing and
transcendence of all that has been omitted by artists.
The age demands violence and we have only abortive
explosions. Do not lose your temper. Let your inside fill
out, until your stomach and brains are so bloated with
pain and strife and despair - till your pores weep tears of
blood, till your eyes sing a song of glass and splinters,
and then let it all go in one mighty atomic fart

99

STUART SUTCLIFFE

UNTITLED
Hamburg Series #90
Oil on paper, 101.5 cm x 79 cm, circa 1960-62
courtesy of The Stuart Sutcliffe Estate

> 66
>
> Interestingly, he never showed any interest
> in the flat, cool, consumerist culture of Pop,
> preferring to pursue an intense inner-vision
>
> 99

FISUN GÜNER

UNTITLED
Hamburg Series #16
Chalk on tissue, 84 cm x 58.5 cm, circa 1960-62
courtesy of The Stuart Sutcliffe Estate

My pictures are still quite conventional in so far as they are two-dimensional. I have only explored colour and shape a little further and there is so much further to push them. What I'm really interested in, is painted sculpture, but this means complete absorption and concentration. Something which needs a great deal of concentrated work for long periods; a complete sacrifice of a lot of ideals

STUART SUTCLIFFE

UNTITLED
Hamburg Series #56
Mixed media on paper, 81 cm x 63.5 cm, circa 1960-62
courtesy of The Stuart Sutcliffe Estate

> His influence has been enormous and the fact that his presence has radiated both the art and rock 'n' roll worlds for over 50 years, is testament to his artistic genius

GILES COOPER

UNTITLED
Hamburg Series #45
Ink and wash on paper, circa 1960-62
courtesy of The Stuart Sutcliffe Estate

UNTITLED
Hamburg Series #29
Collage with oil and ink on paper, circa 1960-62
courtesy of The Stuart Sutcliffe Estate

66

People let us give our soul to our work and let us work with our heart for our cause – and – love what we love – to love what we love!

99

STUART SUTCLIFFE

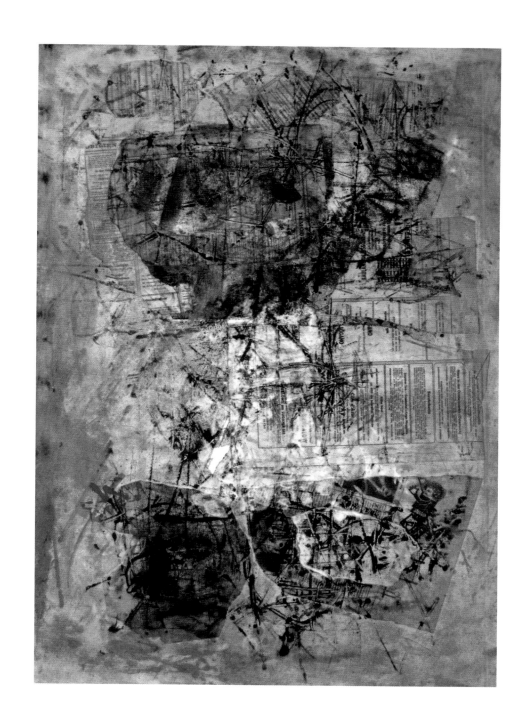

> 66
>
> I do general experiment under this Paolozzi
> fellow. This is a kind of criticism, as it's only a
> general acknowledgement of one's presence.
> This is very confusing at first, even
> frustrating, but eventually this becomes
> necessary to one's peace of mind
>
> 99
>
> STUART SUTCLIFFE

UNTITLED
Hamburg Series #88
Mixed media on paper, 101.5 cm x 81 cm, circa 1960-62
courtesy of The Stuart Sutcliffe Estate

Sutcliffe's slashed red-ink brushstrokes
resonate with me just as much as his
muted thickly coated paintings. They translate
into an aggressive scream that is echoed in
the empty spaces of my imaginary worlds

MARTINA SCMID

UNTITLED
Hamburg Series #10
Mixed media on paper, 78.5 cm x 101.5 cm, circa 1960-62
courtesy of The Stuart Sutcliffe Estate

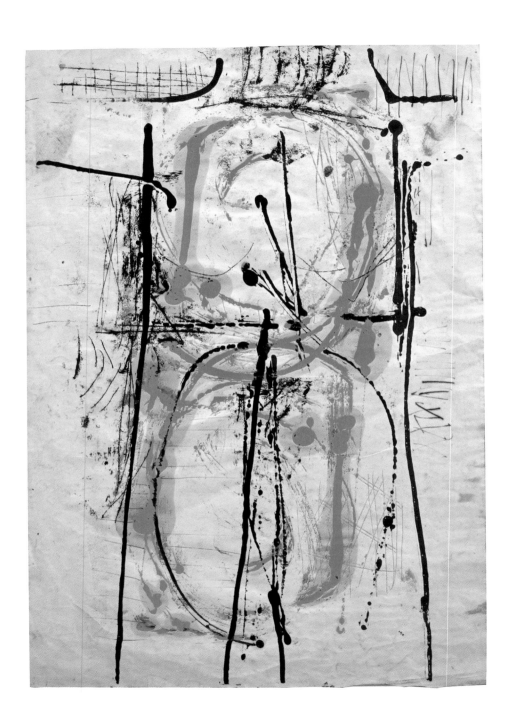

How I long for clarity and yet how I loathe these precise men,
who are never satisfied until they have labelled, ranged and
set aside each separate emotion, ignoring their gradations

STUART SUTCLIFFE

UNTITLED
Hamburg Series #36
Oil on paper, 58 cm x 40 cm, circa 1960-62
Private collection, courtesy of Giles Cooper

"

Abstraction has always had associations with music, also a tendency to draw on disparate and unlikely sources, evidenced through the works of Sutcliffe, and contemporaries that have followed

"

ANDREW BICK

UNTITLED
Hamburg Series #15
Monotype and collage with ink on paper, 100 x 55.9 cm, circa 1960-62
courtesy of The Stuart Sutcliffe Estate

120 121

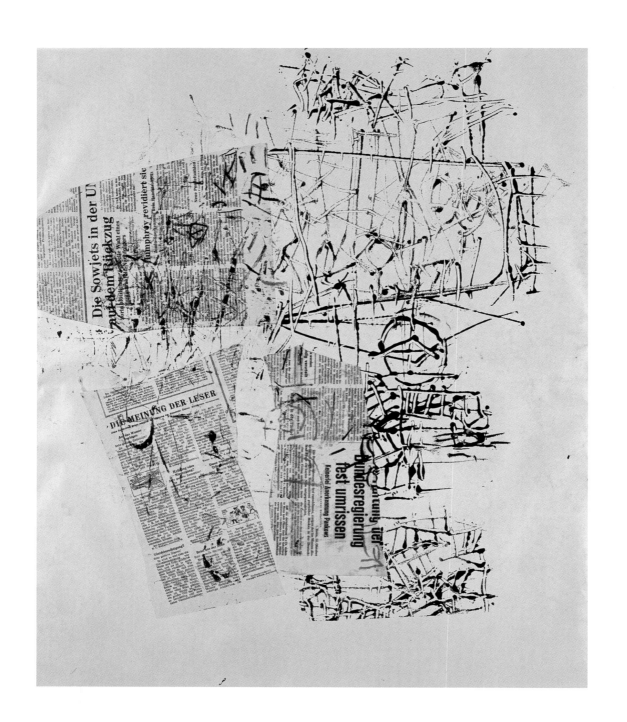

UNTITLED
Hamburg Series #72
Monotype and collage on paper, 68.6 cm x 58.4 cm, circa 1960-62
courtesy of The Stuart Sutcliffe Estate

"

If I stand for five minutes I devour centuries...
the fog, the sieve through which my anarchy
strains, resolves itself into shape. Behind the
shape, chaos... I am suffocated by it. No one to
whom I can communicate a fraction of my feelings

"

STUART SUTCLIFFE

UNTITLED
Hamburg Series #114
Mixed media on paper, 103 cm x 80 cm, circa 1960-62
courtesy of The Stuart Sutcliffe Estate

> **"**
> I have started and things are going quite nicely.
> In a few weeks, I should have a grip on myself.
> My pictures are not so abstract now; vaguely
> figurative and mostly blue
> **"**
>
> STUART SUTCLIFFE

UNTITLED
Liverpool Series #101
Oil on board, circa 1959
courtesy of The Stuart Sutcliffe Estate

> "
> It's been 50 years and Stuart
> still takes my breath away
> "

PAULINE SUTCLIFFE

> **"**
> I take my structures from nature then
> infuse it with expressive colour
> **"**
>
> STUART SUTCLIFFE

UNTITLED
Liverpool Series #87
Oil and mixed media on board, circa 1959
courtesy of The Stuart Sutcliffe Estate

> **"**
> I probably owe a lot to the Celtic love of complicated linear designs
> **"**

STUART SUTCLIFFE

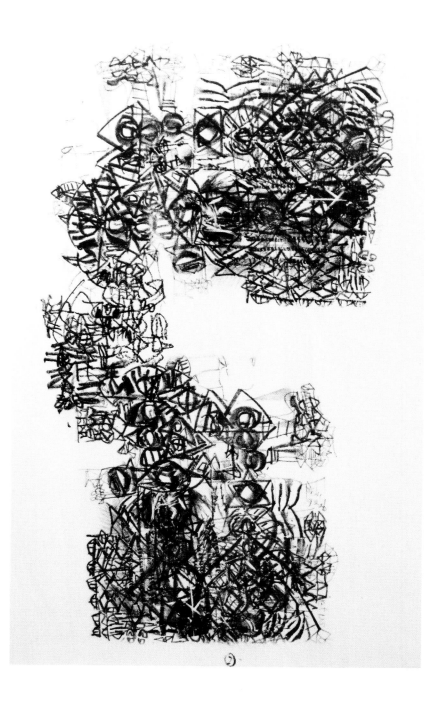

> 66
>
> His life was cruelly cut short,
> but the legacy he left behind was
> his work - and his enthusiasm
> for life, truth and love
>
> 99
>
> CYNTHIA LENNON

UNTITLED
Hamburg Series #910
Lithograph on paper, 68.5 cm x 51 cm, circa 1960-62
courtesy of The Stuart Sutcliffe Estate

The Beatles, Hamburg 1961. Photograph by Astrid Kirchherr
From left to right: Pete Best, George Harrison, John Lennon, Paul McCartney and Stuart Sutcliffe

ARTIST'S RESPONSES
TO STUART'S WORK

Actually it was quite
unrealistic to have considered it,
but for a few moments I allowed
myself the luxury of being a 'rocker'

STUART SUTCLIFFE

Stuart Sutcliffe in his attic studio, Hamburg
On easel: Hamburg Series #3 - see page 90
On floor: Hamburg Series #71 - see page 98
Photograph by Astrid Kirchherr 1961

MICHAEL AJERMAN

Finding an image of a drum set in a shopping catalogue was a godsend, and became the timeless icon that I could stuff, split, and twist, with all my ideas for *In Conversation with Stuart Sutcliffe*. It helped me keep a distance so as not to fall into a blind sense of hero worship for Stuart Sutcliffe, whilst respecting his light that went out too early.

Was the birth of rock n' roll, Robert Johnson tuning his guitar late at night, The Beatles in leather, or Little Richard transferring the sound of trains to a groove? Whatever it is, it feels a long way away. But the echo persists. Rock 'n' roll is very hard to define. Less interested in a contemporary sense of purity, but rather a mutated purity, I have found solace in the sound and imagery of bands like the Melvins and Motorhead. They tour, and they tour hard. Anyone who knows anything about music knows that you can have all the guitar in the world, but if you don't have a tight rhythm (drum and bass). You have nothing. These bands have that.

SLAVE TO THE RHYTHM NO. 1
2011
Watercolour on paper
111.9 x 76.3 cm

SLAVE TO THE RHYTHM NO. 2
2011
Watercolour on paper
112 x 76.4 cm

ANDREW BICK

What marks out Sutcliffe's short career is the European quality within his work, especially at a point when his peers, such as Eduardo Paolozzi, were veering towards Pop Art. Sutcliffe's work is usually described as 'late abstract expressionist', but I see it based in the smaller-scale reflective and analytical build-up that surface painters in Europe were engaged with in the late '50s and early '60s. The association with Nicholas De Staël is about right in these terms, but you would also have to think of Jean Fautrier, Hans Hartung, Wols & Art Informel.

As a young artist Sutcliffe created work that projected an inner emotion, following a path of enlightened vision with explorations into far greater fields than mere paint on surface. The musicality within Sutcliffe's work drew me to the musicality within my own paintings. This, and chance parallels intrigue me; I too sang in a church choir; played bass guitar in a band as a young man; and had a work selected for the John Moores' Painting Prize. There the obvious links end, but I admire his commitment to abstract painting, which evidently he found so important he gave up being in a band for.

This works title, *Heartworn Highway*, is taken from a 1975-76 documentary film on new country and western music emerging in Texas and Tennessee. They are also abstract, playing on the legacies of modernism through combining geometry, the grid, gesture and a complex build-up of surface. Abstraction has always had associations with music, also a tendency to draw on disparate and unlikely sources, evidenced through the works of Sutcliffe, and contemporaries that have followed.

HEARTWORN HIGHWAYS #3
2006-11
Pencil, oil paint, wax and watercolour on wood
48 x 38 cm

HEARTWORN HIGHWAYS #5
2006-11
Pencil, oil paint, wax and watercolour on wood
48 x 38 cm

HEARTWORN HIGHWAYS #7
2006-11
Pencil, oil paint, wax and watercolour on wood
48 x 38 cm

KIT CRAIG

The starting point for this work was thinking about the opposing forces in Stuart Sutcliffe's work and life, his sudden premature death and the subsequent mythologising of the story. Like anything related to The Beatles, his story has been poured over and become part of popular culture mythology. His crucial decision to leave the band and pursue the more solitary pursuit of painting is told from many different viewpoints, but ultimately was unresolved because of his early death. Relating some of these concerns to my practice, the idea of constant decision-making and infinite numbers of different paths to be followed became a focus for the project, exploring it in relation to my own continued investigations into the relationship between drawing and sculpture. The work does not make any specific reference to Sutcliffe but deals with more general concerns, particularly this binary relationship shifting back and forth between an external and internal.

THE IT AND THE OTHER
2011-12
Mixed media
200 x 70 x 125 cm

ANDREW CURTIS

The 'British Invasion' of 1964-66 saw musical acts like The Beatles, influenced by American rock 'n' roll and blues music. They reprocessed and reintegrated these forms into the cultural landscape their inspiration had come from, creating new associations and meaning from an existing presence.

New Empire (Castle Scene) depicts a pair of downed Monkey Puzzle trees outside a house in Kent on the 16th October 1987. The Monkey Puzzle tree takes 150 years to reach full maturity. Because of this it is referred to as a fossil with iconic status. The key to the connection of these iconic trees to this project is the two fallen icons that resonate throughout Stuart's story and that the trees symbolise - Stuart Sutcliffe and John Lennon.

Whilst making this work for *In Conversation with Stuart Sutcliffe* I could only find monochromatic portraits of Stuart but panchromatic photographs of his paintings through Internet searches. One in particular, *Untitled, Rural Scene with Tree*, informed the choices I made for *Castle Scene*. The press image of the fallen trees that I appropriated for this work were taken in the era of widely available colour photography but printed in black and white photomechanical halftone.

Castle Scene is a screen print using a pigment made from finely ground Whitby Jet, a fossil of Monkey Puzzle (Araucaria Araucana). The cultural importance of the fossil and the organism from which it derived symbolises both mourning and celebrated colonialism. Two lost icons appear in this work, forever immortalised through a black and white photomechanical halftone.

NEW EMPIRE (CASTLE SCENE)
2011-12
Unique screen print with Whitby Jet pigment and household enamel on paper, mounted on wood
Each panel measures 88 x 145 x 6 cm

NICK GOSS

bar stools
defunct snare drums
palms
kettle leads
battered amps

The associated detritus of playing in a band.
I wanted to paint an imagining of the
rehearsal spaces and small venues that the
fledgling Beatles would have faced arriving in
Hamburg. The hours spent in liminal/non-
space rooms. When emptied out in the
daytime, these Hamburg venues, like the
Indra or the Kaiserkeller, must have had a
peculiar melancholic atmosphere - spaces
clad in cheap insulating material that offered
limited comfort, but allowed ideas and
musical potential to gestate and flourish.

Stuart Sutcliffe's story is fuelled with
melancholy, an emotive feeling I wanted to
convey through this work.

CASBAH
2011
Oil on two wood panels
Each panel measures 135 x 210 cm

MARK HAMPSON

A few years ago, I bought some brushes to paint the house. Instead, using basic manipulations with studio scraps and props, I made several 'brush bands', visually echoing the look of classic 60s groups. Recently, contemplating Stuart Sutcliffe and his combined legacies as artistic bohemian, image-maker and one of The Beatles accredited with helping to define the band's early image, I decided to reform the brush bands. Whilst remaking and rehearsing them, I spotted a lone brush in a corner of my studio; slightly worn and well-used, his bristled mane was sculpted into a permanent rocker's quiff by old paint, dust and varnish. It instantly triggered a memory of grainy black and white Art School photographs of Stuart that I had absorbed as a young fan. With the help of all my props, Stuart was back. When I came to google Stuart, I realised that, as always, my memory was corrupted and I had constructed a figure from flawed interpretations, merging creative inventions.

My daughter described this brush as 'the cool one'; the details of my invention may have been wrong but the spirit was there. She picked him up and played with him. I dug out my copy of Stuart singing *Love Me Tender*. We all had a dance and, for a dreamy minute, the studio was transformed into the Cavern.

WITH THE BRUSHES (FOUR PIECE SET)
2011
Archival inkjet print
42 x 52 cm

LOVE ME TENDER (THE COOL ONE)
2011
Mixed media on board
20 x 15 cm

THE BRUSHES (FOR STUART THE SPONGE BOB REMIX)
2011-12
Mixed media on board
122 x 122 cm

BLATTOID
2011-12
Mixed media on board
122 x 122 cm

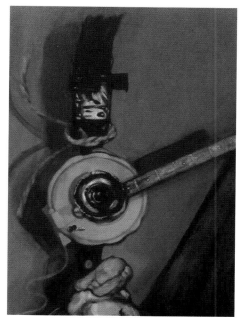

JANN HAWORTH

I have always been haunted by the losses of so many young people that are woven through The Beatles' mythology. It has seemed to me to be disproportionate to what we consider 'usual' for that age group. Sometimes I think the stats are more like a reflection of the war-time loss of young men. Stuart Sutcliffe, Brian Epstein, Mal Evans, Keith Moon, Brian Jones, John Lennon, Michael Cooper, Robert Fraser - all prematurely gone. No conclusions can be drawn but two were shot, others drug-related, some depression, one AIDS - a horrible price to pay for flying close to the sun.

MISSING
(36 PEOPLE, OF ALL AGES, FROM SALT LAKE
AND HOW THEY SAW STUART SUTCLIFFE)
2012
Collage on canvas
50.8 x 50.8 cm
In collaboration with the Leonardo Museum, Salt Lake

IDRIS KHAN

My work for *In Conversation with Stuart Sutcliffe* has a transfixing spiritual quality. I have rhythmically hand stamped the lyrics from The Beatles' song *Hallelujah, I Love Her So* (which is one of three songs on which Sutcliffe was recorded) over and over again creating a spiral shape that appear to pulsate from the central vortex of the drawing. Offering a commentary on the repetition of lyrics that are overplayed again and again can take one out of the physical realm and into the spiritual.

Stuart Sutcliffe's work can be seen as inward expression. I have developed a unique narrative through densely layered imagery that inhabits the space between abstraction and figuration and that speaks to the themes of history, cumulative experience and the metaphysical collapse of time into single moments. These are parallels that could be drawn from the short time Stuart had and the layered image reveals the texture and delicacy of the subject.

HALLELUJAH, I LOVE HER SO
2012
Oil on Paper
50.8 x 55.88 cm

LAURA LANCASTER

For *In Conversation with Stuart Sutcliffe* I have reinterpreted found archive images of Stuart Sutcliffe, translating these into oil paintings. Seated within the tradition of figurative painting, my work investigates the use of the found archive as a catalyst for the creative process. Making works from the anonymous snapshots slides and cine films of strangers, through my intervention the interpretation of this imagery can be manipulated. The nostalgic and sentimental response associated with the family snapshot has allowed an interpretation that allows these images of Stuart to take on surreal qualities.

This work has been approached from the standpoint of a creative practitioner (like Stuart) also engaged with the worlds of art and music (I am a member of several bands). I wanted to use source imagery that seemed to reflect this connection, Stuart's vulnerability and malleability, and engage the interlinking threads between the two creative worlds of which Stuart had such prevalence.

UNTITLED
2011
Oil on board
50 x 40 cm

BACK TO THE AUDIENCE
2011
Oil on canvas
47 x 36 cm
courtesy of Workplace Gallery

BOB MATTHEWS

I began making work with Stuart Sutcliffe's context, influences and relative youth in mind. I was drawn firstly to the ambition and proliferation of youth and of early Art School experience, especially those first few years of intense wonder and wild abandoned visions. I also considered the departure from music and the life that offered, and then began to think more about the musicality of the work itself, the rhythm and structure of his abstractions and the relationship this had to all of my own approaches and distractions.

Trying to tap into my initial impulses at Art School, the experimentation with forms and processes, I then thought more about whether or not I really liked Nicolas de Staël. I wanted to respond to the works of Sutcliffe, respond to the context, the forms within the paintings, the layering and the direct and evident influences, allowing influence to remain a key visual aspect. There is a sense with Sutcliffe's work that we are seeing something not fully formed, the work itself seems constantly at a point of change and because of this it has an unusual clarity.

FORMING
2011
Acrylic paint and Japanese paper on plywood
120 x 90 cm (various parts)

BRUCE McLEAN

Through influence, both artistic and musically since the start of rock 'n' roll in the 1950's I am able to see parallels through my working life to that of Stuart Sutcliffe. I was born 5 years after Stuart and it wasn't until 1985 that I won the John Moores' Painting Prize, an exhibition that Sutcliffe drew acclaim in as a mere student of 19 years old. It's interesting that through his influences and the way his practice was developing into alternative media, we could have taken similar paths, exploring the full reaches of artistic practice that would inform, develop and question the direction of contemporary art.

In 1958, every Saturday at the ice rink, I would listen to rock 'n' roll music while trying to impress girls and smoking Peter Stuyvesant cigarettes. This shaping of my identity helped me to become a modern artist. I was 14 and painted my bedroom in black emulsion paint (which my granny called black emotion paint). In the suburban area of Clarkston Glasgow, all this made me a mini- legend - the original Clarkston Daftie.

I had seen the works of the French artists in *Studio* an International Arts Magazine that my father had subscribed to since the mid-twenties and I was fascinated by the likes of Pierre Soulages, Cesar, Georges Mathieu, Riopelle. At every given moment, I attempted to make a quick Soulages - black abstract lines on white. When I eventually went to Art School at the age of 16, just as The Beatles were surfacing, my inspirational teacher, Sinclair Thompson, introduced me to the works of Nicholas de Staël. I then, of course, started making de Staël type paintings – still-lifes, black on black, grey seascapes with ships in great slabs of oil paint over much under-painting. I sort of knew this was tosh even then, and I am still using much of what I learned as a young artist, as Sutcliffe would have been today, still attempting to be a modern artist, still attempting to inform and question a contemporary art world.

A PAINTING OF A SCULPTURE AND
A PAINTING OF A PAINTING OF A SCULPTURE
2011
Oil, charcoal and acrylic on canvas
200 x 140 cm
courtesy of Bernard Jacobson Gallery

MARILÈNE OLIVER

Sutcliffe suffered severe headaches and, although unconfirmed, his premature death is thought to have been attributed to a brain aneurism. Headspace is based on a set of anonymised MRI scans of a brain aneurism. I combined a number of different techniques to transform the scans into a small sculpture that invites the viewer to contemplate both the beauty of the scans and the mystery of death. The scans have been painstakingly rendered using a combination of tiny dots of ink and drill holes. The drill holes (which catch the light) depict the flow of blood in the brain and, thus, the ball of light, barely detectable at the centre of the sculpture is the aneurism. The tiny dots of ink across the rest of the scans shroud the aneurism in a dark cloud. This combination of points of light in darkness gives the work a seductive, celestial feel. Headspace presents the viewer with a cause of death but, rather than being gory and making us want to look away, it shimmers and invites us to come closer, squinting to peer as far in as possible.

HEADSPACE (ANEURISM)
2011-12
Ink and drill holes in laser-cut acrylic mounted on light box
40 x 30 x 20 cm

FLORA PARROTT

- -

'How I long for clarity and yet how I loathe these precise men, who are never satisfied until they have labelled, ranged and set aside each separate emotion, ignoring their gradations. How to make them see the world of shifting forms in which I live? Now that I begin to isolate my destiny I find it is like those plants which we can never dig up with their roots intact... She's like a rose that has run its dark leaves over the wall to look at the sun.' Stuart Sutcliffe

Ignoring Their Gradations is a response to a letter that Stuart wrote just after meeting Astrid. I was struck by the explosive passion - the clear division that he felt, the inability to find calm or balance and the clarity and frustration with which he viewed himself.

His words make me think of forms repeating themselves, unable to resolve. I imagine beautiful, short-lived, irreversible explosions, extreme, intense combinations of character that have a huge impact on one another but are not sustainable. *Ignoring Their Gradations* is an attempt to explain these ideas by combining materials that react beautifully to one another, with mesmorising results that eventually fade - shapes that twist and turn away from one another, but are so similar that they almost loop back and combine into one.

IGNORING THEIR GRADATIONS (Detail)
2011
Ram's horn, 3D plaster print, digital prints,
tape, OS board, paint, copper nails
approx 2 x 1 x 1 m

IGNORING THEIR GRADATIONS (Detail)
2011
Ram's horn, 3D plaster print, digital prints,
tape, OS board, paint, copper nails
approx 2 x 1 x 1 m

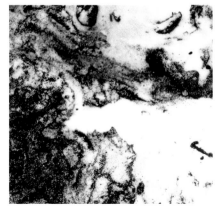

MARTINA SCHMID

Stuart Sutcliffe's paintings and drawings evoke psychological realities that are palpable in their layered shapes and forms. My work attempts to connect the urban experience of the mind with tactile close-up encounters of textures and surfaces.

Abstraction can be seen as a quest to formulate the multi-layered facets of the visual sensual world that surrounds us.

Sutcliffe's slashed red-ink brushstrokes resonate with me just as much as his muted thickly-coated paintings. They translate into an aggressive scream that is echoed in the empty spaces of my imaginary worlds. There is a balance between peaceful contemplation and angry sublimation, which reflects the precarious mental shifts that are required to manoeuvre the man-made built environment we live in.

SINGAPORE GRIP
2011
Acrylic on canvas
25.3 x 35.7 cm

STEVEN SCOTT

Point of Departure reveals subtle levels of assumption and intention inherent in the process of looking whilst also alluding to the notion of options and life choices, acknowledging those made by Sutcliffe in his move to Hamburg to play music and his subsequent choice to pursue visual art; decisions that have shaped his legacy. The two perspectives within *Points of Departure* highlight the alternating paths in which Stuart existed, both subtly different whilst almost mirroring each other as interlinking forces.

Point of Departure consists of two digital images derived from a single monochrome photograph of a waterway in Hamburg harbour. These images are made up of alternate vertical strips of the original photograph and are designed to be installed at 90 degrees to each other so that the single point perspective of the waterway is doubled and seen to recede in different directions. The suggestion of a stereoscopic effect is falsely implied by these dual perspectives, enhanced by a subtle lateral shifting of the elements within each picture. Each image appears to be the complement of the other but, in fact, carries slightly different and conflicting visual information, like the dualistic elements within Stuart's life.

POINT OF DEPARTURE
2011
Digital print
2 panels measuring 43 x 124 cm

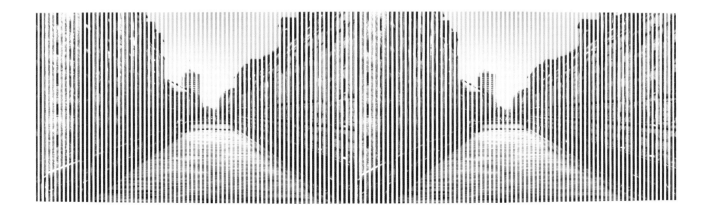

JAMIE SHOVLIN

My work for *In Conversation with Stuart Sutcliffe* takes Sutcliffe's iconic Höfner 333 bass as its subject. Cast against a hazy backdrop, the instrument's headstock glitters under the heavy glare of stage lights. This scene is a recreation of a recreation - the drawing is life-posed from a still taken from *Backbeat* (1994), the film chronicling Sutcliffe's time with The Beatles. Drawn in precise detail, the work celebrates the iconographic link between musician and equipment.

I question how information becomes authoritative and explore the way that we map and classify the world in order to understand it. This work becomes an intimate close up of a story that has been appropriated and mythologised through many sources, highlighting the tension between truth and fiction, reality and invention, history and memory.

UNTITLED (333)
2012
Pencil on paper
28 x 20 cm
courtesy of Haunch of Venison

HOFNER

SERGEI SVIATCHENKO

When I was in sixth grade my parents bought me a black pigskin satchel. It had any number of pockets, a golden lock and a little key. Seen in profile it looked like an accordion. This was where I kept my first Beatles records, and, as far as I can remember, they were *Please, Please Me* and *Meet the Beatles*. Since there was no cover on my copy of *Meet the Beatles* I had to make one myself. This home-made design was a great success, and the cover was later used as the original when exchanging records.

FIVE
2011
Photo collage, signed Lambda Kodak silver paper print,
limited edition of 5 with 2 APs
140 x 100 cm

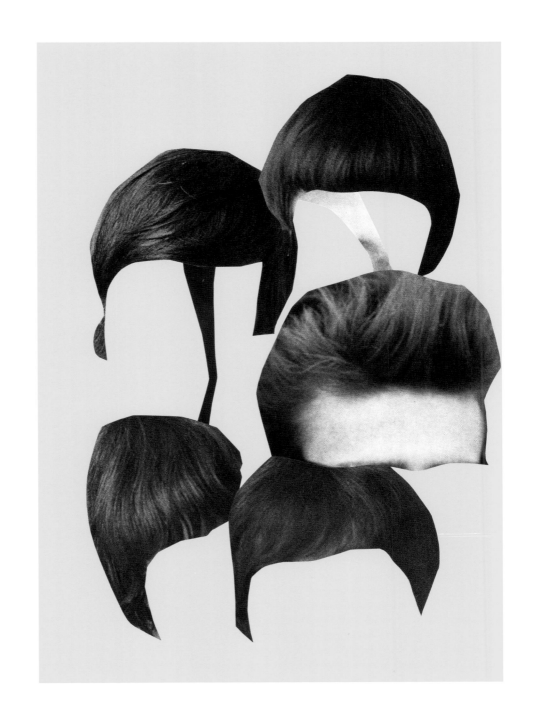

JESSICA VOORSANGER

My work explores popular culture with a particular fascination on celebrity. I often focus on the relationship between fans and their idols, using a range of different media from performance and installation to costumes, painting and mail art.

They Think Art is All About Van Gogh is loosely inspired by the film *Backbeat* (1994), chronicling Sutcliffe's friendship with John Lennon and his tragic demise. The comic book language referenced in the painting style embraces and exemplifies the mythology surrounding Stuart Sutcliffe in the film.

Stuart Sutcliffe (Impostor Series), is part of a larger series of work called Impostors, where participants are invited to 'become' the subject in a form of homage. I supply a costume, wig and portrait of an iconic figure. In this case paying homage to Stuart Sutcliffe.

THEY THINK ART IS ALL ABOUT VAN GOGH (BACKBEAT)
2011
Oil on canvas
92 x 122 cm

STUART SUTCLIFFE (IMPOSTOR SERIES)
2011
Oil on canvas, clothes/costume, wig, mirror and Höfner Guitar
Dimensions variable (painting 20 x 20 cm)

STEPHEN WALTER

- -

In 2008, I produced a whistle-stop 'warts and all' tour of Liverpool where I began to translate its character onto paper, its quirks, idiosyncrasies and stereotypes into a celebration of place. It highlights many of Liverpool's main roads, railway lines, built-up areas and green spaces, with an enlarged section of the city centre. Such a study inevitably drew me towards the story of Stuart Sutcliffe as a figure of cultural significance to Liverpool. It is a fitting tribute that his place is taken alongside all other influential and cultural characters that, from a small town, on a small island, could resonate so loudly throughout the world.

The inclusion of him is a tribute to his memory.

STEPHEN WALTER'S MAP OF LIVERPOOL
2008-09
Archival ink-jet print on fine art Paper
112.8 x 105.5 cm

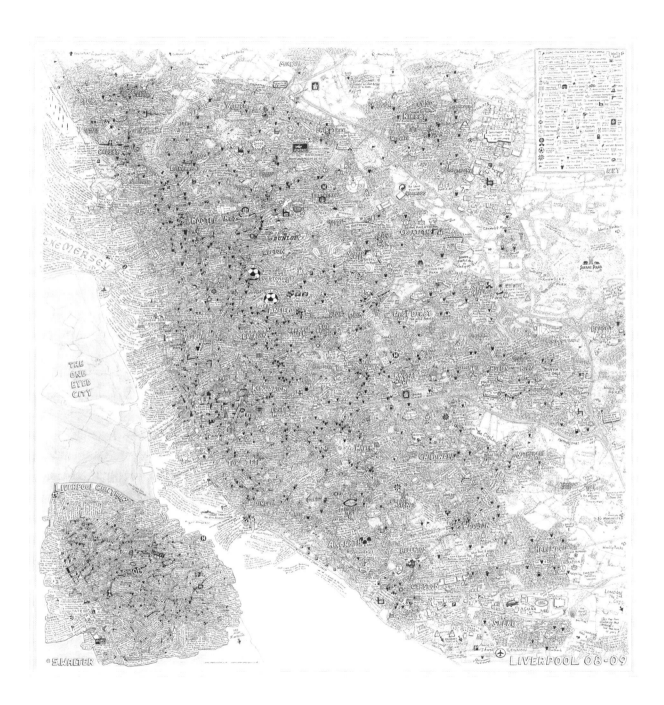

UWE WITTWER

Examining how memory interferes with an image is particularly interesting when the subject is a public figure like Stuart Sutcliffe, where the image is passed not only through the filters of my mind, but also those of the general public. Questioning the relationship between memory and image is central to my work. What intrigues me with Stuart is the interference coming from many angles, from Stuart's history with The Beatles, mixing with the history of popular culture, from an era, which, in turn, had a significant impact on my generation.

My practice deals with what memory does to images and the constant question of what makes an image. *At the Table* refers to an image of Stuart with the other members of The Beatles that I found on the Internet, in the public domain, almost fragmented from a specified story. The shape refers to a misplaced puzzle piece. The blanked-out person at the table is a distraction, a compositional element the painting requires, and also a trap - or incentive - for the spectator to enforce the debate about forgetting and/or substituting elements within the picture itself, and how historical sources can become corrupted through freely available sources of information.

'AM TISCH' (AT THE TABLE)
2011
Watercolour
110 x 160 cm
courtesy of Haunch of Venison

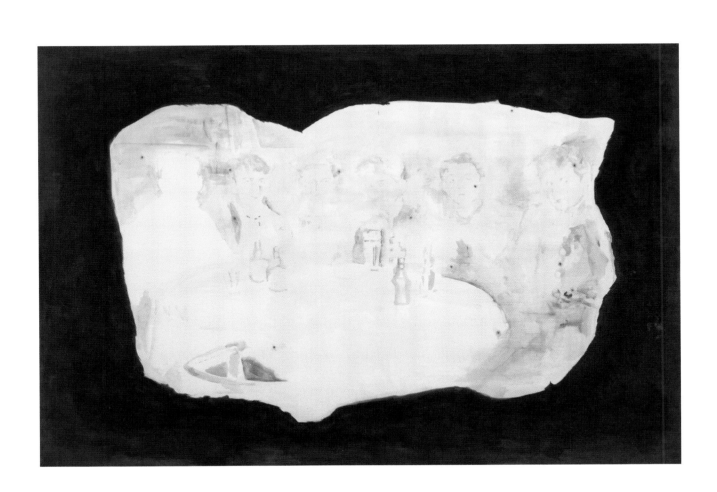

THE STUART SUTCLIFFE CONTEMPORARY ART AWARD

We have been overwhelmed by the enormous response from artists all over the world who have contributed responses to the life and work of Stuart Sutcliffe for this book.

50 Years on, Stuart's work clearly still has a major relevance within contemporary artistic practice. We would, therefore, like to take this opportunity to announce the launch of *The Stuart Sutcliffe Contemporary Art Award*.

This annual prize will be judged by a panel of esteemed judges and full details, including how to submit an entry for the inaugural award, are detailed on Stuart's official website, **www.stuartsutcliffe.org**

There are some who say that Stuart's work may never have been known if he had not been 'a Beatle' and there are others who say that regardless of his part in The Beatles' story, his art would always have found a way to be recognised with huge significance. Whatever the truth, if *The Stuart Sutcliffe Contemporary Art Award* can help new, aspiring talent from around the world, find a way to be known, acknowledged and helped, it can only be a good thing for art and artists, and one that Stuart himself would no doubt have endorsed.

Stuart Sutcliffe in his attic studio, Hamburg
Photograph by Astrid Kirchherr 1961

Stuart Sutcliffe and John Lennon, Hamburg 1961
Photograph by Astrid Kirchherr

I looked up to Stu,
I depended on him
to tell me the truth...
Stu would tell me if
something was good
and I'd believe him

JOHN LENNON

THE STUART SUTCLIFFE ESTATE

Stuart's sister, Pauline Sutcliffe, is the Sole Executrix & Owner of The Stuart Sutcliffe Estate and the Estate owns and operates Stuart's official website, **www.stuartsutcliffe.org**. Please take a moment to visit the site and register on the mailing list to be kept up-to-date with news and developments. There are also opportunities to buy posters, limited edition prints, books, DVD's and much more.

Occasionally, the Stuart Sutcliffe Estate considers selling high-value, original pieces of art by Stuart and memorabilia from The Beatles days in Hamburg. All enquiries should be directed to the Estate's CEO, Giles Cooper, who can be contacted through the website.

Untitled (Hamburg Series #3 detail) circa 1960-62
Stuart Sutcliffe
courtesy of The Stuart Sutcliffe Estate

CREDITS AND THANKS

Giles Cooper, Michael Hall, Pauline Sutcliffe and Diane Vitale would like to thank:

Joyce (nee Sutcliffe) and John Whitelock Wainwright
David and Jean Whitelock Wainwright and Tom, Dan and Steph
Andrew and Allison Whitelock Wainwright and Alex and Megan

Karl Sydow
Anita Sydow
David Leveaux
Iain Softley
Stephen Stegich
Astrid Kirchherr
Klaus Voormann
Ulf Krueger
Vladislav Ginsburg
David Bedford
Christian Furr
Cynthia Lennon
Jacquie Chalmers
Rod Murray
Professor Donald Kuspit
Larry Kane
Yoko Ono
Angie McCartney
James McCartney
Paul McCartney
Ruth McCartney
Olivia Harrison
Hereward Harrison
Tracey Emin
Joyce Brand
Michael Freude
Carol and Ian Sellars
Judy and Terry Mowschenson
Susan Kenny and Zara
Terry Sampson and Shelagh Johnson
Evelyn and Guisha Cantacuzene-Speransky
Peggy Papp
Paul Hunter
Joy Malbon
Matthew Clough
Colin Fallows
Glenn Calderone
Gary James

Rhys Ivans
Annika Larsson
Sherry Liscio
Stephen Dorff
Nick Blood
Cloe Vitale
Elizabeth Rye
Frances Mattola
Nick Karis
Bob Kern
Seth Kelley
Newton Godnick
Maureen L. MacKenzie
The (original) Quarry Men
Graeme Gilloch
Richard Makin
Fisun Güner
Michael Ajerman
Andrew Bick
Kit Craig
Andrew Curtis
Nick Goss
Mark Hampson
Jann Haworth
Idris Khan
Laura Lancaster
Bob Matthews
Bruce McLean
Marilène Oliver
Flora Parrott
Martina Schmid
Steven Scott
Jamie Shovlin
Sergei Sviatchenko
Jessica Voorsanger
Stephen Walter
Uwe Wittwer
Paul King

Jon Stephenson
Richard Piegza
Nick Linford
Pete Best
Adam Robinson
Banksy
Keith Watkins
Sheryl Lee
Jimmy Knight
Ursula Cooper
Damien Hirst
Rye Rahman
Ian Davenport
Vince Power, CBE
Gemma Phillips
Charlie Murphy
Eva Ryn Johnannissen
Alex Hobbs
Vikky Alexander
Jennifer Wilson
Gillian Wearing
Jamie Gazard
Sukhy Hullait
Dennis Reinhardt
Bernard Jacobson
Arcade Fine Arts
Beaux Art
CCA&A Gallery
Edit & Post Soho
Green Screen Soho
Hales Gallery
Haunch of Venison
Josh Lilley Gallery
Mirvish Productions
Payne Shurvell
Tintype Gallery
Workplace Gallery
...and finally to Martha and Charles Sutcliffe

...and a big thank you to everyone who engages with the importance of Stuart Sutcliffe. Through all of us, Stuart's legacy lives on

Design by Media Junction
www.mediajunction.co.uk

Printing by John Good Ltd

Photograph (opposite) of Stuart Sutcliffe by Astrid Kirchherr c.1961

66

Bye for now...
don't worry about me...
I'm very happy in so many ways...

99
STUART SUTCLIFFE